W9-ABJ-894

NATURE'S WAY

ALSO BY ED McGAA

Mother Earth Spirituality

Rainbow Tribe

Native Wisdom

Red Cloud: The Story of an American Indian

Eagle Vison: Return of the Hoop: a Novel

NATURE'S WAY

Native Wisdom for

Living in Balance

with the Earth

ED MCGAA, Eagle Man

HarperSanFrancisco
A Division of HarperCollins*Publishers*

HarperCollins books may be purchased for educational, business, or sales promotional use. For information please write: Special Markets Department, HarperCollins Publishers, Inc., 10 East 53rd Street, New York, NY 10022.

HarperCollins Web site: http://www.harpercollins.com
HarperCollins®, ■®, and HarperSanFrancisco™ are
trademarks of HarperCollins Publishers, Inc.

FIRST EDITION
Designed by Joseph Rutt

Library of Congress Cataloging-in-Publication Data is available upon request.
ISBN 0–06–051456–6
04 05 06 07 08 RRD(H) 10 9 8 7 6 5 4 3 2 1

To my nephew David Ressl and his son Matt and the thirty-one other Sun Dance pledgers at the Thunder Valley Sundance, near Rockyford, Pine Ridge Oglala Reservation, 2003; mostly all young men who will carry on the tradition. And to Angela Wozniak, a dear, supportive friend for nearly half a lifetime.

CONTENTS

Acknowledgments   ix

Introduction   xi

ONE   WISDOM THROUGH OBSERVATION   I
       Lesson of Eagle

TWO   FIND AND PRESERVE THE MEDICINE   20
       Lesson of Bear

THREE BALANCE IN ALL THINGS   50
       Lesson of Lion

FOUR   ONE AMONG MANY   71
       Lesson of Wolf

FIVE   DEVELOP INTUITION   105
       Lesson of Orca

SIX   SEEK TRUTH   129
       Lesson of Owl

SEVEN STRIVE FOR FREEDOM   155
       Lesson of Tiger

EIGHT HEAT   182
       Lesson of Cottonwood Tree

NINE   THIN   206
       Lesson of Deer

TEN   GONE   226
       Lesson of Buffalo

ELEVEN TOO MANY   254
       Lesson of Rat

       Notes   275

ACKNOWLEDGMENTS

To Mark Salzwedel, to whom I am once again grateful for being my editor;

To Renee Sedliar, whose patience and insight have frequently been amazing in the revisions of the manuscript;

To Reverend Cheryl Downey and Reverend Malcolm LeFever, for their tireless and insightful research and writing in the final four chapters, as well as for their encouragement, advice, and editing;

To Reverend William Stolzman, who went out into Nature's Way as a Jesuit priest and took part in Sioux ceremonies with respect and admiration;

To Joe Thunder Owl Brewer (deceased) of the Mdewakanton Sioux Tribe, traveling companion on many expeditions;

To Sonny Hare, Yankton Sioux, for his deep cultural knowledge and our shared language and warrior experience; and

To Dr. Beatrice Medicine, Lakota Sihasapa, for her support, wisdom, and knowledge.

INTRODUCTION

The term "Native American," the most recent gloss for North American aborigines, is now in disfavor with many tribal groups and individuals. The National Congress of American Indians, a powerful self-interest group, has passed a resolution opposing its use at their most recent convention. Throughout the historic Indian-white interface, such names as "North American Indians," "Amerindian," "Indian-American," and "First-Americans" have been in vogue at various times. In this essay, I use "Native American" and "American Indian" interchangeably. As for the focus of the essay, the Lakota, who are often labeled "Sioux," "Teton Sioux," "Western Lakota," and "Dakota" in the anthropological literature, I use the term "Lakota," for I am referring to the Western Sioux who speak the Lakota dialect of the Siouian language. I also use designations such as "Rosebud Sioux" to indicate the reservation as a social system to which one assigns oneself. This is accepted procedure by most Lakota Sioux.[1]

I concur with my close friend and aunt in the Sioux way, Dr. Bea Medicine. I also will use phonetic pronunciation of the Sioux language. The English language uses the more practical phonic system. Why Siouian language has been reduced to the nonphonic method is indeed frustrating and extremely misleading for ordinary laymen.

I am an enrolled tribal member of the Oglala Sioux, also known as the Oglala Lakota. My tribe's history goes back to when our tribal grounds were in the Carolinas. After centuries, we finally ended up on a reservation in South Dakota, one of the last Indian tribes to be sequestered, five years after a battle you may have heard about involving a Colonel George Custer in 1876.

I believe that it is because of my tribe's willingness to relocate and adapt to new environments that it has maintained its freedom to practice its rituals and traditions without too much dilution by an entity I will refer to as Dominant Society. In simple terms, Dominant Society is reflected in the beliefs and practices of the largest governments and religions. While indigenous people such as the Sioux tend to honor Nature, Dominant Society tends to view the natural world as an endless resource to be exploited.

I do not expect you to trade your set of beliefs for mine. I do not have all the answers. But in my tradition, we ask more questions and we share our honest observations. Hopefully, once you have completed reading this book, you will know what I know, and I am fairly sure you will see that a spiritual path that honors Nature is the only way out of the serious crises facing our planet. I call that path Nature's Way.

In this book, I attempt to portray how Sioux and other Nature-respecting societies have believed and practiced. Through their examples, I hope to show how Dominant Society can avoid disastrous consequences, overcome religious intolerance, treat women and men equally, preserve our environment, and live in peace. We can then progress onward to solving humankind's most serious problems.

It has been the tradition of our tribe to honor Nature in all its forms.

Unlike Dominant Society, we regard more than the adult males of our tribe as valuable. Along with the Iroquois, we developed a form of democratic governance that truly honors the wisdom of all, including women, children, animals, plants, stones, and unseen spirits. As one holy man always used to tell me, in every being and in every event "there is a teaching." I believe Nature's Way is democratic. Democracy that respects secularism and views Nature as sacred is the strongest approach toward saving the planet.

I do not write from mythology when I reflect upon Native American spirituality in this book. In my opinion, mythology leads to superstition; and superstition has proved fatally destructive to many millions down through time. It is ironic, then, that Dominant Society accuses Native practices of being based on myth. Honest observation, which is what this book (and Native American spirituality generally) is grounded on, *cannot* be myth.

I write from real happenings, experiences I have witnessed, as well as from the wisdom I have learned from Sioux holy men I have been fortunate to meet personally. Many of those lessons were learned during the time of the brave Dr. Martin Luther King Jr. His catalyzing efforts for truth inspired renewed tribal-based efforts for social and religious freedom. We Sioux sought the return of our own spirituality after a century of deprivation. The U.S. government unlawfully, unconstitutionally banned our belief system in the late nineteenth century, through the coercion and lobbying of the Christian missionaries. Not until 1978 was the ban on our religious practices officially reversed by the United States Congress.

The rise of Dominant Society, the desacralization of Nature, and the complicity of institutional religion speak clearly to the most urgent needs of our time. If we hope to address those needs successfully, we need to sound a call for spiritual awakening, to create a new global culture based not on dominance over Nature for economic and political gain, but on values that endure for all times and all people.

One of the Sioux holy men I had the good fortune to know was Chief Fools Crow, also Oglala Lakota. He had some profound advice on what a person should do in order to be a force of positive change in the world. That advice? Become a "hollow bone."

> To become a clean hollow bone, you must first live as I have, or if you have not done this already, you must begin to do it. You must love everyone, put others first, be moral, keep your life in order, not do anything criminal, and have a good character. If you do not do these things, you will be easily tricked, and will become a bone for the powers of evil.[2]

Nature's Way is divided into two sections. In the first section, I will lead you through some lessons represented by animals and even a tree, to help make your "bone" clean and hollow. Each lesson builds on the previous one, leading you to sharpen your spiritual power. With that grounding, you will be ready to face the information in the second section. In that section—the final four chapters of the book—the consequences of the desacralization of Nature become very clear and very disturbing.

I tend to tell stories, and I may seem to wander a bit within each chapter, but I've tried to tie things up in summaries at the end of each chapter to help you extract the meanings. This is a cultural teaching method among the holy men with whom I have studied.

Another of those holy men was Chief Eagle Feather, a Sichangu Lakota. I was thinking one day about what he would say about my writing this book. Probably something along these lines:

"The Wahshichu [white man] has brought all this down on himself because he thought he knew so much but in reality was playing with big trouble. For what has happened to our people we could easily say, 'Let him perish in his own greed-made waste.'

"I don't think Chief Fools Crow or the Black Elks would approve of such an attitude from us, however. It would allow that fancy college word to come into the picture. What is it? Ahhh, *ego*. Yes, we would be picking up that false word *ego* and trying to say, 'I told you so.' It would doom us too in the end. For survival of all, Nephew, for the Generations Unborn, we have to share our knowledge and change the Wahshichu."

Then he would probably pause and add, "Or at least give it our best try!"

Occasionally, you will be introduced in these pages to another Native American teaching method known as *Iktomi*. Iktomi are traditional clowns or contraries, and I have a couple from England that visited me from time to time during the writing of this book. I put up with their jokes because sometimes they made a worthwhile point.

I will also refer frequently to a prophecy made by a Sioux holy man named Nicholas Black Elk in the book *Black Elk Speaks*, which was first published in 1932. I was close to the interpreter of this book, Ben Black Elk. His father, Nick Black Elk, spoke only Sioux, and John Neihardt, the author, spoke only English. Ben spoke both languages fluently and conveyed to me, from his father's vision, the future appearance of four horses, each of a different color, representing different calamities that would soon face the Sioux Nation and the world at large. My own father spoke of the same horses, but that's understandable since Ben used to come visit our home often. Because they are such serious threats to Mother Earth, I have drawn the parallel to the reference in the Bible to the Four Horses of the Apocalypse.

It seems clear now that the Four Horses of the Apocalypse are indeed on the horizon. A return to the old values of Nature's Way does not seem to be very likely, and yet it is an absolute necessity if the two-leggeds (humans) are to survive. The destruction will not come from space aliens, a volcanic eruption, a giant meteor impacting Earth, or a man-God that appears in the sky. These are our most popular predictions, and specific dates have been projected down through time.

But doom dates come and go without these external threats materializing. It seems clear that humans are now bent upon destroying each other. One method is our stubborn insistence that God is speaking through a single ideology only—ours, and no one else's. But there are other methods by which we are destroying ourselves. We are presently destroying the very nest that we live in by ignoring the sacred within Nature!

Let us begin the process of healing our world by learning the first and most important lesson toward gaining our spiritual power. Eagle teaches us to observe as we go forward into Chapter One.

ONE

WISDOM THROUGH OBSERVATION

Lesson of Eagle

Eagle is the symbol of observation. The Sioux consider it to be the creature that best symbolizes immense wisdom. It learns from all that it sees. It is the eyes of the all-seeing *Wakan Tanka*, the Great Spirit, the mysterious unknown entity that created all things. When the Sioux see an eagle flying, they are reminded of Wakan Tanka's observation of their actions—both what they do and what they don't do, both good deeds and bad. Those actions are stamped into the memory of time and within your memory and mine, and within the memory of others whom we have helped or harmed. The memories of all those others have "observed" us.

MEMORY IS OUR SPIRIT

The Sioux believe that lies, deceit, greed, and harm to innocent others will never be erased, and neither will good deeds of generosity and caring. Dominant Society, on the other hand, leans toward the "forgiveness" theory, which claims that bad deeds can be purged. Daily life seems to bear out the Sioux perspective: victims do not readily forget horrible atrocities committed against them simply because the perpetrator has somehow been "forgiven." With greater consciousness of the long-term consequences of human decisions, the Sioux avoid a host of problems. We do not harvest natural resources beyond reasonable need or without replacing them. We do not enter into commitments (such as parenthood) without a clear intention to make good on them. We treat others with dignity and compassion, recognizing that any enemy can become our ally over time. Realizing that we will be answerable for all our harmful acts—at least in the Beyond World, where all have memories—we strive always to be tolerant and considerate.

THE CONSISTENCY AND PURPOSEFULNESS OF NATURE

Nature, with its seasonal parade of events, demonstrates to us that it is both repetitive and consistent. When we go out into Nature and take a walk, when we observe and enjoy the world around us, we know that we can trust and depend on Nature's actions. We know that although occasionally the Earth will shake, we will not fall off it. Within the boundaries of where they have risen before, the rivers will continue to flow. And only if we live near one of the few active volcanoes will we have to worry about the mountains posing any threat to us; they will continue to collect the life-giving rains and send them down to us. Nature's beauty is a gift we can enjoy: we might feed a squirrel or just look at one; we might observe a flock of geese or a flight of ducks; we might sit on a park bench or drive a thousand miles to Yellowstone Park or the Black Hills of South Dakota; we might don a mask and snorkel and put our head under the water and look at reef fish, marveling at life in another natural medium. *Ahhh!* What a spellbinding, amazing observation: a joyous, colorful reef!

Nature is also very deliberate and truthful. The Sioux believe that when we observe Nature directly, as Eagle does, we are observing natural entities precisely as the Ultimate designed them to be; all the actions and reactions of Nature are deliberate. If we are watching frogs and turtles starting to hibernate for the winter, we know that they will not be milling around atop the ice next month. If we see a pair of robins in the springtime making a round nest, we know that soon they will be laying eggs within; they do not create the nest for its decorative effect upon a maple tree. A school of salmon out in that vast ocean will go directly to the stream they were spawned in, and not to another. A pair of buck deer will fight over the privilege of mating with a harem of does, not to impress other bucks with how macho they are.

Animals have unique designs and programs that can be observed and learned from. Because of these designs, they don't waste energy on purposelessness or imbalance. Some animals are carnivorous; others are omnivorous; still others are herbivorous. You won't find a cow eating meat out on the range where lush grasses grow. And if a great white shark is nearby, I suggest you stay out of the water, unless you have a perverse desire to be its lunch.

THE FREEDOM TO THINK

The more we experience of the world around us, the more reward we will enjoy right here, let alone when we enter the "pearly gates" of the Beyond. The higher the plane of knowledge, the more of our own kind we seem to be able to associate with here, and that's no doubt even truer in the Beyond. The mind is limitless in its capacity to receive and glean information. We cannot have been given such magnificent brains just to passively observe Nature. Clearly, we are meant to think, analyze, deliberate. And yet humans seem to have some sort of fear (or is it plain ignorance?) of exercising the simple freedom to think. Why are we so prone to let others do our thinking for us—to lead us astray and control us? Creator has placed no limits upon our minds other than around that which is obviously mysterious—like how far is up, how far is down, when did time begin, and when will it end?

I believe that Creator is telling us something by allowing us so much freedom and giving us the ability to retain all that we observe. We were meant to gain as much knowledge as we can, and that's what I intend to do. I believe that the knowledge and insight I glean here during my time on Earth will go with me into the Spirit World. We carry with us the bad some have done to us, and the good—but we also, more importantly, carry with us our experience. I would hate to go into the Spirit World with nothing but a little knowledge and a weak assurance that all will be fine. Lack of gathered wisdom and experience would limit my freedom no differently than does the clipping of an eagle's wings.

LEARNING TO OBSERVE

We all start out in life as great observers of Nature, but in the process of indoctrination into Dominant Society, some of us seem to lose that childlike wonder and awe. We begin to discount Nature as a mere resource to be exploited. We start to ignore the many voices of Nature—and even their urgent warnings.

During my formative years, I was raised in the magical Black Hills of South Dakota. Although my tribe, the Sioux, legally own the Black Hills by U. S. treaty, the Hearst family (who owned the Homestake gold mine) were more influential than a tribe of Indians. I was fortunate to have Nature all around me when I was a growing child. The four-legged, finned, and winged ones that resided within the Black Hills and out to the Great Plains and the remote Badlands were free within their natural setting. I did not view them as captives in a zoo and consequently was afforded rich insights into their habits and habitat. Stored in my memory, stamped on my mind, are many scenes that I experienced as a child and on into adulthood that would look quite impressive if they were placed on canvas or captured in a video.

There was a big brown trout that lived in a pool among the roots of a towering cottonwood not far from my home. I would sneak up to the old tree by Rapid Creek and peer down into that shaded hole before joining my friends for a swim farther upstream. The scene was more than just a painting. That fish was the largest trout I had ever seen. I noticed every movement of his fins as he waited for quarry to come by. An eerie feeling came over me as I stared down into that shaded hole. The water was so clear, it was like a lens allowing me to view that trout's world below the surface. Maybe the trout sensed my innocence, my awe, and my respect—sensed that I would do no harm. To this day I am impressed with these clean freshwater fish. I go fly-fishing often and release most of my catch.

The more we appreciate the life and world of any being, the more difficult it becomes to kill it unless our own survival is immediately threatened.

LISTEN TO YOUR MOTHER!

The Sioux refer to the Earth as *Ina Maka* in the same way that we sometimes refer to it in English: Mother Earth. She is the one who gave birth to all creatures, and it is through her that we learn what the Great Spirit or Creator intended for us. I was taught that the white man made his Creator (God) in his own image. Many medicine men and medicine women have taught me that it is actually Nature's Way that is reflected in us, in those who observe it.

I meet so many people who have so many misconceptions and just plain lack of knowledge about their rich past—a past that revered and respected the wildlife, saw our animal brothers and sisters as relatives. In fact, an Indian might consider these memories of the Creator's direct creations—the *Wamakaskan*, or animal world—as spiritual paintings, because they reveal a deep, living depth of Creation. Each animal has its own power or gift to convey, because they were so endowed by Wakan Tanka. Does not a mountain lion tell us that we can become independent and walk the lonely chasms of change undaunted? Does not a portrait of the owl, the eagle of the night, tell us not to fear the dark or mysterious places? Surely the beaver conveys a serene security and pace brought forth by a steady endeavor for those of us fortunate enough to find our own bliss. And yes, we all need endless scenes of the freedom of hawks, eagles, wolves, and the great orcas of the seas to forever implant a resolve that we must never lose our connection with the vast, soothing solitude of Nature. Each winged, four-legged, and finned creature has a meaning to convey that can be beneficial to our intricate two-legged lives. Even a common field mouse or a disciplined, dedicated Badlands ant has a message to convey if we will stoop to search for and study it.

NOTICE WELL

Animals are the innocent ones, the truthful ones, who follow obediently as Creator intends. Is the Great Spirit telling us something for our own good? "See, here is what I have made. Notice well that all these truthful ones live in harmony among and within themselves." Maybe God, the Great Spirit, is telling us this: "Notice well that my creations do not take more than they need. Notice that they care for their young and do not abandon them. Notice that they do not overpopulate; and in the rare cases that this happens, Mother Earth steps in to severely curtail that species!" (Remember this harsh fact very well!) "No species controls this world of the Wamakaskan."

These are teachings that I have learned by simply watching and observing. They reveal much of Creator's natural way, a way that can be discerned by a Nature-oriented intelligence, by a mind willing to throw aside ego, greed, and the foolish supposition that Human is superior over Nature.

NATURE AS A HOLY BOOK

I come from a tradition of Nature observers who did not learn how to observe Mother Earth from textbooks or sacred scriptures. We simply paid careful attention ourselves, or heard stories from others who had watched and learned. Our elders passed on their knowledge from Nature—present and past.

What was helpful to remember from the past was taught to following generations, and what no longer served us was let go. So as a tradition we honored the wisdom of past observations but did not make it rigid and unchangeable, as if the only way to be had been set generations prior. As Nature shows us if we observe, Mother Earth both changes and stays the same.

As a child, I heard a constant drone from the all-knowing white man who taught the Sunday catechism class that reservation youth were forced to attend. He spoke definitively of who God was and what He wanted. Though my father advised me to heed the white man's message, he gave it little credence. "No one knows who God is," he would say. "Only a damn fool would attempt to tell you that." He would wave at the sky and tell me to look around me. "Indians would tell you that it was too big to know." He would place his hands in his pockets and shrug with resignation, adding "but it is a white man's world now. Indians are passing on. You'd better listen to those priests. You will just make yourself a bunch of trouble if you stick to the old Indian ways." I learned from both my father's awe of God and his observations that our world was changing.

SIX POWERS AND FOUR WINDS

Greater entities have also had an influence upon me, especially as I have become older and think more in philosophical and spiritual wonderment. The Six Powers (north, south, east, west, Father Sky, and Mother

Earth), the Four Winds, the Four Elements (air, fire, Earth, and water), and on out beyond to the heavens, the farther galaxies, the black holes, and unfathomable space—oh, such Mystery leads one to unanswerable thoughts, but yet one *can* think! Adventures and revelations from ceremony also have influenced my speculations. This knowledge, coupled with the idea that the Great Spirit will teach through its own, direct creations, has become my "book," my scripture, but it is too vast ever to become fully attained in printed form.

I would have to admit that I have spent more hours immersed in the bosom of Mother Earth than I have at any other activity. Yes, I have received some soul-filled, highly important supplements from mentors and diligent writings. That information has been beneficial indeed, and I could not have written a word without such fortunate material and teachings. But it is Nature herself that gave me a solid background when I was a mere child spending days upon days out upon her. Swimming almost every hot day in a Black Hills lake or stream, fishing for trout, roaming the plains hunting (mostly rabbits, which we always ate), searching the Badlands for fossils, dodging rattlesnakes—in all these activities and more, I learned about Nature.

I also learned from seeking the wily ringneck pheasant in fall cornfields. The Dakotas are dotted with such fields—corn, hay, soybeans, along with shelterbelts of trees and other seemingly endless cover. The many sloughs, creeks, and gullies are edged by brush, hedges, weeds, thicker weed beds, thicker weed stands, and cattail clusters. One of the delights of Dakota living is experiencing a pheasant eruption anywhere from a couple roosters to a hundred from a crowded slough full of cattails. That sight gives a person a pretty good idea of the power and complexity of Nature.

Yes, endless cover for game birds is about as close to Nature as a person can get. Corn-fed deer, rabbits, and also predators such as the coyote, raccoon, possum, fox, hawk, and owl can also be found within areas whose human population growth is minimal to none. By comparison, these teachers are much harder to find in areas where the rapidly growing population constantly paves and covers Mother Earth.

In the absence of Nature as a teacher, those who live in urban areas are forced to get a secondhand account from films, television, and written materials. To see the value in experiencing Nature directly rather than indirectly, imagine the difference in your learning experience if you entered a lecture hall for a class and a knowledgeable teacher started an hour-long video and then left instead of delivering the material in person and being available for interaction.

LEARNING FROM A TREE

Children do not observe as adults do. As a child, I never thought of the stately cottonwood that watched over "my" trout as an example of endurance, but it is. Have you ever wondered why few cottonwoods fall during extreme winds—winds that blow over oaks, elms, and maples? It is because the cottonwood has supple branches that sway and bend with the storm, allowing the wind to blow through it. Somewhere on my adventurous Nature trail I learned to appreciate not just the cottonwood's shade but also its wisdom: sometimes a two-legged has to give a little and not stand so rigid.

There were many things I didn't give much thought to as a boy. For example, I never thought much about my older brother purchasing my first fly rod for me. Decades later I would buy a rod myself for a small boy, a grandnephew, and take him to the same spot on the stream that my brother had showed me. It was only then that I realized how grateful I was that I had had someone older looking after me.

I am in the process of teaching this young one now, as I did my own children, how to enjoy a wondrous trout stream. With the eyes of an older adult, I recognize the cottonwood's endurance as a truth about the heart of parenting, and its "giving and bending" as a truth in my heart that allows me to be grateful for my older brother. I had a good, kind, hardworking, dedicated father—an older man—but he was attached more to ranching, horses, and the lifestyle of cowboys. He had broken many a horse, and even though that task is dangerous, he rarely was hurt. He was also an excellent roper, and he braided quirts and bull-whips. Fly-fishing and modern sports sparked no interest in him.

As a child I was most interested in play not much different than that of young mountain lions, wolf pups, and bear cubs. I liked to fish, but my goal wasn't food or competition. I was content, even when I became fairly proficient with a rod, not to try very hard to catch my particular trout. If I saw that he was there, I would most often bypass that hole, believing that he was just too wise to be caught. Besides, I had a certain unspoken affinity for him.

I spent many days, many summers on that beautiful stream, catching fish for my parents; and when I was not fishing I was immersed in the deep pools, somehow oblivious to the cold mountain water on hot July and August days. Teachings came gradually, almost automatically, to me, as they do to all children raised in Nature.

A RABBIT'S STRENGTH AND WISDOM

My parents also liked to eat a cottontail rabbit or two. My brother, who was old enough to be my father, would take me out hunting, and I learned where many of the quick little creatures could be found. I once viewed a pair of golden eagles teaming up on a wily jackrabbit in the Wasta cedar breaks close to where Rapid Creek empties into the Cheyenne River. The Cheyenne courses through western South Dakota, and midway across the state it empties Badlands alkali into the Missouri, where walleye and huge northern pike lie within its estuaries.

The day we saw the eagles, my brother motioned for me to crawl up to his vantage point behind a clump of sage on the rim of a bluff to watch them slowly drive the jackrabbit from one cedar tree to another. The rabbit was too wise to make a run for it in the open; instead, it dashed from tree to tree. How clumsy the eagle looked as it waddled in under the low-branched cedar trees while its mate fanned its wings, ready to take after the prey. Rabbits may be vulnerable creatures that people can catch and eat, but they have been given their own warrior strength and wisdom, in opposition to eagles.

CREATION'S EXTENDED FAMILY

As a child, I gradually came to think of the trout and the jackrabbit as members of my extended family. In fact, *all* creatures—two-leggeds, four-leggeds, finned ones, and winged ones—become dearer to me and teach me more the more time I spend with them. Anyone who has had a pet—especially those who had a pet as a child—or who has had a profound meeting with a wild animal in Nature will know what I mean. As we go back through our memories of experiencing Nature, it is often the encounters with wild animals that are the most impressive.

Have you ever rounded the corner of a corral and there come face-to-face with a bobcat out for its evening hunt? I have, and the experience will never leave my memory. The bobcat's eyes, wide open, seemed to look straight into my soul, my spirit. A frozen moment in time. One look. Bobcats are incredibly fast—this one seemed to vanish into thin air. And yet even a split-second encounter like this brings knowledge. It teaches the kind of seeing that animals in Nature commonly use. When an animal stares at you, you're left with a sense of having been read to your depths.

I have seen deer, buffalo, coyote, elk, bear, moose, and even the spooky antelope all at close quarters. Though my first encounters came when I was a child, such scenes continue to be painted annually within my memory as I fly-fish those clear Black Hills streams. West of the Black Hills, heavy industry is rare for a considerable distance. Little if any acid rain falls on these streams, though in many streams in the eastern United States acid rain is such a problem that stocked trout can't reproduce and feed sufficiently. I can lift up a simple rock in the Black Hills streams and smell cool moss. I can see a whirligig beetle or a rock-worm nymph scurry and wriggle, or watch flies dance up from the waters when the temperature reaches the mid-fifties due to a winter Chinook, during what the white man sometimes calls "Indian summer." Trout leap and splash when the flies dance.

A heavily racked deer poked his face out of the edge of a South Dakota cornfield one day while I was walking a dry creek covered with pheasant tracks. Somehow, he knew that I was only pheasant-hunting. He stood there for some long moments and simply stared at me. Enraptured, I took in the surrounding scene with all my senses. A starling flock cackled, and the sound of changing fall blew down from a railroad embankment in the background to rustle drying corn with hanging ears, while my regal friend with his commanding horns surveyed me handsomely. I tend to see lots of big-racked bucks in the fall, no doubt because I always try to get "way back in there" when I pheasant-hunt—about the only hunting sport that I do anymore. In the Dakotas, there are thousands of acres that have been returned to their natural state through the Conservation Reserve Program. Pheasants, songbirds, and related wildlife abound. I hope that the government doesn't abandon this program that returns the land to Nature's Way.

Along with the bucks that I see annually, several arctic terns come back each spring. Returning to one of my favorite ponds, they dive-bomb schools of bullheads and rest for several weeks or often a month before going on toward the top of this planet. They are so streamlined and effortless in flight that it's easy to understand how they can cover such great distances in their travels.

Oh, and my good friend the turtle. We have known each other for quite some time now. He likes me because I helped him once when he was caught in some wire near his pond. He used to always sunbathe on a particular rock by a spot where the cows would come and drink. He had been missing from that rock for a while, so one day I stopped to look for him. Whether I was curious about him, or whether some spirit or force made me do it, I don't know. On two previous occasions I had been told by police officers in squad cars that I should quit stopping beside the pond because there wasn't enough room to get my car completely off the road and onto the shoulder. I stopped anyway on this one particular day, and I found Mr. Turtle trapped in some wire. I set him free and dumped the wire into my trash can.

To this day my friend is still there in the summers, even though the cows are now gone, displaced by houses. And though what I have to say about him is not very exciting, I just could not leave him out. My friend Turtle has not seemed to grow much for as long as I have known him, but otherwise he seems to have a healthy life. I enjoy the many bright colors I can see on his underside when I am up close to him. Just seeing him on his flat rock always gives me a special feeling. Indeed, we are *Mi-takuye Oyasin* (related).

SPIDER MARVEL

Even the smallest of creatures have much to teach us if we are willing to observe with care. The spider, for example, offers a lesson about divinity itself.

Those who follow Nature's Way believe that the Great Spirit manifests itself within and through all of that which it creates. Even a tiny spider building its web can be a manifestation if we have the sense to recognize such an example as an engineering and architectural marvel. What placed that ability to perform into such a tiny, seemingly insignificant creature? What about all the rest of the millions and billions of other insects, four-leggeds, finned ones, and flying ones? Most all species perform unique functions totally diverse from those of the other species, and *all* perform skills beyond the ability of humans. We certainly cannot spin a spider's web, nor can we endure the long ocean swims of the polar bear or take flight with the eagle.

If we thoroughly explore Nature, we can see that Creator obviously favors diversity. We creations are diverse as night and day, yet we are all related and interdependent because of the Mystery of the great unseen force that bestowed so many attributes, gifts, and powers within even the tiniest of creatures. Even within our own species, our minds, memories, and personal experiences make us diverse from each other.

THE BLESSING OF EAGLE

Of all my animal relations, however, it is Eagle who has taught me the most about learning through observation. As a former combat pilot who spent a great deal of time high up in the air, I am in tune with the influence of Eagle. Eagles have very keen eyesight, and even at great altitudes, they can choose to scan many square miles or zero in on the sudden twitch of tiny prey hundreds of feet below.

A pair of eagles hovered over my friends and me as we built a sweat lodge some years back. It was at a time when eagles usually were out hunting fish along the river, so we were surprised to see them at all. When we left the site to gather more saplings for the frame, they stayed, hovering even closer to the lodge in our absence. The manner in which they flew and the interest they seemed to display imparted to me a sense that they approved, that they felt we were doing a good act. Since then, that little lodge site—a small church place, if you will—has had some strong and rewarding ceremonies.

It is important to have an openness to the animals that share an endeavor or event with you, for they may have a message, even a blessing, for you. Sharing endeavors with an animal can produce enduring connections, as with that trout I visited repeatedly as a boy. Much can come back to us in spirit if we honor and respect an animal's presence.

Even in the more densely populated areas, one occasionally sees eagles, both bald and golden. The golden eagle (which looks, when it's on the ground in the distance, like a man walking) is now much more prevalent than when I was a youth. We used to see it only in remote Badlands ravines or in the Cheyenne River breaks. Having discovered the taste of pheasant, the bald eagle is also on the rise: it now frequents cornfields near the Missouri River and its tributaries, feeding primarily on dead birds. On more than one occasion I have surprised a feeding bald, which in turn set my heart to racing: the sight of a bald suddenly rising in front of one is startling.

They don't always avoid humans, though. These birds seem to have an almost spiritual sense for whether a human visitor intends to harm them or not. They rise and circle above to watch the person; and as long as he or she keeps on walking politely, they circle on back behind to resume feeding. Occasionally, they land on a telephone pole or tree, if one is nearby, to watch the visitor. A hawk or an owl will generally fly away when a person enters the scene, but not an eagle—providing it senses that it can trust the intruder.

The last thing in the world I would do is harm an eagle. I don't believe in superstitions, or at least I attempt to downplay them, but I have succumbed totally to one superstition: never harm an eagle! I don't want the kind of bad luck, misfortune, *pejuta shi-cha* (bad medicine) that allegedly can happen to one who ignores that warning.

THE EAGLE IN THE CHICKEN COOP

My father told many stories of the past. I now have the chance to pass down a story myself—one centering on an eagle. Growing out of my own observation and learning, it is not one of his, but it happens to demonstrate what a spiritually strong and wise person he was, though I rarely saw him enter the white man's church.

I was but a young boy when my father found a golden eagle starving to death in a coyote trap. Its leg was badly mangled. He fetched a blanket from the car so as to capture the big bird with the least harm to himself and it. The rescue was successful, but my father received a lifelong scar

on his forearm from the eagle's claws. We took the eagle home with us
and attempted to nurse it back to health in the chicken coop.

We had a big orange-colored rooster that was so mean he would
chase anything—even us kids. This rooster had never lost a fight and
wasn't afraid of people or dogs or any of the usual suspects.

The eagle sulked in the chicken coop, looking out at us, and at a
changing audience that included the rooster, through an iron gate that
covered the opening. We used a smaller hole beneath the gate to pass
jackrabbits through, but the eagle would not eat them. Ordinarily chickens would pass through this opening, although now they stayed away
from the chicken coop because of the eagle.

My father was worried about the eagle losing its strength, confined
in that small space. Maybe the big rooster had similar thoughts, because
one day he went jauntily through the opening. I guess he must have
thought that he could whip the eagle, since in his experience he could
conquer just about anything he came across. Some people, even some
countries, are like that, making ill-advised decisions to go off and fight a
force much larger than themselves.

Ill-advised doesn't begin to describe that rooster's cocky intrusion. All
of a sudden there was nothing but orange feathers in the chicken coop.
The eagle had swooped down on that rooster so fast he probably did not
know what hit him. The big golden eagle ate the rooster, leaving only his
head, his feet, and a pile of orange feathers. From then on the golden devoured our rabbit offerings with relish. He became so healthy and strong
that the Hill City zoo offered one hundred dollars to my father.

This was a large sum of money in those days. Most people, especially poor people like we were, would have taken the offer, but not my
father. We were poor, but we had dignity and a spiritual respect. My father took the eagle back to the Badlands and released it. *Freedom!* The
eagle circled high above my father before it flew toward some distant
buttes. Over the next months and years my dad would occasionally go
back to that place and hold up his big cowboy hat, waving it at the

buttes. Often the eagle would see him and fly toward our place, circling over my dad in greeting.

My father was proud of his scar and of the fact that money could not buy the eagle. The eagle's acknowledgment of my father was an indication to us that the spirit forces of the world were pleased that we had set the eagle free and had not succumbed to the material goods we could have bought by selling it.

This story of my father fairly well illustrates why I had a great respect for him. He taught me to honor Eagle and ourselves by not compromising, for any material reason, the time-honored sacred relationship humans have with Eagle and other fellow creatures; and to nurture a spiritual regard for the freedom of that most majestic of Mother Earth's creatures. I also observed that my dad lived a healthy life all the way up into his seventies and enjoyed life right up to the end, when he finally succumbed to a sudden and swift heart attack. (Not a bad way to go!)

TOOLS OF OBSERVATION

Observation of Nature is a key first step on the path I call Nature's Way. Although nothing can replace our own five senses, in these modern times we have a powerful tool for observing Nature—science. Maybe with all the new discoveries in communication and electronics, including the Hubble Space Telescope, we can finally break free from the foolish superstitions that have besieged us down through the centuries.

Another valuable resource in observing Nature is all the knowledgeable elders who have come before us—those who knew a deep respect for Nature and who bore few superstitions. These elders' words and experiences live on, thanks to the written word and modern technology. Their beseeching ceremonies (rituals asking for help and guidance from the Spirit World) are additional great teachings for those seeking to move ahead on Nature's Way—a path that is no doubt as old as planetary man and woman when they first began to communicate and observe the vastness surrounding them. Direct observation backed up by modern science and elders who observed and learned from Nature is a strong combination for a truthful spirituality.

WHAT DO WE LEARN?

We northern Indians say that Creator is benevolent. We have far less fear of our Creator, it seems, than do people of other faiths. When I observe the simple towering rose bush that grows in my front yard, this flowering plant speaks to me: it tells me that Creator appreciates the kind, delightful beauty that I see presented to me on long summer days. The world is covered with radiant, pleasing flowers. And guess who designed them?

Creator also causes my blood to clot when I cut myself. And when badly injured, I faint, as most people do, becoming temporarily removed from the excruciating pain. How kind Creator must be to arrange our bodies to be able to comfort us in this way. Yes, we have to have the pain to warn us and to keep us from overdoing it while we heal, but we are given relief when the pain is most acute. I observe such things and realize that Creator has a "tough love" form of kindness.

Even death, which we may view as a personally sad event, can be seen as compassionate and caring to us and the Earth, if we achieve Eagle's distance and observe from the perspective of bodies beyond our own and times beyond our life span. If we didn't have death, we would have no room left on this earth for others. It would be so crowded that we would no doubt wonder, "Where have all the flowers gone?" Each succeeding generation would not have as much of Earth's bounty to enjoy if no one ever passed on.

I could go on and on with examples to prove from observation that Creator is truly benevolent. The benevolence that I see all around me gives me a tremendous amount of confidence and helps me enjoy my time on Earth. Just as a child who respects kind and considerate parents and doesn't live in fear is eager for life's adventures, I feel free to explore unknown areas and habitats of this benevolent sphere. My sense of wellbeing also keeps me from fearing any Spirit World that may lie beyond.

A sense of wellbeing and confidence is contagious. If people are confident and believe that their Higher Force is indeed kind and considerate, they become more pleasant to live with, and hence those who surround them can experience a higher harmony. Life then becomes more fruitful. And it all begins with direct observation.

In summary, observing all of Creation from the perspective of Eagle is a never-ending source of the wisdom and knowledge of Creator and bountiful Mother Earth. Such has been the practice down through time by many indigenous peoples not bound by dogmatic human rules. As we learn more about Mystery and the lessons of truth in Nature, we become more sensitive to distortions and falsehoods and less willing to put up with them. As we observe, we learn of the diversity and commonality among Creation's designs, acknowledging the sacred gifts and reflections of the ultimate Designer. Each creation can teach us of Creator and make a deep impression on us, if we but observe it with the sacred eyes of Eagle, who teaches us to acknowledge with grateful hearts the sacred gifts of Creator and Mother Earth.

The next chapter explores the lesson of Bear, who has much to teach us about healing. Bear medicine uses gifts of the Earth and the philosophy and wisdom of Nature's Way to heal both body and spirit.

FIND AND PRESERVE THE MEDICINE

Lesson of Bear

Though shrinking in numbers and endangered in some areas, Bear is a symbol of power in cultures the world over, and a strong totem for those who seek Earth's medicines and healing powers. Bear's claws dig into Mother Earth for her healing herbs and roots. Bears seem to notice herbs that other animals don't pay attention to, and dig these for their own use.[1]

In fact, a bear's natural senses are specially evolved to allow it to find and survive on both plants and animals, including nuts, berries, fungi, insects, and small animals. Researchers think that bears may have color vision, as humans do, which helps them find food in the undergrowth, and bears' eyes mirror the moonlight, giving good night vision. It is believed that bears have better hearing than humans, perhaps in the ultrasonic range, and a much better sense of smell (seven times greater than that of a bloodhound), the latter due to an expanse of nasal membrane that is 100 times larger than that of humans. Like snakes, bears can also detect intimate environmental information through the chemically sensitive Jacobson's organ on the roof of the mouth.[2]

To the Sioux, Bear has always been the "chief" of the animals when it comes to herbal medicine. Black Elk gave Bear the credit for his powers to cure with at least two hundred herbs. Bears tend to prefer acorns, Juneberries, and cherries, which are three natural elements often compounded when making medicine. Despite those preferences, bears seem willing to eat *all* herbs. Because of that healing diet, Bear is considered by the Sioux to be almost invulnerable, a strength much admired and desired by warriors through the centuries.[3]

Through prayer and song, the early Sioux gained Bear-like knowledge and discernment to "tune in to" and gather leaves, stems, fruits, and roots when those things were at their peak strength and could most potently impart their healing gifts. When Sioux medicine people performed a healing ceremony, they would often drum and move in a circular fashion to show that they were in tune and in harmony with the natural forces. They believed that being in tune with Nature was the greatest preventive medicine for both a healthy mind and a strong, resilient body.

Today the modern Sioux use both reliable medicine people and the Public Health Service, because they recognize that both ancient and modern wisdom have their place. The development of the healing arts continues today in part because of the groundwork of ancient healers, but also because of new medicines discovered.

EARTH'S DWINDLING HERBAL AND SPIRITUAL MEDICINES

Many medicinal plants have been discovered by Human, and there are untold more yet to be discovered throughout the world. Unfortunately, we are losing many such plants—both those we know to have medicinal value and others whose properties we do not yet know. In the tropical rain forests, for example, we are losing hundreds of plant species as the forests are being cut down. There are too few of us doing something to help preserve these disappearing medicinal gifts from Mother Earth. It is Earth's biodiversity that ensures that Human continues to have the many products essential for daily life, such as food, fuel, fibers, and medicine.

In the United States almost 25 percent of the drugs currently in use come from plants. According to the World Resources Institute, "Of the top 150 prescription drugs in the United States, 118 were originally derived from plants, fungi, and other species."[4] Plant-based anti-cancer drugs provide both an economic boon ($250 billion in economic value annually in the U.S.) and a promise of new life. One such drug is Taxol, which is commonly prescribed for the 24,000 women who are diagnosed with advanced ovarian cancer each year. Taxol is derived from the Pacific yew, a species that grows in the old-growth forests of the Pacific Northwest and that was considered, before the discovery of its health benefits, to be a worthless weed tree. Those who are recovering from transplant surgery find benefit from the gift of an obscure Norwegian fungus that produces cyclosporin, an important suppressor of the body's immune response.[5] In the interior scrublands of Florida, on a small protected area of only 300 acres, a rare herb once considered worthless was discovered to have health benefits. Now that herb, Lake Placid mint, is used as a potent antifungal compound and as an ant repellent. The rosy periwinkle flower found in Madagascar has been successfully used to treat several forms of cancer, including Hodgkin's disease and childhood leukemia. And a recently discovered vine in Africa may be a key to treating those who are suffering with AIDS.[6]

Yet the overwhelming majority of plants, fungi, and microorganisms have not yet been investigated—nor will they ever be, if current trends continue. Of the 250,000 known species of plants, only 5 percent have been analyzed for their medicinal properties.[7] Who knows what cures are awaiting discovery in the remaining 95 percent? Potential new antibiotics like penicillin, cures like quinine, all-purpose medicines like aspirin, and powerful painkilling drugs like morphine could be found in as-yet-undiscovered plants—but not if those plants become extinct. The World Resources Institute reports that every time we lose a species—and we are losing a lot—we lose an option for the future; we lose a potential cure for AIDS or a virus-resistant crop.[8]

We are also losing the spiritual medicine taught in Nature's Way: to seek the truth and be truthful; to carry a positive attitude; to have and show an appreciation of Creator's gifts; to acknowledge and maintain a relationship to the spirits of the Spirit World; and to develop humor. We must find and preserve those healing tenets. Bear medicine teaches us to find, take, and preserve the medicine that Earth provides—whether that be herbs and modern-day drugs or Nature's wisdom. We may have to dig with "claws" to find spiritual medicine that has been neglected in our way of life or been buried in history, but find it we must—and then we must preserve it to restore harmony with Mother Earth.

MEDICINE AS A LIFESTYLE

The old-time North American Indians were quite healthy. Queen Victoria commented on their robustness back in 1877 upon meeting a contingent of Lakota Sioux brought by Buffalo Bill Cody: "I am sixty-seven years old. All over the world I have seen all kinds of people; but today I have seen the best-looking people I know."[9] Their good health is no mystery, of course. They took healing medicines directly from their environment. They enjoyed endless miles of freedom. They did not pollute their environment or subvert Nature's Way for their own greediness. They did not have taxes, traffic problems, pollution, congestion, drug problems, or alcohol abuse. The North American Indians knew how to appreciate what Creator provided. They cultivated the medicine of humor and were relaxed with close family members and with tribal ties. They did not clutter or impede themselves with untruthful behavior toward one another. This congenial ecology (both human and environmental) was powerful medicine and added to their good health and longevity.

In today's world, we tend to think of "medicine" as an herb or pill we ingest when we are ill. To the early Native Americans, "medicine" meant the ingestion or application of a healing herb, but it also encompassed all attempts to bring healing balance to what was out of sync in their bodies, minds, and spirits. From that perspective, the deepest effect of plant medicines is sometimes not the particular physical or chemical effect on the body but the spiritual openness it enhances. In other words, an herb can do more than what is apparent.

Likewise, medicine can be different for different people, though their symptoms are the same, because each person is unique. Sometimes, though, one medicine may be appropriate for an entire tribe. That medicine might be information, insight, or guidance from dreams or from experiences in Nature, attained through communication with the Spirit World by each individual or through a holy person.

Sometimes medicine is a process, or a struggle, or a test to stretch and grow in spirit. Sometimes medicine is simply speaking and/or hearing truth. It is always a teaching in harmony with Creator and Mother Earth, with experiences often told in stories and passed down by the holy ones and leaders.

Organized religion, in contrast, purports to offer good medicine, but it exacts a huge toll, both individually and collectively. I believe that organized religion set the computer back a good millennium! The suppression of science by the Christian Church in medieval times is one of the most serious offenses that has occurred against humanity. Because of the suppression of the advancement of scientific knowledge, certain critical inventions were most certainly delayed. Cases such as Galileo being convicted of heresy and imprisoned by Church leaders for daring to suggest that the Earth revolved around the Sun instead of vice versa were, unfortunately, not rare.

Humanity paid other horrible prices for medieval organized religion, including the torture and death of millions of women based on falsified devil association, as well as the expulsion of Jews and other ethnic groups based on religious dissimilarity. The Spanish Inquisition, which targeted first non-Christians and then later, during the rise of Protestantism, non-Catholics, is only the most infamous and dramatic attempt on the part of a religious majority to rid a region of infidels. The stifling and distortion of truth and the massive dispersion of lies during the Inquisition (and similar purges) promoted disharmony and deep divisiveness, resulted in grossly painful and inhumane acts, and stamped fear into the DNA of every European—especially the women.

People who get religiously carried away and commit unnatural and inhumane acts are not limited to the lunacy of the Middle Ages, unfortunately. In Afghanistan at the recent turn of the millennium, the Taliban rigidly enforced incredible religious rules via their religious "police," publicly beating and even stoning some women to death over the slightest supposed "Koranic" infraction. The Jim Jones sect that drank poison in Guyana in a mass suicide in 1978 was likewise "unnatural"— not in harmony with Nature—as were the "Hale-Bopp comet suicides" by another recent group of religious extremists.

RECOGNIZING TRUE MEDICINE BY ITS EFFECTS

Each of us needs to take great care not to fall in with a misdirected group. We need to guard against the herd instinct that seems to increase as we grow in numbers and proximity. Humans are individual and must work to remain so. Bear teaches us to discern the medicine we find by using all of our bodily senses to tune in to the truth, to search through the underbrush of confusion and lies for the kernel of authenticity, especially when others attempt to keep us in the dark. We must ask, Is this group or teaching "natural" or "unnatural"? That is, is it in harmony with what can be observed in Nature? Is it appreciative of Spirit's gifts? Does it seek the truth and value truthfulness, or does it claim to have the answers already?

Obsessing on only one way or one truth is neither observant of Nature's Way nor appreciative of Spirit's gifts or truth-seeking. Such narrow obsession can ultimately turn on a person like a hungry bear. For instance, if some group's course spells out an "unnatural" ending, interested seekers should back away. That group is hungry, and its followers will become prey. Bear wisdom encourages us to look for the truth, even if that search reveals our own ego's false need to obsess on one single truth. We must look continuously for truth, for medicine that appreciates and honors the life that Creator has given.

REVEALING SUPPRESSED TRUTH

Many readers have undoubtedly seen, over the past few years, a news photo of Kathleen Soliah, a former member of the Symbionese Liberation Army (SLA), a group that in the 1970s engaged in various terrorist acts, including the attempted murder of police officers in California. Kathleen Soliah disappeared into society before she could be prosecuted for her involvement with the SLA, changing her name to Sara Jane Olson, turning responsible wife and mother, and becoming an active member of the local St. Paul, Minnesota, community. She is now imprisoned for crimes she committed with the SLA several decades prior.[10] In one photo I saw, she was at trial with three of her former alleged accomplices (all of them in orange prison garb). It is a stunning picture. To me it is a warning to our future-bound youth and should be captioned, "Be Careful Whom You Pick as Friends."

But Sara Jane Olson has had many supporters. "What is to be gained by exposing her past?" some pious peacemakers have asked. "Let bygones be bygones! Hasn't she showed that she's a good human being and a productive member of society? What good can come from tarnishing her good character? Isn't it better to forgive and forget?" Like Bear seeking healing herbs, though, we need to look for the medicine of truth. Hiding real history or ignoring historical facts is negative in relationship to harmonic progression. Distorting history is an insult to the human race. There is nothing "wrong" or "sinister" about stating truthful facts about organizations, modes of thinking, mythologies, or painful happenings caused by certain religious beliefs and dogma. What's wrong is that some people are incensed when such facts are brought to light, even when done so for the purpose of learning and encouragement.

Creator allowed us a perceptive memory. Suppressing information of actual happenings is an unnatural act; it is creating a dishonest account of history, which is contrary to the consistency of real truth. What we can learn from the past should never be obscured or obliterated, no matter how painful or negative. On the contrary, we need to do all we can to dig up and discover the authentic past and learn the truth. We need to recognize when we as individuals or groups do not own up to our past actions or otherwise cover, hide, or lie about ourselves and our behavior, so that we can live more in harmony with truth.

DEDICATION TO TRUTH

The Sioux knew the importance of a dedication to truth and passed on everything that they learned from historical experience—both positive and negative. The truth was preserved in a sacred way through pictographs, songs, and stories. It is through those words and pictures—especially of times of struggle: war, illness, and starvation—that later generations could know and learn medicine from the past. The tribe, as witness and bearer of the truth, would never knowingly harbor untruth or act as a group from the basis of falsehood or disharmony. One of the greatest crimes, among the Sioux, was to lie in front of one's tribe and the Great Spirit.

Bear medicine encourages all upon the planet to discern and expose false ego and false superiority, which persuade some people that they can cover up or distort the truth because they are "better," "wiser," "more intellectually blessed," or "more important" than the rest of the world's citizens. From the political shenanigans of Watergate to the Holocaust, from tribal eliminations in Europe and Africa to Al-Qaida and modern terrorism, we have witnessed and continue to deal with the negative effects of global actions based on the lies of false ego and false superiority.

The worst of all of these human ideas is the one that states that a single people (tribe) was chosen by God to lead all others, subdue all others, save all others, and kill reluctant others if need be. That practice has been ongoing for the last several thousand years and continues in the politics of the war on terrorism. Where has it gotten the human race as a whole? In a whole heap of trouble!

A WORLD OF VICTIMS

False ego and false superiority have turned a large portion of the human race into victims. Suffering at the hands of egocentric wrongdoers—controlling individuals, insulated corporations, corrupt politicians, agents of war, and other purveyors of human disaster—victims of false superiority seek truth and justice but more often than not cannot find it. They go to their graves disappointed, often in agony for being falsely persecuted.

I believe that victims of untruth will clamor to set the record straight even after their death—and will finally be able to abolish falsehood in the Spirit World. I firmly believe that all truth and true justice will prevail in the Beyond. Why do I state this? Because I "wish" it so? Definitely not! Rather, because I have observed the disharmonious consequences that result from untruthfulness and injustice in this life. Falsehood and deceit inevitably violate the harmony of Nature's Way, inspiring in those humans who recognize the violation a deep passion for real truth and justice.

Nature herself is supremely honest, and that should be indication enough of what prevails in the Beyond. It is honest because the four-legged, winged, and finned ones fulfill their true natures in innocence, as Creator designed them. For instance, if an animal is going to attack, it is honest about that intent, showing all the appropriate signs and signals. It does not pretend to befriend its foe, then attack. Likewise, a female that is in season engages in behaviors that make it clear her intentions toward the male of her species.

Animal motivation is as straightforward as animal behavior: an animal does not attack another based on false accusations or hearsay or prejudice or select a mate based on false promises. Nature is humble; it does not try to be anything other than what Creator created. It does not wrongfully persecute victims or foster lies to get ahead or to grab more than what it needs. If a mountain lion encroaches on another's territory, the truth is that it is after food it needs; it is not invading based on historical lies, unjust sentiments, or greed.

PRESERVING NATURE: THE SOURCE OF MEDICINE

Native people were able to trust the assumption that Nature was indeed honest and would dispense only true, unadulterated justice should the need arise. One thing Nature was adamant about was that she desired to be preserved. The Indians therefore endeavored to work with Nature, and they managed to preserve it.

For example, buffalo were a staple for many tribes of North American Indians. They were honored as sacred, and all pieces of the animal had a use. Nothing was thrown away—not even the tail, which was used as a fly brush or whip (among other things), or the bladder, which was used as a water pouch. Failing to use all of the animal was a violation of the gift of that creature's life; and if you wasted it, Creator might not send you another.

Because of this respect, buffalo were not disrespected or greedily overhunted, despite herds of at least 40 million. It was not until they were overhunted and dishonorably wasted by the white man in the 1800s that they were almost brought to extinction. When the railroad went through (and trains were sometimes delayed a whole day or more while buffalo crossed the track), white men began advertising killing buffalo for sport. White men with guns would simply shoot from the train until all the buffalo were dead. Other white men relentlessly hunted down the animals wherever they roamed on the plains, often killing just for the skins or the tongues. In fact, sometimes they killed them and left them to rot intact.

Nature's law demands that we protect her abundance, that no creature be disrespected through greedy overhunting and waste. The penalty for violating that law is great harm or loss. Heeding that law, North American Indians managed the forests of the upper Midwest through periodic and partial burnings, preserving the continuity of ample areas of thick underbrush vital to the sustenance of many animals. Without thick underbrush those animals would have died or moved on, and with them the larger animals that preyed upon them, both of which provided food and sustenance for the Indians themselves.

Nature's law calls us to understand and protect relationships in the web of life, supporting and preserving the harmony within each ecosystem. The Indians recognized the importance of the web, heard Nature's plea for protection, and worked to preserve the environment that Creator had given them.

It is not always easy to hear Nature's message to us. Studying and preserving the spiritual teachings of Nature require focus. The leaders of organized religions definitely are not students of Nature. They are too busy studying the philosophy and politics of today's Dominant Society. The materialistic and television-famous religious parrots of that society are not spiritual or environmental leaders. They *cannot* be, because they fail to bring the medicine of true harmony and justice to us and to the Earth. Indeed, many of their teachings contradict harmony. These religionists do not and will never have the power to bring the sort of world harmony Mother Earth once knew, and that Native Americans experienced on this continent. And until these so-called leaders spend time immersed in Nature, their message will not change.

But leaders of organized religion are not alone: few Westerners in today's world are students of Nature; few hear, and fewer still heed, her law. When people amass great wealth, as the majority of Americans have (when measured against global standards), possessions dominate their focus. In the old days people were so immersed in Mother Nature that a goodly portion of their focus on her teaching was all but automatic. Unfortunately, modern society is geared toward urban living, placing most of Mother Earth off limits when it comes to earning a living. Very few people can make a living from hunting or fishing. In the old, old days, centuries ago, open Nature surrounded a hunter. Not one single fence had to be crossed. A hunter abided daily in natural freedom that a businessperson might now taste but briefly on a four-day fishing trip. The hunter-gatherer-fisher not only was immersed solidly in Nature's fold but was totally dependent on her on a first-line, direct basis. That situation placed early humanity in a much closer perspective to all that she has to teach.

ACCESSING THE MEDICINE OF NATURE

An important lesson of Bear is that medicine is found in Nature. As we have seen, that medicine consists of more than just the herbs themselves. A natural environment is itself a great medicine because of all it has to teach us.

Unfortunately, the time most of us are able to spend within the confines of Nature's jurisdiction today is severely limited. Though we may feel the lure of a few fish or of big game during hunting season, more and more access to Nature is controlled by the wealthy, who erect barriers to keep the rest of the world from infringing on their newfound possessions. Nature's solace, so inherently common to Indians, even in recent centuries, is becoming something only the rich can afford. We are trapped in a vicious cycle. Those few who have time, money, and access to enjoy Nature are too materialistic to penetrate deeply into her spiritual teachings, while the majority of the world, especially the youth, are deprived of their inherent right to access Mother Earth's teachings for themselves. Neglect perpetuates neglect.

"So what is the answer? What is the cure?" we desperately ask. We seek medicine. We seek the teachings of Creator and Mother Earth. We seek ways to live in harmony with what Creator has provided.

I received a teaching from a Sioux holy man named Bill Eagle Feather that addresses the human quest. The experience he and I shared contained rich medicine for Nature's Way and helped form my understanding of life, death, and the Spirit World.

THE TEEPEE IN THE WATER

Once I sat beside a bay with Chief Eagle Feather. A teepee was behind us, and we saw its reflection in the water in front of us. That evening he would conduct several Sweat Lodge ceremonies for a workshop of Hunkpapa Sioux anxious for the old way to come back. We had just built the lodge and were taking a few minutes of well-earned rest.

Chief Eagle Feather pointed to the water and exclaimed, "Nephew, now there is a teaching." This was his customary way of beginning something that he felt was important for a person to know. "That teepee reflecting in the water, it is telling us something the Almighty wants us to know." He pointed back at the tall canvas structure supported by lodge poles and then pointed out to the water. The reflected teepee stood out clearly in the Missouri River backwater before us. "If you go dive into that water, Nephew, you will not find that teepee." He would always start out with something that was, like that statement, basically simple and obvious. "If you walk over there and look in the water, you will see yourself." He paused and asked, "Now what does that tell you, Nephew?" Knowing that I didn't know the answer, he continued.

"That teepee in the water tells us first that there is a world beyond. Some say the Spirit World. Next, it tells us that we have a home in the Spirit World. But if you want to jump in the water now, you will not find it." He stood up and motioned for me to follow to the water's edge. When we looked down in the water, we saw both our reflections.

He pointed at my shadow, now long as the sun pursued its downward trail to the west. "Ho *wana* [Now], what is that?"

"My shadow," I answered.

"Oh huh," he grunted. "When you die, you will no longer have a shadow. Your shadow will then go into the teepee's reflection through the teepee's door, and you will have found your home!"

I followed him back to the teepee and we sat down in front of it. "All these things are simple, Nephew, yet they are way beyond the *wah shi chu*." (He used the Lakota Sioux term for "white men," but that term can easily be understood as "Dominant Society," from his perspective.) He paused and looked around sourly. "Creator did not need to make reflections or shadows, for they seem to be of no use for us." His look brightened. "You will come to learn that every little thing the Creator makes, no matter how unimportant it seems, has a teaching. Some have powerful teachings, like I just told you."

A pair of horses in a corral beside an old abandoned missionary church nickered above us. As we looked toward them he added, "That church up there could never convince the Indians there was a Beyond Life for all of us." After a moment he added, "Not like our own way can do it!"

He had given me a lot to think about. I turned to him with a question. "So when I die, Uncle—my shadow will go into the teepee door and I will be in the Spirit World?"

"Oh huh," he echoed with a brief laugh. "That won't be for a while yet. When you look at some of our peace-pipe bundles you will see the two teepees on them. The teepees have doors. One is for when we come into this world. The other is for when we go into the Spirit World. One reflecting the other. A holy man gets you ready for the Spirit World. At least he lets you know that there is one because he believes that." He grunted harshly. "Some damn fools think no such thing exists."

I remembered many Sioux peace-pipe bags that bore that same symbol, even though artists had severely altered the various designs through beading or drawing. "Artistic license," I thought. Yet there was a commonality. The pair of teepees on the medicine bundles were always opposite. One reflecting the other.

"A life here: the teepee behind us represents our home. Life beyond: the reflection in the water tells us we have a home beyond and someday we will all go there," I offered.

Chief Eagle Feather seemed pleased with my reply. He smiled broadly before speaking with authority. "You are learning, Nephew. Tomorrow night we will do a *Yuwipi* [a ceremony described in Chapter Six]. After the *Inipi* [Sweat Lodge, described in Chapter Five] tonight and the Yuwipi, you'll be pretty well convinced there is a Spirit World!"

STRENGTHENING CONSCIENCE

Living life with an awareness of consequences both here and in the Spirit World—that is, seeing both the teepee and its reflection—is one of the greatest of all medicines. People sometimes refer to that awareness as conscience.

Eagle Feather suggested that the path from one teepee to another—that path we call *life*—is just a part of experience. What goes on in either teepee is a mystery. If our journey continues into the Spirit World, it seems highly probable to me that the earthly process of seeking and finding justice is reflected and will carry over into the next realm. If we are allowed to take with us our memories, we will be free forever in the Spirit World to chastise all who wronged us; and conversely, we will be chastised by those whom we have wronged. Traditional Indians—those who believed in the old ways—feared no divine judgment. They lived with only the certainty that they would leave their body behind at death and be left with their memories.

This concept explains why the old-time Indians had a much more serious view of their conduct while upon this earth. When people believe that they will have to answer throughout eternity for serious wrongs, they are far less prone to commit such wrongs upon innocent others while they are in this world.

The old-time Indians definitely believed that a Spirit World exists. In addition to evidence of it in Nature, they saw signs of it and contacted it through their ceremonies. The white man's ceremonies, from my experience, frankly do not have this form of power.

CEREMONY AS MEDICINE

Our highest reverence is for the Great Spirit, the Creator, but we also realize it is Nature that Creator placed here for us "in order that we may live." Therefore we hold many ceremonies out in Nature and upon Mother Earth to communicate with Mother Earth and all her Forces and to be closest to what Creator has created as we beseech to the Higher Powers it has made for us, and, of course, always, we include the Creator, Wakan Tanka (Great Mystery, Great Spirit, among many respectful and acknowledging terms). When we surround ourselves with nature as in Sweat Lodge and Sun Dance, the more natural, God-created harmony we feel within as we beseech. These ceremonies, touching both the spirit of Nature and the spirit of Human, are medicine, bringing healing to individuals and communities.

White man, on the other hand, sets aside holy spaces, usually indoors, for ceremonies. Blinded by lack of knowledge, perception, and experience of Nature, white man cannot touch the Spirit World. Therefore the white man's ceremonies lack the healing power of medicine. Separated from Nature by a vast chasm, followers of Dominant Society make light of whatever harm they do here on this planet. They do what they will and then move on by merely asking for forgiveness. This fairytale marketing is quite effective, I admit, but many who rely on forgiveness may be in for a big surprise if the truthful elements of Nature hold true in the Spirit World.

Peter Catches, a Sioux holy man, once journeyed down into the Spirit World in a Sun Dance vision. "Drunks were there," he said. "They were reaching out for a dancing bottle before them. Women who had abandoned their children were wailing. The lonely cries of their children could be heard." It would seem that these spirits, who had cared little for their offspring when they had the chance, are now with their own kind; and their dwelling does not seem a particularly refreshing place to be.

"Go back and tell them what we suffer," he was instructed by the tormented spirits.

All you Ku Klux Klan members, hate groups, child molesters, and women beaters, go way over there! All of you religious fanatics, you whose egos told you that you knew everything yet who did not observe what was in front of you, go over there! All you harmful ones who had many victims: those whom you made suffer, they are waiting for you over there, because they have not forgotten their suffering. Your so-called forgiveness cannot erase that!

Forgiveness—that is the medicine that white man tries to offer through his ceremonies. But the forgiveness that some religions offer has no long-lasting benefits. It may make the wrongdoer feel better for a while, but it does not change the consequences of bad behavior. Even if the wrongdoer forgets, the victim cannot. Look at nature: even the animals have memory. Ever seen a mistreated dog? Ever seen one that had much love and affection? The two sorts of dogs react differently, do they not?

While victims may not forget, they must move on. It is good medicine to maintain a positive attitude. We must not let those who have harmed us cloud our worthy pursuits and interests. I will continue to return to my beloved trout stream and pheasant field with happy thoughts as long as my body is willing and my loyal four-legged companion, Rex Dog, stays with me.

Though we may not take comfort in forgiveness, we can live more fulfilling lives here and in the Beyond by avoiding the need for forgiveness. We are advancing in the direction of the great entity that is our Creator when we attempt to probe, investigate, ponder, wonder, and learn from Creation. Going out and exploring Nature has a much healthier ring for me than sitting in a church singing, "Praise you, Lord. Praise be to you, God. Hosanna in the highest." I thank the Great Spirit for allowing me to observe, but I have to get out into this vast world and do the observing.

SHAPING OUR "DISK OF LIFE"

This exploration gives us healing medicine, but it is part of a much higher quest. I have made a personal discovery that affects me daily: I believe that we shape and form ourselves every day of our lives, and that this freedom of action or inaction develops, molds, and actually creates our spiritual entity—our individual spirit or what some refer to as the soul. Yes, what we do today, what we did in the past, and what we will do in the future creates, reshapes, and reshifts our spirit. And that process does not end with our last breath. We will carry on our self-creation once we enter the Spirit World.

Inside us, within this unique spirit (soul) that each and every one of us has been given, within this creation to which we contribute, lies our character, our record, our background, our reputation, our knowledge, and the mysterious spirit that Dominant Society refers to as one's "soul" and Native Americans refer to as one's "spirit." As we move through life, it becomes far more than just a memory bank of observation. It builds and changes with the various virtues and vices and lessons we encounter as growing adults.

I call that soul/spirit the "Disk of Life," because I believe that this term makes it easier to identify and understand the internal process of ongoing change, development, and self-creation. Just as we would alter a computer disk, we expand, alter, and transform our own Disk of Life, our circle of growing knowledge and related experience.

What I add to my Disk of Life is very individual, because every one of us has different experiences and hence different observations. We react with other members of our society, and sometimes we react similarly, but nonetheless we react as distinct individuals due to separate influences. Even two people who profess the same philosophy, have the same interests, develop the same tastes, and share the same backgrounds end up having different life experiences, and these enter and transform their Disks of Life. These experiences and observations affect their thought processes, opinions, suppositions, questions, conclusions, theories, prejudices, stereotypes, ideas, and, yes, even spirituality or religion. As a result, these two individuals, so similar in so many ways, shift out of agreement with each other in reference to some major or obscure point of life.

Because of the uniqueness of each individual Disk of Life, I tend to question what learned men tell me and am uncomfortable with just accepting teachings with an attitude of "blind faith." What works for them may not work for me. Bear supports this attitude, teaching us to do a little digging beneath the surface, a little scrounging through the under-cover of what we are told, so that we can find the food and medicine we need. Teachers who are wise do not mind such scrounging; they welcome a questioning attitude rather than condemning searchers for their independent investigation.

If I thought I could receive a more powerful contact in another religion, I would certainly change. But I have experienced far too much response in Nature's Way for me to ever change now. Considering the many close calls I have had, the close brushes with death I have experienced, I believe that some powerful contact in that Spirit World has definitely responded to my beseechments and prayers!

NEAR-DEATH EXPERIENCES AS MEDICINE

Death is an essential part of Nature. I believe that I have used up my initial nine lives and am somewhere into the next nine. Each time I have come close to death, the experience has left quite a memory. Bill Eagle Feather would say it was a teaching. Among my flying experiences, I have crashed a huge Phantom jet on the end of a runway, landed a jet among waiting fire trucks with both main tires blown, crashed a helicopter at night, and lost an engine, resulting in an open-field landing, besides experiencing anti-aircraft fire and SAM missiles in Vietnam combat. A few blizzards almost got me. (A person has some fairly serious thoughts when wandering through a whiteout.) I have even been shot a few times.

Fear of death when crashing in an airplane is different from blizzard-death fear. In a crashing airplane, everything happens so fast that all a person can think about is trying to keep some semblance of control. I have been involved in several crashes, and I *concentrated*; that's about all I *could* do. Being lost in a blizzard (on the ground or in the air) is different—it's a long, steady, fearful experience, regardless of how long it takes to be rescued or find a way out.

I hate to admit it, but I have had a bad blizzard close call as a hunter—and a really stupid one at that! I didn't have a compass, a lighter, or a pack of matches with me. That's sheer stupidity! A close death in a blizzard is far worse, in my opinion, than a close death by crashing, because I had plenty of time to think about my stupidity and its ramifications. I thought about my kids and other loved ones, and I felt pretty bad that they were probably going to miss me.

On one of my close calls I foolishly went out alone in bad weather to pheasant-hunt. I was fine for a while but then lost my way, wandering lost in the blizzard for over an hour. I was fortunate that my dog got me out. That was a close one! It brought me right up to the Door, and I had to do some serious reflecting. I faced death with a "Well, this is it" attitude. At first panic set in, and for a few moments I succumbed to it, but then I got a grip. There I was, lost as can be, and the snow was swirling down; everything was white. Whenever I turned into the wind, I couldn't see a thing. I was starting to get cold, and it was only a couple of hours before nightfall, when the temperature would plummet. All I could do was try to use my resources, lighten up any unnecessary weight, and then face whatever happened. In my case, to conserve energy I threw away a pheasant, a wet glove, and all of my spare shells except those that were in the Benelli shotgun. I kept the gun, thinking that maybe I could signal for help with it. It had a sling, which made it easy to carry, allowing me to keep my cold bare hand in a jacket pocket.

I was starting to get chilled and everything was white. I paused in a shelterbelt (a line of trees and undergrowth) and made some promises to Creator and the Six Powers. As I stood quietly, something said, "Follow your tracks." It wasn't spoken; the words just came into my mind. I don't want to give the impression that God was speaking directly to me, yet this thought wasn't of my own making—at least it did not seem to be. Maybe it was. Who knows?

Anyway, I proceeded to follow my tracks, which had led me into a freezing slough. My golden retriever picked up on my plan and went out ahead, backtracking in front of me. Occasionally he would come back and roll playfully nearby. Maybe he was telling me that he still had strong energy and that I should not give in to fear. The snow was really coming down by this point, and it was hard to see. I kept my head down and followed the dog's fresh tracks. Slogging along in that way for what felt like hours, we got out safely. My advice? Never, *never* hunt without a compass and adequate matches and lighters, and start backtracking immediately if you find yourself in bad snow. I bought a reliable compass the next day and now follow my own advice.

Had I had matches or a lighter with me that day, I would have built a large fire in a depression in the shelterbelt and waited out the night. Without that alternative, the cold was penetrating. I had already started getting serious shivers from the swirling wet snow when I left my future up to my dog (and the spirits). I was cold enough that I began to contemplate what it would be like to die, and what it would be like for those I left behind. It was the severance of relationships that seemed to bring my most unhappy thoughts. When I finally made it back to my car and sat in it, warming up, I got the shakes—not from fear but from the wet cold I had spent too long in.

I have also had a number of near-death experiences that were just quick scares, over with almost before they'd begun. Nothing can give a person a greater scare than to leap across a fallen log and land beside a coiled rattlesnake while out cottontail-hunting. Fortunately, when that happened to me it was autumn and just a little too chilly for the snake to be aggressive. Instead of striking, he crawled languidly back into the rotting hollow of the log.

We have all had close calls in auto crashes or near-misses in those infernal machines. I have been more fortunate than some others: so far, I have spun around a few times, left the road more than I care to admit, and even collided a few times—but I have not yet been hospitalized for an accident.

One time black ice south of Des Moines sent my northbound pickup spinning across the snow that divided the two directions of

Interstate 35. I could see a semi-truck coming south toward me, and on my second spin we collided. I bounced back to the median with my box pretty much in shambles but little damage to the semi. I was in a big Ram V-10. It's lucky that I hit a truck rather than a car, as I would have done considerable damage to a smaller vehicle. And there was another bright side: the semi actually kept me from going off into a ravine. I believe that if we are appreciative of the Spirit Forces, they look after us. My many lives are proof enough for me. Many a reader has a different story to tell in this regard, and some of you have had time confined in a hospital bed to contemplate seriously what you are going to do with your life. I may die tomorrow, but that semi blocking the ravine enabled me to finish this book. Maybe a good project sharpens the spirits' vigilance.

One near-death incident had a most unusual ending. En route to South Dakota for opening day of pheasant-hunting, I fell asleep. I was behind the wheel on the freeway, heading west across Minnesota. I dozed off and veered to my right down into high grass. I was heading up the side of the opposing slope when I woke up. The grass was high enough that it had slowed the car considerably, but now the grass was impacted in the rims of my car. The car went to two wheels and almost rolled before I could take control. Then it fell with a thud and I steered it back to the highway.

A sign whizzed by as I merged back onto the freeway. It read: Okabena. Needing to stop and calm my nerves, I took the exit, driving up the incline and parking the car off to the side. I thanked the spirits by making a sign that the Sioux call "the power of the hoop" (or the medicine wheel)—a circular motion executed by my shaking hand. I drew an imaginary circle out in front of me, then inserted the Four Directions with a downward movement within the parameters of my imaginary circle for north and south and a horizontal movement for east and west. "Spirits!" I acknowledged.

My dog was in the backseat of my minivan, and I turned to pet him with a still trembling hand. Being up on two wheels about to roll over was still in my mind. All of a sudden, as I looked back past the dog, I saw a pair of pheasant roosters flying in the distance. Minnesota pheasant season always starts before South Dakota's, and this got my attention— and fast. I hurriedly loaded my shotgun after dragging it from its case, and Rex and I drove down the road. The pheasants had landed near a small creek. We had no more than stepped from the car when one rose and I hit it. It went across the creek, and Rex went after it. Another one rose at the fence and I hit it also. Nothing better for getting over a near-fatal crash in a hurry than seeing a pair of pheasants!

Seeking adventure does have its perils, I know, but always thank the Spirit World when you have a close call, and the spirits will return to help you in your next encounter. I hope I have proven this point.

HEALING OUR WOUNDED CONFIDENCE

We Sioux and some other tribes have spirit-calling ceremonies in which spirits enter and help us, and we are quite convinced that the spirits' involvement is allowed by Creator—which all the more cements our feelings and beliefs that Creator truly is benevolent. We have observed these spirits, we have felt them within us, and thus to us they obviously exist. The difference between them and the white man's spirits is that ours primarily convey knowledge. They may have some intervening power when we face danger, but that is a mystery; we do not observe spirits at work in those cases as we do in a ceremony. Having met death over and over, having survived with little or no injury, I cannot help but believe that some force intervened. Mathematically, I have had too many close calls without serious injury. Even in my childhood I had some close calls that could have been fatal.

I am not complaining, mind you. I am extremely thankful, and I am confident as I move forward upon my life's quest. Confidence from believing that the spirits are with you can be a powerful medicine. Chief Crazy Horse believed that the spirits were with him when he rode into battle. He wore a small stone behind his ear in acknowledgment. His confidence helped him be successful in his combat endeavors.

THE MEDICINE IN GRATITUDE

When we discover that a hurt child is safe, find a lost treasure, or experience a feeling of protection, we should immediately thank the Spirit World. The sentiment of gratitude is more important than the words chosen. "Thank you, spirits," is my simple and seemingly effective refrain. We have all had a close call or two out on the highways or walking paths—it is a busy world—and each instance of protection warrants our thankfulness. When an accident almost happens but is averted, I do not stop and build a shrine of thanksgiving, but I do exclaim, loudly and with appreciation, "Spirits!" Then I settle down and more calmly express my profound appreciation. I often make the sign of the power of the hoop as well. My spirit helpers or guides seem to be well aware of this symbol, which states that we are truly all related. Appreciation is a strong ingredient in establishing a close relationship with these guides.

Back a few generations, if a hunter brought a large animal back to a hungry winter camp, a camp facing hard times, the group's holy person might decide to give a thanksgiving ceremony as a community acknowledgment of gratitude and to express appreciation to the Spirit World. If it was a time of plenty—in summer, for instance, when snows did not restrict travel and food was in abundance—a formal presentation to the Spirit World was generally not made if a hunter brought an animal back to camp. Thanks were given informally only; if the camp celebrated more formally in days of abundance, they would be in ceremony continuously! One could surmise that the Spirit World probably has common sense!

HUMOR AS MEDICINE

I would like to make available in this book sufficient information that anyone interested can advance in the rich medicine of Nature knowledge. The reader will benefit from old, proven knowledge, which indeed did spawn a happier and more balanced society. Laughter and congeniality among a people—traits common among the North American Indians and other indigenous groups—are strong indicators that something rich exists within a lifestyle/culture. A particular form of spirituality indeed must be extremely wholesome if its proponents exhibit humor and genuine pleasantness. When people have less to fear because of their spiritual concepts—when, for instance, they don't have to dread the Afterworld—that spirituality pleasantly permeates their everyday activities. Why shouldn't modern Human be intelligent enough to bring back a rewarding lifestyle that was here before—one that encouraged and promoted laughter?

Chief Fools Crow made a point about the healing power of laughter: "Another thing medicine people need is a good sense of humor," he said. "You know that I enjoy life and like to laugh. Laughter breaks the tension. It is a very good healer. And, it keeps us from taking life too seriously."[11]

When Native peoples were continually surrounded by nature, they had a much more relaxed existence than we know today. A study conducted in Australia indicated that hunter-gatherer groups found much more time to play and pray than their more "advanced" counterparts.[12] The adults sometimes amused themselves by watching the play of children, and there was much laughter among them.

Humor can foster health in those who rediscover the power of its medicine. We must learn from those who practice it: the indigenous of the world, as well as the creatures of Nature—the four-legged and winged ones who enjoy innocent, honest humor. Like Bear digging herbs and roots, we must scavenge for humor. We must develop it as a spiritual strength at the heart of our way of life. Nature can teach us if we pay attention.

I plan to go so far as to include some Iktomi (Indian humor) in these pages—maybe a few excerpts spawned by Trickster Coyote—in the hopes that some small degree of happiness can reach into lives that were made shallow, cold, or even frigid by a humorless childhood. All beings should have the privilege of laughing. Most Nature-respecting people I have met across the world have had a rich sense of humor. I hope that this writing can reflect that.

"What is an Iktomi?" you ask. Those familiar with some Native terminology may also ask, in the same breath, "What is a Heyoka?" thinking that there exist similarities. A Heyoka does things contrariwise. In other words, he (or she) does the opposite of what you would expect him to do. He is a trickster or a clown. The old Heyoka were simply clowns, making people laugh at their antics. At our powwows in my youth we had Heyoka clowns that danced backward—that is, danced in the opposite direction of the other dancers. When the drums had finished their beating and an announcer had begun speaking, the Heyoka would still be out there, dancing merrily. Sometimes a police officer would be asked by the announcer to go out and "remove those Heyoka so I can get on with my announcements." Sure enough, though the police officer would wind up being chased by the clowns. Yes, Heyoka are definitely contrary.

An Iktomi exists more in storytelling. The listener puts together his own imagery as the story gets told. Iktomi often comes in the form of a bumbling spider or a mistake-prone, "cunning" coyote that gets himself into all sorts of merry trouble as he attempts to outwit everybody. Coyote and Spider also have traces of contrariness.

Well, anyway, I have a couple of contraries that are doing their utmost to sneak into this book. My two contraries, if I allow them in, will be from England, of all places. Why? Because they are contrary, aren't they? Why should an Indian writer have to have Indian-only contraries, especially if he is introducing readers to his contraries? You must remember, contraries do not do what you expect of them, and they are not likely to be from where you think they should be from. You might expect them to be all mischief, for example, but they may surprise you and come up with some interesting information. You just cannot figure out a contrary, so it is best that you do not even try. They do drive some strong points home, though, once in a while. They like to lure people into areas that they have never thought of before and then surprise them with a new teaching.

My Iktomi detractors are mischief-makers, although they do project a few dead-centered puns every once in a while. I will do my best to keep them from interfering with this book, but bear in mind: one cannot always outwit a contrary. Their names are Finkley Finkworth and Finchley Beaverbrooke; and I tolerate them because, as intellectuals, they can occasionally help me. This subject can get pretty dry at times—world doom, straitlaced churches, and stiff clergymen! Finkley and Finchley may have to jump in once in a while to lighten things up. As we carry on toward planetary destruction (if we don't change our ways), we need some humor to brighten the path. I am sure we have the blessings of Chief Fools Crow and Chief Eagle Feather in this particular area, and John Fire (also referred to as Lame Deer) as well.

Finkley Finkworth and Finchley Beaverbrooke (of the House of Beaverbrooke and Beansworthy, no less), insisted that they become contributing authors. They hereby offer us a quiz:

What should be your tribe's reaction to the Pilgrims stealing a corn cache when they first came ashore?

A. The tribe observes the intruders with little discussion, presuming them to be hungry.

B. A loudmouth suggests that the tribe go out and kill the interlopers, but he is ridiculed by the wise men, who state that the Pilgrims' conduct will not endanger the tribe's survival.

C. A quartermaster type for the tribe prepares a set of calculations confirming that other, remaining caches of food are sufficient to allow the tribe to comfortably make it through the winter.

D. A peaceful chap suggests that the tribe merely watch the intruders and report on their ongoing activities, since the tribe considers itself more than adequate to repel any acts of aggression from the "new people."

E. All of the above.

Finkley stated, on reviewing the options, "Why would such a 'warlike' people keep the strangers alive through the next several winters—as we know they did—and even teach them how to plant crops? That would not be a normal reaction of a warlike people—at least, not unless they were planning on fattening them up to sell in some nonexistent slave market."

Finchley commented, "What if the situation were reversed? Let us suppose a particular tribe were to 'flee' America and sail an oceangoing canoe up the Rhine, Thames, or Seine and steal a grain cache (no corn, but oats or rye) after landing. (Which their Great Spirit doth provide, of course.) Which country would have reacted in a warlike manner?"

A. Germany (Finkley's pick)

B. England

C. France (Finchley's pick)

D. All of the above (My pick)

Well, such is an interruption when contraries pick at your work. I doubt that their test will seriously affect the world—though maybe that is their intention (no one knows). Maybe they are fooling us by coming across as harmless at first. We should be on guard!

From the humor of contraries to the memory of a beaten dog, there is abundant medicine right in front of us in Nature's teachings, each like a healing herb for us. Like Bear we become stronger the more we find and eat. Sometimes we need to dig a little deeper, especially when seeking medicine of truth, because false ego and false superiority strive to cover it up. But Nature's Way provides essential teachings about harmony with Mother Earth and Creator, reminding us to seek truth, be positive, appreciate Creator's gifts, relate with the Spirit World, and have humor. We need to heed all these teachings to bring balance to ourselves and to the planet.

Chapter Three takes a look at one particular medicine: the medicine of balance. This is the lesson of Lion.

THREE

BALANCE
IN ALL THINGS

Lesson of Lion

In all of Nature, lions are one of the most credible examples of equality. Both male and female lions hunt, and both care for the young. Both lion and lioness are free individuals within a pride, which is an "extended family" of related females and their dependent cubs (supplemented with temporary groups of resident males). Though now limited to the African veldt, the range of the mighty lion once reached far into Europe.

Male lions, during their short-term residence with a pride, maintain a hierarchical system of dominance within their group. Providing egalitarian balance, the female and her "sisters" do not participate in that hierarchy. There is no dominant female to control reproduction, so females are free to breed synchronously; and many in the pride do typically give birth at the same time. These mothers form a nursery and band together to share nursing responsibilities and to protect the cubs from new males, neighboring females, and other dangers. Individual mother/child bonds are acknowledged and honored, however—for example, when feeding on a kill. Because of the male's predisposition to infanticide, lions within the pride keep their distance from young cubs (and are sent away by lionesses if they venture too near), but they take on more of a paternal role as the cubs get older.

QUEEN OF THE VELDT

Protective and hunting roles are complementary between lions and lionesses. Males protect the pride from strange lions, while the females protect their hunting territory from other lionesses. From a hunting perspective, the female lion is the "queen of the veldt." Females capture the majority of the mid-size prey for the pride, often using group strategy for the kill, while males kill large prey for the pride, largely through sheer strength. While the male lion will often roam alone, killing his food for himself, the female lions stay in a group for more successful protection of the pride, sharing food with all and therefore getting less of each kill to eat.

The lioness lives a life free from suppression and inferiority and enjoys the cooperation of all her pride members and male coalitions. She is not only balanced in regard to the dominance dynamics of the males, but also balanced within herself in regard to her dual role as nurturer and aggressive hunter/protector.

In Iroquoian society, where Mother Earth is revered, women voted as equals with men long before universal suffrage became a rallying cry in Dominant Society, and in some matters held greater responsibility. How many human societies treat women with respect and offer them equal access to rights and privileges that men enjoy? Not many! In Sioux society, the major possessions—principally, the lodges—were the woman's property.

Because the world at large does not get enough exposure to feminine principles such as acceptance, emotional expression, and peacefulness, we have moved too far from center and are therefore contrary to Nature's (Creator's) plan. Humanity's patriarchal track record is dismal at best. We need to remind ourselves, as individuals and as a culture, that aggression and intimidation are not our only options when something does not go the way we want.

A NATURAL BALANCE IN OLD EUROPE

Far back in time, before 3500 B.C.E., a civilization known today as "Old Europe" lasted for millennia in what is now Yugoslavia, Czechoslovakia, and an area extending down to Crete, over to Palestine, and up to Istanbul. In this egalitarian, Nature-based, and Nature-respecting civilization, described by Riane Eisler in *The Chalice and the Blade*,[1] the Earth Mother concept was entwined within the culture. With no limiting Bible or Koran to label women intellectually inferior or to cast blame for some mythical "fall from grace," women played strong political, religious, and social roles, and "feminine values" were pervasive.

The art did not idealize cruelty, weapons, or power based on violence. Men were not adorned in their graves with military ornaments (shields, swords, and so on). There were no lavish "chieftain" burials that required the sacrifice of wives, concubines, or slaves, as was recorded in ancient Egyptian culture. In fact, the burials of the women were as ornate as the men's; and, if the grave size and types of artifacts discovered within are considered, some women were apparently even more exalted than their male counterparts. This was a balanced, egalitarian society in which women had power, position, and respect. The warrior-think, man-only-think perspective that we sometimes think of as essential to an advanced society was not evident (or was at least subdued).[2]

It would appear that an Eden did exist after all, and this one lasted much longer than the ages of Christianity and Islam added together. This was not like the Christian mythological Eden (if there ever was one); although if peace and prosperity are a measure, it was an Eden without a doubt, lacking the degree of war and strife that we in these modern times repeatedly experience. Like lionesses in a pride, the women of Old Europe were involved to an extraordinary extent in the design and management of their society. The big cats roamed the region in those days, and the Old Europeans, like the Iroquois, may well have been strongly influenced by what they observed; the lioness, the queen of the vast lands, no doubt garnered Nature-respecting attention.

This past culture continues to be verified in many ongoing archeological digs and studies, all of which bear witness to a commonality of positive values. The history of Old Europe, this long-lasting, peace-loving society, is one that European descendants should make themselves aware of. After its fall, Europeans shifted from a peaceful partnership to a society of dominance and strife; and much of value was lost in that transition.

It appears that Old Europe found what the North American Indians later cultivated for millennia. The Indians kept their society alive even longer, however. Both societies interrelated the Earth's role with that of society, balancing male and female energy, as does the lioness in her pride. The cooperation that exists among lions in a pride is evidence that those who hold female and male energy in balance are likely to be more peaceful than those who favor one over the other.

North American Indians (along with most indigenous people) had an important model of peacefulness: they considered Creator to be benevolent. Nature herself supports this view of divinity, as opposed to the wrathful male God of today's Dominant Society. Hundreds of thousands of buffalo in the early days, multicolored sunsets, whirling brooks, snow-covered mountains, a rainbow arching across the Great Plains, a hummingbird sipping nectar—all these are beautiful, restful, pleasant scenes that nurture the human spirit. God made and created every one of them!

The nurturing and protective lioness and her pride provide another example of Creator's benevolence. While hierarchical males provide food for the others after they have eaten all they want, egalitarian female lions provide food generously and with care for one another's cubs and the pride; and they protect against potential cub-killing rampages on the part of adult males, whose instinct is to assert dominance over other males (including other males' offspring).

Societies that ignore the lesson of Lion and become rigidly patriarchal engender fear, wrath, and punishment. They become aggressive, forcing themselves upon other nations, dominating the opposition, and subduing movements toward peace and kindness. As they grow and spread, they bring horrible suffering to many of their citizens.

THE RETURN OF THE CONTRARIES

"Yes, but what of natural disasters?" Finkley interrupted. His Iktomi sidekick, Finchley, added, "You're romanticizing God if you don't mention the tragic natural disasters that have befallen Human since the caveman days."

I had to agree with them to a degree, but the blame for most such disasters has to be shared. "Well," I pointed out, "people created their own chances when they built Pompeii below the volcano that eventually erupted, and they do the same today when they build in the tornado belts caused primarily by warm Caribbean air merging with advancing cold fronts from the north. 'Tornado Alley' states are going to become more disastrous as people increasingly populate and build in these areas. The same holds true for coastal cities facing hurricanes."

Finkley offered a scholarly smirk. "The volcano happened to be Mount Vesuvius. It buried the city, *totally* buried it. Nature can wreak tremendous havoc at times."

"Yes," I conceded, "but some areas of the world are prone to *specific* disasters. Knowing the risks, humans have had plenty of time to take precautions, not overly inhabit such areas, and build accordingly. Creator often gives us sufficient warning of trouble, especially if we look at the disaster history of an area." I thought for a minute. "Besides, it is almost miraculous how many people escape from most disasters. You read about it all the time."

Both Iktomi were unconvinced but seemed contented with the point they had made. I remain of the opinion that far, far more benevolence than evil (in the form of natural disasters) comes from Creator's Nature.

A SHARED PATH BEFORE PATRIARCHY

When we think of Creator as a definite Mystery, honestly and entirely unfathomable in its ultimate essence, it is difficult to see how any group of people can claim private "ownership" or a "chosen relationship" with that unknowable God, and more difficult still to see how they can use that alleged relationship to justify patriarchal dominance over others. Allegations such as "My God even looks like us and not your people!" and "My tribe is chosen" and "We are the master race, selected by God" have led to (and continue to bring) serious tragedies for the human population down through time.

The discovery of the existence of Old Europe, with its lifestyle paralleling that of many indigenous groups, is serious evidence that our destiny on earth need not follow the disastrous path we seem committed to; we *can* now make a major diversion. European descendants should no longer find it difficult to identify with American Indians (or with the later Celts, for that matter), for their pasts are truly similar if we reach back far enough! Old European society offers proof that Europe at one time did harbor a deeply Earth-respecting existence.

But that existence has been lost, at least within Dominant Society. Nature was gradually separated from its sacred component over the ensuing centuries, and that fact has culminated now in our planet's current disastrous environmental and humanitarian crises. The roots of this separation can be found in the abandonment of the Nature-based Goddess religions and cultures that existed in Old Europe and throughout the Fertile Crescent of the Middle East over 3,500 years ago.

Despite this claim, I am not advocating a Goddess religion as our current solution. If I were to advocate any religion, it would have to be a balanced one. Although the early Goddess religions *were* balanced—they were egalitarian and integrated with Nature rather than women-dominant—the gender-specific label "Goddess" leads to misunderstanding today.

Perhaps it was their very balanced, peaceful ways that led to the demise of the early Goddess religions. When warring nomadic patriarchal groups invaded from the north, spurred by an emphasis on male might and aggression and armed with iron-tipped spears and iron swords (rather than the bronze of the region), they helped the early Hebrews, with their one male God, to eradicate the various Goddess- or Earth-centered religions and cultures. With these changes, the groundwork for the demise of a sacred attitude toward Nature was set, and the fates of both women and Nature became tightly linked.

The rejection of the spiritual power of Nature can be seen in biblical stories that influenced the most basic thought of Judaism, Christianity, and Islam. In the Book of Genesis there are two accounts of creation. The first tells that man and woman were created at the same time and are equal in their responsibility to care for the Garden of Eden; the second tells us that Eve was created as an afterthought to Adam from an insignificant rib. Traditional interpretations have tended to support the second, thereby linking negative ideas of women and Nature. The story teaches the hierarchy of God over man, and man over woman and Nature. It shows us Eve's weak will against the temptation of the serpent; her deceitful persuasion of Adam to eat the forbidden fruit; and the expulsion of Adam, Eve, and the serpent from the Garden of Eden.

Ironically, the serpent was one of the main symbols of the Goddess religions that thrived in the centuries prior to the patriarchal religion of the Hebrews. Prominent archeologist Marija Gimbutas informs us that the snake and its abstract derivative, the spiral, are the dominant motifs of the art of Old Europe.[3] Riane Eislar clarifies further: "Clearly the serpent was too important, too sacred, and too ubiquitous a symbol of power of the Goddess to be ignored."[4] By accepting the counsel of the serpent (the Goddess) and tasting the forbidden fruit of the Tree of the Knowledge of Good and Evil, Eve and Adam were initiated into the knowledge of the secret that "only the gods knew"—the secret of Creation in sexual and spiritual awareness. According to Merlin Stone, "In each area in which the Goddess was known and revered, she was extolled not only as the prophetess of great wisdom, closely identified with the serpent, but as the original Creatoress, and the patroness of sexual pleasures and reproduction as well."[5] When the snake, a main symbol of the Goddess, was thrown out of the Garden, so was the Goddess—and, ironically, so was Nature herself!

Hebrew writers wrote the second story around 400 B.C.E., possibly with an ulterior motive: to warn Jewish men and women against participating in the once-flourishing matriarchal and Nature-based Goddess religions, so as to facilitate the successful separation of Nature from religion. Dire, severe consquences evolved from these Hebrew stories, resulting in the downgrading of women and the retreat from Nature's balance. Native stories did not degrade women! Humans became far less peaceful. This simple tale began a long history of blaming woman (and by extension the Nature-based religion of the Goddess) for the fall of all humankind in Eve and Adam's expulsion from the Garden of Eden.

As the countries of Old Europe and the Fertile Crescent eventually transformed into patriarchal societies, Goddess religions, with their foundation in Nature, disappeared. Instead of woman being viewed as working hand in hand with Nature to nurture life, woman (and Nature) came to be regarded as merely the passive "soil" in which man would "plant his seed." Now man and his male God controlled the power and mystery of both woman and Nature.

Ultimately, the Genesis creation story had terrible consequences for women. Though women functioned as leaders in the early Christian Church, and the Goddess Sophia was honored in ceremony and ritual by other sects, by the end of the fourth century powerful literalist interpreters of Christian scripture had relegated women to second-class status. Women were no longer seen as equal partners with men, but as seductive descendents of the evil Eve, because of whose sin "even the Son of God had to die." According to Augustine, a Christian Church Father writing late in the fourth century: "What does it matter whether it is a wife or a mother, it is Eve the temptress we must beware of in any woman."[6] Clearly, by that time the banishment of the Goddess and her Nature-based religion was complete.

There is a holy day for modern Christians that honors St. Patrick, who we are told drove the snakes out of Ireland. Such claims Human doth make! I have always doubted that a mere man could alter what Creator made. If there are no snakes in Ireland, it must be because of Nature. That is the case in New Zealand, where there are at least no *poisonous* snakes. What St. Patrick's Day really celebrates is the victory of Christianity over the Nature-based religion of the Celts. It is a modern result of the negative religious and cultural attitudes toward the Goddess concept, women, and Nature—attitudes that were spawned so many centuries earlier. Another, more far-reaching result of those attitudes are our ecological crises, which reflect the domination of Nature and women by men.

In early 2002, Bernard Lewis wrote an article in the *Atlantic Monthly* entitled "What Went Wrong?" In it, he tells of an entire civilization, Islam, that sacrificed its forward progress (if human rights, standard of living, and individual freedoms are valid standards for measurement)— all in the name of hoarding power among males. The lack of basic human rights, especially for women, in the Islamic world demonstrates a vast gap between it and Europe to the north. Worse, that lack, along with various religious and cultural practices, precipitated a drastic fall for the Islamic empire, which once surpassed the Western world in the fields of science, technology, and the humanities. Lewis writes: "By all the standards that matter in the modern world—economic development and job creation, literacy, educational and scientific achievement, political freedom and respect for human rights—what was once a mighty civilization has indeed fallen low."[7]

SEPARATION OF CHURCH AND STATE

Lewis further states that a principal cause of Western progress is the separation of church and state and the creation of a civil society governed by secular laws. Islamic society, on the other hand, is governed by patriarchal religious law—and perhaps that was its downfall. As Lewis points out, keeping women in an inferior position in society deprived Islam of "the talents and energies of half its people and entrusts the other half's crucial early years of the upbringing to illiterate and downtrodden mothers." Children raised in such a society "are likely to grow up either arrogant or submissive, and unfit for a free, open society." Lion teaches the medicine of exposing the young to strong and balanced female involvement. Lewis, it seems, would agree: he emphasizes that the future of the Middle East will be greatly influenced by the "success or failure of secularists and feminists" there.[8]

Many in the Middle East blame a variety of outside forces for the troubles there. Like Lewis, I am more inclined to look within: the denial and subjugation of the female half of the area's population is contrary to what we observe in Creator's balanced Nature, and regional chaos is the consequence. Here is a prime example of a whole religious society (the largest in the world!) being commandeered by religious fundamentalist extremists and forced to go backward. Patriarchal clergy distorted early Islamic thinking, fostering rules completely contrary to Nature, and then brainwashed fanatics to carry out their dictates. Like the hierarchical male lions, those clergy control what is "fed" to the people, taking what they need first.

THE CELTS AND NATURE'S WAY

On the other side of the coin, there emerged into recorded history in the sixth and fifth centuries B.C.E. a society called the Celts; they did not produce a written history of their own, but they had a strong oral tradition. By the fourth century B.C.E. the Celts were at their peak, and by the beginning of the second century B.C.E. they had migrated and, in the words of historian Peter Ellis, "founded settlements and outposts across the entire European continent, from northern Spain to Turkey, from the British Isles to the shore of the Black Sea."[9] Much has been learned about the Celts from various sources, all of which confirm that Celtic tribal society was relatively egalitarian, democratic, and in harmony with Nature. Ellis describes that society:

> The Celtic tribal system was a highly sophisticated one. The good of the community was the basis of the law. . . . Chieftains were elected as were all officers of the tribe. Women emerged in Celtic society with equality of rights. They could inherit, own property and be elected to office, even to the position of leader in times of war. . . . Tacitus observed, "There is no rule of distinction to exclude the female line from the throne or the command of armies."[10]

Is it not possible that the Celts were either related to or strongly influenced by the advanced civilization that Eisler speaks of in *The Chalice and the Blade*? Perhaps that earlier society migrated or shifted westward when the patriarchal intruders came down from the northeast with their advanced weaponry. The word *Celt* comes from Greek and Roman writers, who used it rather indiscriminately to refer to the various tribes that occupied Europe to the north and west of them. Physically, the Celts were taller and lighter-featured than people in southern Europe (though there were dark-haired Celts), and they often had blue eyes.

The Celts shared with the Old Europeans a belief in the immanence of the spirit world and the immortality of the soul. Classical writers, who often denigrated Celtic spirituality as superstition, frequently commented on the Celts' intense obsession with spiritual matters. Celtic scholar Anne Ross notes that "the Celts were so completely engrossed with, and preoccupied by, their religion and its expression that it was constantly and positively to the forefront of their lives."[11]

CELTS IN EARLY AMERICA?

Just as the Celts may have grown out of, or been influenced by, the Old Europeans, might the early Celts have influenced the spiritual insights of the Native Americans? Or how about vice versa? There are certainly striking similarities between the two worldviews, as shamanic practitioner Tom Cowan notes:

> Like American Indians, the Celts lived in diverse, scattered tribal units, sometimes banding together for specific trade or military purposes. As peoples who practiced an indigenous, earth-centered spirituality, the Celts and Native Americans share many animistic beliefs and practices, along with a common attitude and respect for the land and the spirits of the land. . . . Like Native Americans, the Celts suffered from the advance of other settlers. . . . Eventually the majority of the Celts were defeated, absorbed, or pushed westward by an advancing, militaristic Roman civilization.[12]

The idea that Native Americans might have been influenced by the Celts is supported by a December 2000 article in *National Geographic*, which indicates that the magazine has finally shed its Bering-Strait-only theory and now suggests that some migration from the east also brought early settlers across the Atlantic.[13]

Who were the first Europeans in the New World? Was it Leif Eriksson and his Vikings, or was it the legendary Irishman St. Brendan of the Misty Isles? Actually, it was probably neither. Recent archeological finds in New England indicate a European settlement as far back as 800 B.C.E.! The evidence is threefold: first, in an ancient complex of stone buildings; second, in scores of tablets inscribed with a writing matching that used in western Europe around 800 B.C.E.; and third, in American Indian words that parallel those used in western Europe at that time. Researchers studying this data have concluded that the adventurers who crossed the Atlantic over 2,800 years ago were Celts.

The Celtic identity of the structures has been established through the science of epigraphy—that is, the study of ancient inscriptions on stone. Barry Fell (now deceased), a former Harvard professor and past president of the Epigraphic Society, identified the inscriptions as Ogham, a system of cipher used by Celtic people over 2,500 years ago, and was able to translate them. Dr. Fell's research is conclusive in dating the Celtic presence in North America.

Some of the inscriptions found and translated identify graves; others taken from the oracle chamber are religious writings; and still others specify land boundaries. Some two hundred stone chambers have been found in New England, many of which are constructed in the form of Druidic astronomical calendar observatories. Together, they suggest a Celtic settlement in the New World at the time Ogham was in use in Europe—that is, about 800 B.C.E. Further, a study of local Indian words and place names has revealed Celtic roots. Other methods, such as the identification and dating of pottery, tools, and implements found at the site, have also revealed the settlement to be Celtic, matching items produced in the Celtic regions of western Europe during the Bronze Age.[14]

Maybe influence flowed *both* directions—from the Celts to the Native Americans and back again—over as much as several millennia, with traffic going both west and east across the Atlantic. If the Celts were in North America as early as Dr. Fell's research suggests, it is highly probable that early traders returned to pre-Christian Europe with many of the values of the New Continent (later to be called North America). That exchange would explain why certain North American tribes have traces of physical resemblance to Celtic/Nordic features. Walk through the Rapid City, South Dakota, airport and study the remarkable photographs that hang from the walls. As you look at the pronounced features of full-blooded Sioux veterans who defeated Custer at the battle of the Little Big Horn, you might think you were looking at a slightly darker than usual group of war-bonneted Celts or Vikings!

Some northeastern tribes have features very unlike those of western tribes and even more unlike those of northwestern coastal Indians. Traces of Celtic and Viking influence may explain why northern tribes look different than southwestern tribes, such as the Navajo and Pueblo. One has no difficulty in discerning a Sioux from a Navajo or a Tlingit. Maybe in addition to an inspirational tradeoff of values and spirituality between the Celts and the Sioux/Iroquois—a sharing of the best of what these Nature-respecting peoples had to offer—there was also a sharing of genes. The appearance of the Sioux and Iroquois people—lighter-skinned, taller, and heavier-boned than their southern counterparts—suggests some intertwining of the blood.

I believe that this possible sharing of bloodlines and almost certain sharing of cultures shows that the paths of Native Americans and European Americans came from the same place: a place of equality for both men and women. That reminder of Nature's Way is the lesson of Lion.

THE GHOST FROM THE OLD ABBEY

That common origin in a more natural relationship between the sexes was clear to me when I visited England in 1994. I visited the Great Circle at Stonehenge and had a fascinating dinner with Philip Carr-Gomm, Chief of the Order of Bards, Ovates, and Druids. His book *The Druid Tradition* explores a spirituality that parallels the Native American Way. There are many startling similarities between Native American and Druid teachings and practices. The Spirit of the Circle, the Spirit of the Stones, and related stone circle (medicine wheel) ceremonies, along with Vision Quest and Sweat Lodge, are reflective of a possible intertwining past. In addition, the Bards, Ovates, and Druids use the term "Great Spirit."

Following the Carr-Gomm meeting, my traveling companion, Morgaine Avalon, and I stayed at an inn that was built on the grounds of a former abbey. I had been forewarned in America by friends that a ghost or spirit stayed there. It would often "play" with guests, my friends cautioned. I purposely chose to stay at this inn, because the Native spirit ceremonies I have been exposed to have made me fairly invulnerable to any fear of ghosts or spirits. The latter term—*spirits*—is our preference, rather than Dominant Society's *ghost*.

Sure enough, about midnight, an ephemeral form appeared at the end of my bed. I had been waiting for it and probably would have been disappointed had it not appeared. (Now, I wish to give readers the indulgence that I may have fallen off to sleep, in which case all of what I experienced was a mere dream—quite a realistic one, I might add.) At first the "ghost" seemed to want to scare me. I felt that my covers were being pulled, and I noticed that Morgaine's covers were also pulled down, though she remained fast asleep. I bolted upright with my peace pipe and *wotai* stone (a beseechment tool also called *wotawe*—more on that in Chapter Five), which I had taken to bed with me purposely. I simply pointed my pipe at the ghost and told it (quite truthfully) that I was not afraid of it and it should pass on to better things in the Spirit World. I do recall introducing myself and explaining what I believed spiritually. I actually ridiculed it for engaging in such foolish antics to scare poor tourists.

This is all fairly zany, I know—and as I said, it could have been simply a very realistic dream. In any case, I somehow sensed that this spirit was a former priest and a celibate, maybe because I had been told the history of the converted abbey earlier. As the spirit and I talked, I patted Morgaine and asked the spirit if it had ever been with a woman. It moaned as if in pain. My senses were a bit befuddled—after all, I had had very little experience talking with spirits, and though not afraid, I was certainly apprehensive—so I really cannot give a precise description.

I kept command of the conversation, however, despite my apprehension. I asked it if it had ever had offspring, and again it seemed somewhat pained. It retreated backward for a moment and then slowly advanced to hear what else I had to say. I explained that our Sioux holy men believed in balance of the sexes and that they did not have to give up being with a woman to be spiritual leaders. Thinking of the pain that my question about women had caused, and my sense that it had been celibate, I told it that it had been lied to by its leaders and deprived of an ordinary life. I added, "Maybe that is why you are still here without any closure in your life." I sensed that the spirit understood some truth in what I had just said. It retreated again, this time with finality, and I felt that it was passing to a Spirit World beyond.

I finally went to sleep, and the next morning I woke up with my peace pipe and wotai stone still beside me. All that day things went well, and I felt as if some force was paying beneficial attention to our journey. I thought often about my conversation with the spirit, realizing that the scene I remembered clearly could have been mere imagination but suspecting that it was more.

The following day, after a morning meeting with the noted Celtic author Geoffrey Ashe, I beseeched at the Tor in Glastonbury with my peace pipe and four colored stones of Black Elk's colors. It was a beseechment of appreciation: we simply wanted to acknowledge that Nature's Way still lived on, as our meetings with Philip Carr-Gomm and Geoffrey Ashe suggested. Things went so well following the simple ceremony at the Tor that I suspected the Celtic spirits were quite pleased with our gesture. Later that day I met with Robert Stewart, an authority on Merlin, King Arthur's seer. His comments also supported a connection, a powerful one at that, between the two Nature-respecting spiritual cultures on opposite sides of the Atlantic.

Morgaine and I had to connect with a flight out of Gatwick airport later that evening, and we had to do some traveling on a tight schedule to reach Gatwick on time. On a drive that could have been extremely stressful, every traffic light was green and I navigated the potentially confusing roundabouts with ease. When we got to the terminal, I was disappointed to discover that the rental-car offices were not at the airport proper, as most are in the United States. Heading in the direction the signs pointed, I stopped at a gas station—*petrol* station, I mean—to fill up the car. A pale, ghostlike figure in an old-fashioned taxi pulled up beside me. "Hello, old chap," he volunteered. "Having a bit of trouble, I presume."

I looked more closely at him and saw that his clothes looked as antique as his taxi. "You got that right," I said. "I have to deliver my rental car before catching a plane, and I'm running a bit late." (When you have been in England a few times, you seem to pick up the words—"a bit" this and "a bit" that.)

"Don't worry, Yank. I can solve your problem. What company are you renting from?" I told him and he added, "Follow me."

We were at the rental office in no time and seemed to sail through the check-in line. By the time the paperwork was finished, he had transferred our bags into the front of his cab—a rather peculiar but effective arrangement. We then sped to the airport, calmed by his repeated reassurances that we had plenty of time. When we got to the airport and pulled up curbside at our airline, Morgaine reached into her purse and counted out a goodly amount of English money. With his fare and a healthy tip in hand, he waved us goodbye with a broad smile, though he could not drive off for all the crowds and other cabs surrounding him.

After we had gone only a few more steps Morgaine found some more pound coins. Preferring to give them to our good Samaritan rather than exchange them for dollars, she handed them to me to take back to him. I turned to run back to the curb but his cab had totally disappeared. We were dumbfounded as to how he could have gotten away so quickly. Could he have been the "ghost" from the night before? Maybe we will find out in the Spirit World. I was honest with him is all that I can say.

From my observation, he had had little balance in his previous life, and perhaps he had lacked the knowledge to move on instead of scaring innocent tourists in a lonely room. Maybe I instilled the knowledge he needed. Did he now recognize a balance of cultures and want to extend his appreciation? Or was he a Celtic spirit or former bard of long ago who simply appreciated the fact that someone from the New World was connecting to the similarly balanced beliefs of the Celtic Way? Mystery—it is all sheer Mystery!

Maybe the Atlantic Ocean was not such a barrier, after all. An article by Mary Lou Skinner Ross sheds some light on practices common on both sides of the Atlantic. This extensive presentation, published in my previous book, *Rainbow Tribe*,[15] allows us a window to compare egalitarianism in both Sioux and Celtic life. Women readers especially will breathe in a refreshing, invigorating spirit, a newfound vitality that may lift them toward a balanced, equal-gender "Manifest Destiny"—an outcome that is long overdue if this planet is to be saved!

Maybe early inhabitants of the Misty Isles gained premonitions, through Druidic ceremonies, of the sacrificial Inquisition that was to come. Knowing of the continent across the Atlantic, perhaps they chose to make a timely exodus, as the Sioux did from the Carolinas. We Sioux avoided a similar, annihilating "Great Inquisition" by listening to our spiritual connection and hastily leaving our homeland. The Celtic hypothesis suggested here would have northern Europeans boating across the Atlantic long before the Pilgrims and joining up with some of my Native ancestors.

THE CELTIC KEEPERS OF BALANCE

Within the Celtic culture, the spiritual leaders were known as bards. Their role was similar to that of the medicine people and record-keepers of the indigenous North American tribes. Both males and females, the bards took on their role in the interest of the tribe, preparing themselves through years of study. That extensive process presumably weeded out power-seekers, who would not have tolerated such self-sacrifice simply to be in the priesthood, leaving a more democratic, power-sharing clergy. The inclusion of women in the priesthood also suggests a high value of true democracy. Although European men have proven repeatedly throughout history to have a difficult time including women within social and religious structures, the Celts' strong connection with and respect for Nature led them to lioness-like democratic values, not unlike those of the Iroquois and the Sioux.

Unfortunately, the Celtic way of life did not prevail. Roman leaders and English kings eager to put humanity over Nature destroyed the records of Celtic Earth knowledge, to the detriment of modern two-leggeds.

A DUPLICATE CREATION

Perhaps that Celtic wisdom is not truly lost after all. Native Americans, with their similar affinity for Nature, are able to reach into the "sacred mind" of that earlier time—or perhaps the "sacred mind" is reaching ahead through Native American knowledge. It is the same Nature that both groups—Celts and indigenous Americans—were studying, after all. As was noted earlier, it is not so remote a possibility that the ancient Celtic and Druidic wisdom was transferred, at least in part, to the northeastern tribes and then to the Lakota/Dakota Sioux, who trace their roots back to the area where the Celts first landed and explored. Maybe natural values were a sort of duplicate creation, since both cultures learned from Nature. Who knows?

My main concern is not who started Nature's Way and kept it alive, but the simple fact that it *was* discovered—and was appreciated and practiced for a long time on both sides of the Atlantic. We all have to come back to it eventually, incorporating the balance of women into our patristic orientation. We will lose the planet if we do not study and learn from Nature's Way.

I wish that there existed a tribe of Celts on some remote United Kingdom island untainted by the proselytizing Christians who, after hundreds of years, successfully stamped out the last vestiges of Celtic culture and religious practice. I would certainly go there to work on this book. Perhaps then non-Indian readers would feel more "at home" in their search for Nature's Way. Native Americans, who have had so much taken away from them by European intruders, would not have to feel or fear that again the whites were taking something more—this time not their land but their culture. Perhaps my encounters with the Druids and ghosts of England is the most affirmation that the Great Spirit will offer me about our shared past in an equality and balance demonstrated by Lion.

Fear that Nature's Way will be erased by Dominant Society, as so many other indigenous beliefs and practices have been, often causes Native Americans to close doors to non-Indians who are searching for a better way, despite the commonality of belief and ceremony that we have seen in Native American and ancient European heritages. And that fear is legitimate: some non-Indian seekers feel drawn to adopt Indian holy places for their own use. Many Indians resent and fight the public's access to their sacred places and ceremonies because of the sense of intrusion that results. (This dilemma will be discussed further in Chapter Six.)

Like lionesses in their pride, Chief Fools Crow, Black Elk, and Bill Eagle Feather encouraged all people of all races and beliefs to share wisdom and help anyone who respects Nature's Way. The planet is in such a dire state that knowledge for its salvation must be passed on. Lion medicine teaches us to work toward that salvation in the balance of masculine and feminine energies in our lives. Time is of the essence if we are to reclaim the balancing power of woman—and Nature—on this Earth. We had it once, and Nature is readily available to teach us how to find that medicine again.

The next chapter, Chapter Four, explores another concept that will contribute to Earth's salvation: the concept of one among many. That is the lesson of Wolf.

ONE AMONG MANY

Lesson of Wolf

Wolf is a misunderstood animal. Yes, it is a predator; but, as I must remind my two-legged friends, we are too. When we walk into a McDonald's or stalk the aisles at the grocery store, we are just as much a predator as Wolf.

Wolves hunt mainly through group effort and are extremely loyal to their pack. When a single wolf happens to find a wounded animal, it rarely closes in on the unfortunate creature, even though the wolf has the advantage of killing the animal and feeding itself first. Instead, the scout returns to the pack, bringing the others the message that wounded game is nearby, and all of the pack who can hunt set out promptly and feed as one. Some of the wolves then take back food for the pups, waiting back at the den. Scout wolves also return to the pack to communicate approaching storms, herds of game, and dangers such as nearby humans.

The Sioux respect the ways of Wolf. They value warriors; but not those who would take more than their tribe needs, because they can see how the pursuit of unrestrained self-interest has led much of the rest of the world into cycles of war and antipathy. The Sioux also value the messenger; and they are one of the few tribes to survive through sharing their culture and wisdom, not keeping to themselves with foolish superstition and a dangerous sense of superiority. They managed to travel through history carrying their old peaceful ways, keeping those ways intact and in tune with Nature into the very recent past century.

Like wolf scouts, those of us who know the dangers ahead must take responsibility for warning and teaching others. Those of us who see the signs of environmental imbalances on Mother Earth must not be silent as if we were one alone. Indeed, we are *all* one among many in the environmental crisis our world now faces. We are each an essential connection in the web of life, and as such, no one is superior; no one person or country can live only unto itself and survive in balance with Nature.

Like wolves, we must work together to survive, but we need truthful, responsible, knowledgeable, and non-egocentric leadership and communication. Leadership in Nature's Way is epitomized in the leader of a wolf pack: the alpha male relies on others, understands that he too is just one among many, and he recognizes that the good of the many comes before any short-term gain motivated by self-interest.

A VISION OF LEADERSHIP WITHOUT DOMINATION

The Sioux believe that the story of Black Elk and his vision, mentioned in the Introduction, demonstrates the power of a similar spiritual leadership. Black Elk's vision constitutes the powerful core of our Sioux Nature spirituality today—a visionary teaching that brings to this present time the ancient values of Nature's Way.

That vision was given at a time when the Sioux tribe enjoyed the freedom of the Great Plains. This was over a century ago, but several years before the famous battle at which the Sioux defeated Colonel Custer. A young boy named Black Elk (referred to in later years as Nicholas Black Elk) had a vision that took him into the Rainbow Covered Lodge of the Six Powers of the World. The first four of these powers—West Power,

North Power, East Power, and South Power (the Four Directions)—all spoke individually to the boy in his vision; then Father Sky and Mother Earth spoke to him. At the end of their speaking, a Blue Man of destruction and corruption appeared. Native traditionals believe that this Blue Man is now wreaking havoc upon the earth and that, unless he is confronted by Human, will cause us to lose the planet. A more detailed presentation and discussion can be found in my book *Native Wisdom.*[1]

The challenge of confronting and subduing the Blue Man is daunting, especially when so much of the world is unaware of the danger. It is hard to be one among many when the many don't share our views. Sometimes the initiative to lead is stifled by the desire to "not make waves" in the community. At other times there is actual danger in standing up for change, even when we know in our heart that it's best for all. Wolf teaches us to balance our responsibility to lead with the good of the many, so that all are cared for in the pack but the pack keeps on moving and thriving.

Often when we are the lone one among many, the Spirit World sends a courageous helper to help us fulfill our duty. For example, for a long time Black Elk was afraid to reveal his vision to his people. He kept it in his heart for years, until his tribe had become captives and been herded onto reservations. It is my supposition that helpers from the Spirit World brought an honest white man to him to catalyze his courage to tell his story. John Neihardt, a writer, entered Black Elk's life and put his story down on paper, to be conveyed to the world in the book *Black Elk Speaks.*[2]

THE SIX POWERS

We have all observed and experienced the guiding forces that revealed themselves within Black Elk's vision—the Six Powers—whether or not we know a single page of what was revealed. Let's look at each of those powers in turn:

West Power (Black)

We acknowledge the life-giving rains from the west as the power to make life. Thunder and lightning have the power to destroy, but we realize that more life than death transpires with each rain. As the sun goes down in the west, darkness comes to the land. Thus the color for the west is black. Spirits who enter ceremonies have fewer distractions if it's dark when two-leggeds seek to communicate with them; therefore, spirit-beseeching ceremonies are usually held when the West Power has allowed darkness to come forth. The Spirit World is associated with the West Power in this regard but is not confined to a direction.

North Power (White)

We think of endurance, cleanliness, truth, rest, politeness, and strength as associated with the North Power. The cold north has Mother Earth rest beneath a white mantle of snow. She sleeps and gathers up her strength for the bounty of springtime. When the snows melt, the Earth is made clean. When Native people wintered over somewhere, often confined to a small area for a lengthy time while they waited for the spring thaw, they learned to be extremely polite and truthful with each other. They kept clean by using the sweat lodge to take winter baths and to beseech to the Spirit World. The power of the cold white north taught them to endure. The cleansing white goose wing Black Elk received in this great vision emphasizes endurance and cleanliness.

East Power (Red)

The third power brought Black Elk the red pipe of peace. Peace begins with knowledge. To have peace, one must first become aware of knowledge, which comes forth out of the red dawn, the east, with each new day. When knowledge is discussed and considered, with various people sharing their thoughts, observations, and needs, that knowledge can become wisdom. As an example, a widow can add much wisdom to a council that is considering whether to make a war or planning to send out a war party. She can tell of the loneliness of the children, and of her own grief, when their father (her husband) was slain during the last war party. Likewise, when lands are to be taken from a people by financiers or politicians, the people's voices should be heard.

Here again, we see the function of the messenger or scout in Wolf society. Communicating knowledge of what's happening can help a group make wise decisions for the people's interest—decisions that adequately compensate anyone hurt by the general good. Especially when sabers rattle and threats are made, wisdom can lead to understanding, and understanding can bring peace to the land.

The pipe of peace and the red dawn that brings new experience each day are symbolic of knowledge and wisdom coming together in this day and age. We are in an early stage of the age of communication. We have already seen great progress in bringing important information and knowledge into people's homes and lives; and we have wonderful new tools that will enhance communication still further—mysterious radio waves, television signals, the Internet, and much more—which give us optimism that our planet can be saved from past practices of destruction. The red dawn rises to bring a bright new day—and another, and another—promising that we can add knowledge to our lives as long as we walk this planet. And if we hope to save our world, we have no choice but to communicate truthfully and fully. We have seen what can happen when humans refuse to communicate: ethnic cleansing, war, and fanaticism, both religious and secular.

South Power (Yellow)

Medicine from roots, stems, herbs, and fruits are associated with the South Power. As we saw in an earlier chapter, many species are beginning to disappear, and some of these medicines will soon be lost.

The sun rises higher and higher as the South Power advances with summer. Eventually plants such as corn and wheat bring forth golden kernels that will sustain much life through the long winter. Abundance is the primary gift from this power, for it makes all things grow, and creatures are allowed to take that which grows. In earlier days, buffalo fattened on endless grasses in the summer. During the heat of those days, buffalo hunts provided meat that was cured in the hot, blowing wind and saved for the long winters to come. During this time of plenty, dances and gatherings of thanksgiving were common. Being thankful for what we receive, as the plains dwellers were, adds strength to our search for sustenance, provision, and shelter.

Sky Power (Blue)

When Father Sky spoke to Black Elk, he promised that the things of the air would be with Black Elk to help him in his struggle. Could these "things of the air" include the vast open space of communication that now encircles the globe? Could it include the many satellites that beam back video and radio waves so people can see and talk directly across the skies? What the Sky Power said affirms the advance of more peaceful people upon the earth, because the promised things of the air *are* helping to promote peace and harmony; it's happening right before us.

Earth Power (Green)

Mother Earth, the sixth power, is the provider. She is our home. Not long ago it was unfathomable that mere human could alter or harm such a powerful Mother. Black Elk's vision took place over a century ago, yet Mother Earth focused only on the Blue Man, for obviously she visualized the serious threat way back then. She showed Black Elk the danger that was confronting the Earth: this danger was the Blue Man of greed and deception, a force that was already harming all living things. This Blue Man symbolizes the corruption, insensitivity, greed, and ignorance that threaten to engulf the Earth.

The message of Earth Power is that the Blue Man will wreak great destruction, using lies and untruths. If he is not banished, all creatures, including two-leggeds, will perish. Untruth is the Blue Man. And he roams every byway of this land. Every day we observe great deception by those who lobby our political leaders in Washington with disregard for the environment and the needy among us; we see deception among political leaders themselves as they profess to care about others but look out for their own interest first; and we see deception much closer to home, as we all struggle to hold untruth at bay. The Blue Man works through anyone and everyone who has forgotten that he or she is one among many.

As the situation worsens, more eyes will be opened to the evils of falsehood, and eventually the old ways of real truth will *have* to be accepted in order to finally destroy the Blue Man. Hopefully, that will happen in time for the planet to regain its old harmony. Religious fundamentalists will no doubt keep on praying, ignoring the problem and waiting for miracles, but the only realistic and workable solution is to return to the values that have been shown to work—values based on a love and respect for Mother Earth. In the meantime, some tragic consequences will transpire, because the ozone layer and the population spiral simply cannot wait.

DEALING WITH THE BLUE MAN

In Black Elk's vision, the Six Powers attacked the Blue Man but were beaten back. At that point, they called on Black Elk for help. The Six Powers, in their pleas to Black Elk, demonstrated the need for two-leggeds to destroy the corruption, lies, and greed of humankind, because

it is these traits and behaviors that, in turn, are destroying our envir -
onment.

Black Elk was persuaded by the Six Powers and, in his vision, attacked the Blue Man. His bow changed suddenly to a spear, allowing
him to kill the Blue Man. I interpret that changing of the bow to a
spear—a change that gave Black Elk the ability to destroy the Blue Man—
as symbolizing the new knowledge about Mother Earth that he had
gained in his vision. Is that same natural knowledge—Nature's Way—the
spear that we can now use to save the world environmentally? Can Nature's Way give the world a more peaceful, one-among-many perspective, freeing us from war-fomenting greed and my-way-only organized
religion? The answer to both questions is yes: if we simply listen to and
watch our Mother, we can learn to be peaceful and Nature-loving, and
we can then devote to the environment the energy that we used to
waste on fighting with other individuals, groups, and nations.[3]

Everyone is free to choose his or her own interpretation of the Blue
Man and of the weapons needed to combat him. We shall wait and
watch how the succession of new political administrations in this land
will deal with the incarnations of the Blue Man that surround them
daily. I expect little from our elected officials, but I hope that they prove
me wrong. I have more faith in the people rising up with a renewed,
Nature-based spiritual imagery and thereby destroying the Blue Man.
Maybe if enough people realize and accept Nature's Way, a grassroots
movement might take hold. One thing is clear: if we continue on our
present course of unconcern, the dreadful consequences approaching
will force disastrous change regardless.

SPIRITUAL POWER IN DOMINANT SOCIETY

As it is now, unfortunately, those who lead Dominant Society in the
realm of religion can tell us very little about the spiritual power within
Nature, for Dominant Religion purposely ignores Nature. Do you think

Billy Graham, Pastor Bob of the Crystal Cathedral, the Reverend Falwell, the pope, your local pastor, a gathering of misogynist monks way off in some monastery sitting atop a secluded hill, or Pat Robertson is going to teach us about the spiritual connection between us and Mother Earth? They would have to admit that they know nothing of Nature, because for centuries the Christian Church has been preaching totally the opposite: "It's all right to subdue Nature; in fact that's our human calling" has been the Christian theme.

I was watching a Sunday service on television a few years back. I believe it was Pastor Bob of the Crystal Cathedral—you know, that huge mansion of a glassy church that was always one of the mainstays of what I used to jokingly call "polyester hour"! (Hey, they've said and written far worse about us "heathens and pagans"!) It was a special Sunday that day I watched, for there was to be a gala unveiling of four statues—four men all larger than life. These statues were to last on throughout civilization, on into several millennia at least, barring some great exodus or abandonment or destruction.

Naturally one statue depicted Pastor Bob in all his Sunday-robe finery, holding his "Word of God" Bible, of course. Another statue portrayed Billy Graham, the third displayed the Most Reverend Bishop Sheen of the Catholic Church (or is it Most Right Reverend Bishop Sheen?), and the fourth was—well, I forget who the fourth fellow was, but he was a man, of course, and white. Each statue was draped with a cloth prior to the ceremony, and as each was unveiled, sighs and swoons murmured forth from the audience. Ah yes, the fourth statue was none other than Norman Vincent Peale. All figures carried a Bible and looked exactly like the real-life versions of all four men. My Iktomi friend Finkley termed them the Mount Rushmore of organized religion.

When Columbus sailed, not one statue was sculpted of any leader, political or spiritual, by the Nature-respecting peoples of the northern portion of the new hemisphere he was heading for. Not even warriors who had gone off to war rated a statue (or any other imagery, such as a bas-relief on a cliff wall) for future generations. Maybe not many wars had existed out of which to make war heroes. Aside from a few inscriptions on a few canyon walls—inscriptions that are mostly drawings of resident animals—indigenous Americans didn't harbor a need for glorifying the self. (Central Americans were more inclined toward inscriptions, however. Statues and bas-reliefs were numerous, although the majority of the figures depicted were spirit concepts or lesser gods responsible for certain endeavors, rather than effigies to departed or living humans.)

The reason North American Indians didn't glorify individuals as Dominant Society does is that they believed in the value of "one among many," a philosophy that doesn't call for singling out any one person for special glorification in his or her physical likeness. You should have seen how Pastor Bob beamed when he unveiled that one statue. *This is me! This is me!* That he was able to keep himself from jumping up and down like a little boy with that beaming face is a real tribute to his composure. I thought he was going to hop right out of that fancy black cloak he wears. Good thing he didn't. That might have diminished his living image!

Think of it. We're talking about millennia of leaders, down, down through time, and an entire continent of people—the American Indians (at least the northern portion)—that had a view opposite that of Dominant Society. They weren't egotistically moved to go out and start pounding on a piece of stone to shape it in their likeness: "Look at me! Look at me!" They had the time, most certainly, but their pursuits were directed more toward contemplation for the mind than toward egotistical effigies of mere humans.

HUMAN'S GLORIFICATION

Perhaps the best way to encapsulate the model of Wolf's "one among many" leadership is through the concept of humility. That is something we don't see too much of these days. Post–Native America is a society that glorifies and honors humans, with monuments as large as carved mountains and as small as commemorative postage stamps. Presidents have sold pardons and the nation's timber reserves to receive exorbitant donations for monumental self-sufficing presidential libraries. Millions of smaller monuments—grave markers of various shapes and sizes—take up valuable aesthetic space across our lands. Think of it. At one time a person could travel from ocean to ocean in North America and not stumble across a single statue or grave monument blemishing a far more aesthetic scene: Nature.

"One among many" is a lesson not only for human responsibility toward others but for our responsibility to Nature as well. It teaches us not to deface, detract from, disrespect, or dishonor one another, the community—or Nature—for self-gain or self-gratification. No one is superior to another or to Nature. This perspective fosters a set of values different in many respects from that of Dominant Society. If we follow this road—Nature's Way—we must expect abrupt change in our life. We can make choices that support our natural values, and each of those choices will bring an incremental change: for example, we can forgo the egotistical carving of our name on granite at death, freeing up six feet of precious Earth for future generations by getting cremated. If we choose *not* to follow this road, that won't exempt us from change. It's only a matter of time before we'll *all* have to start making adjustments, regardless. Our very survival will demand change.

THE NEED TO MOVE AND ADAPT

Another lesson that Wolf teaches is the need to move and adapt. Wolves keep a close eye out and move the pack often, seeking greater results and less danger. Their temporary dens were echoed in the teepees and other temporary structures built by Native Americans. It is this adaptability that has kept Wolf and his indigenous two-legged brothers and sisters from harming Mother Earth, because they have seen her bounty as endless. Dominant Society, on the other hand, came from a very

crowded and territorial European environment. Because of that, the first
white settlers built the first fences on the continent.

Until they were isolated on reservations and given what were often
the least desirable lands to live on, the Sioux survived by being mobile
and adapting. By the time Columbus set sail, other adventurers had already been up and down the coast of what would come to be called the
Americas. The Sioux at that time were called "Dakota," which means
"friends or allies." One among many, they were in the Piedmont area of
what would later be called the Carolinas at mid-millennium, and then
soon they were on the great move westward. In the north were the Iroquois, the most powerful of the group (in actuality, they were a united
confederacy made up of five organized tribes); the next most powerful
tribe was the Cherokee, who lay to the south of the Piedmont and enjoyed lush agricultural lands; the Shawnee were west of the migrating or
soon-to-be-migrating Sioux.

These powerful tribes had a basic commonality of social values and
religious and spiritual beliefs. Their "one among many" philosophy was
reflected in their openness to and practicing of common ceremonies
among the tribes. Indians were of the belief that they should (and would)
adapt to whatever ceremony seemed to work the best for spiritual communication, regardless of which tribe it was borrowed from. Chief Eagle
Feather, a Sioux holy man, was not averse to borrowing from things
learned in his travels. "Chief Sitting Bull had a saying," Bill Eagle Feather
would mention at his gatherings. "When you see something that is better, pick it up and take it along; but do not be afraid to keep the best of the
old ways, especially those which have been tried and proven. The old
chief also said to put the best of the two together, the old and the new,
and go on." Eagle Feather would add, "We Sioux do this with ceremony.
What comes out better for us, we pick up and go on."

Sweat Lodge, Vision Quest, and an annual tribal thanksgiving to the
Great Mystery or Great Spirit were ceremonies most tribes held in common. I also suspect that a powerful prediction ceremony for calling on

the Spirit World was held in common by most large tribes. The Iroquois, Canadian Chippewa, Pueblo, and Sioux to this day still hold this ceremony. It has differing names and is conducted in dissimilar ways from tribe to tribe, but the basic outcome is the same. This ceremonial borrowing and adaptation demonstrates openness to the spiritual experiences of other groups, undefiled by a sense of superiority. It also reveals a willingness not to be possessive, conservatively rigid, or closed to any but their own tribal tradition. Because the tribes agreed that they were one among many, there was no divisiveness around who communicated "correctly" with the Spirit World.

Just as the Indian tribes, while dignified people, did not assume superiority, likewise they did not feel in any way inferior to European society. "One among many" means not feeling inferior to others as well as not looking down one's nose at them. My favorite historian, Jack Weatherford, tells of the writings of Baron Lahontan, a French ethnographer who lived with the Huron tribe. The Hurons decried the Europeans' obsession with money—an obsession that compelled European women to sell their bodies to lonely men and compelled European men to sell their lives to the armies of greedy men who used them to enslave yet more people. By contrast, the Hurons lived a life of liberty and equality. According to the Hurons, Europeans lost their freedom in their incessant use of *thine* and *mine*.

MASTERS OF OUR OWN VISIONS

One of the Hurons explained to Lahontan, "We are born free and united brothers, each as much a great lord as the other, while you are all the slaves of one sole man. I am the master of my body, I dispose of myself, I do what I wish, I am the first and last of my nation . . . subject only to the Great Spirit."[4] Weatherford explains that Lahontan's writings rested on a solid base of ethnographic fact: the Hurons lived without social classes, without a government separate from their kinship system, and without private property. Demonstrating the lesson of Wolf, the Hurons valued the equality and the lack of greedy, self-centered possessiveness of "one among many."

"One among many" exists wherever liberty and equality thrive without the overriding need for materialistic possessions, divisive social classes, and ownership of Nature—a need rooted in greed and obsession. "One among many" respects the needs of the tribe or community, elevating those needs over the ego's wants. And it acknowledges the basic imbalance of being self-serving or enslaved to anyone or anything.

FICTION OF THE MAGNA CARTA

The concept of "one among many" encompasses all the basic freedoms inherent in modern democracy. American anglophiles occasionally point to the signing of the Magna Carta by King John on the battlefield of Runnymede in 1215 as the start of civil liberties and democracy in the English-speaking world. That document, however, merely moved slightly away from monarchy and toward oligarchy by increasing the power of the aristocracy. It continued the traditional European vacillation between government by a single strong ruler and by an oligarchic class.[5]

In reality, the Magna Carta was a power tradeoff between the king and the land-owning barons. It was not the basis of equal rights for all, nor did it reflect the value of group responsibility inherent in "one among many." No provisions for free speech, freedom of assembly, an elected leadership, or the freedom of movement within the forests to hunt for food were included. These freedoms were unheard of when the early colonists first settled in America, yet America's history books solidly proclaim the Magna Carta as the birthplace of civil rights! Most historians either deny or ignore the fact that the North American Indians had these great social benefits already in common use for the inspection of the likes of Benjamin Franklin, George Washington, Thomas Jefferson, and Thomas Paine, who then incorporated these freedoms into the U.S. Constitution and Bill of Rights.

MISLABELING THE INDIANS AS "WARLIKE"

Contrary to later stereotyping promoted by the aggressive, invading white man—himself very warlike—the Indian nations were not especially warlike. Too many facts and values ignored by white society prove otherwise. A nation cast by an invading force back upon other nations, as the Indians were, always has to fight for survival, and thus it can be accused of being warlike—especially if doesn't lie down and submit but fights back. We basically peaceful Sioux were always termed "warlike" by white historians because we *did* fight back, and rather effectively—but only after migrating thousands of miles to avoid conflict. Fighting for survival is not the same as being warlike and materialistic—adjectives that fit the invading white man far better. There are times when "one among many" requires fighting for the preservation of one's very existence.

It is interesting that Wolf, basically peaceful and group-oriented, has endured similar negative stereotyping by the white man. He has been labeled as dangerous to humans—even "man-eating"—just as Indians were labeled warlike. The fear-mongering has been so great that many wolves have been killed for no good reason—the justification being, of course, the safety of white society. And yet both Native Americans and wolves were peaceably practicing "one among many," fighting for survival only when forced to.

The American Indians were quite satisfied with their hunting bows and spears in the field of combat for centuries. Historically, all of the many neighboring tribes seemed to feel the same. The wary Europeans, on the other hand, constantly improved on their weaponry, because the various neighbors had equivalent values and pursuits.

Furthermore, Indians practiced what is called "coup" upon the battlefield, something that was unheard of among Europeans. If an Indian touched an enemy on the battlefield, the informal rules of combat often required that the man be retired from combat and sent home, very much alive but nonetheless vanquished.[6] "One among many" means not taking more than the tribe needs, and what tribe needs to take human life?

Trade routes peaceably connected tribes as one among many across North America. These trails could not have been planned, built, and maintained if the tribes were constantly fighting. Trade items from the ocean were often found great distances inland, indicating that the tribes were circulating freely. The tribes had been on this continent, peaceably coexisting for the most part, for thousands of years before the overpopulating Europeans came on the scene. Their ability to be basically content with their lot allowed a relatively peaceful existence compared to the constant warfare found in European society. "One among many" is simply not conducive to a warlike presence.

NATIVE HOSPITALITY AND THE PILGRIMS

If the Indians were so warlike, why would they have allowed the Pilgrims to land and then settle? They certainly were given provocation to attack, given that the Pilgrims' first act was to steal an Indian corn cache ("which the Lord hath provided!" the Pilgrims wrote in their ship's log). Think of it! A bunch of hairy, unwashed people showed up on the Indians' beloved shores and immediately stole a stored cache of corn that the tribe had preserved and placed away for the winter.[7]

And yet, rude as that was, the newcomers were one among many from the Indians' point of view, and the strangers *needed* the food out of desperation and a lack of local survival skills. The Indians could not deprive these newcomers of food if the weary travelers were starving, much less wage war against them. In fact, if the Pilgrims had not been so rude as to steal the food, the Indians would have probably offered it to them! If an Indian had been as desperate for food as the newcomers, he would simply have asked for help. But people who come from a truly warlike and materialistic culture do not trust the many, and therefore they feel justified in taking (or, more precisely, stealing) from and even warring against their neighbors.

The Siouan-speaking people trace their recent history back to the East Coast, where the invading white man first settled. As white society began to encroach on Indian territory, all of the tribes struggled to maintain the strength of "one among many" as their "oneness" was lost, assimilated, given up, or otherwise destroyed by the invaders. Maintaining a Native identity was especially difficult, though, for those tribes who remained in the east. For instance, the Wacama (a Sioux tribe) that did not move west, became subject to Dominant Society. Located in North Carolina now, they no longer retain their Native language, have lost their culture, and are Christianized, according to the tribal chairwoman I spoke to. "Our last Siouan speaker, an old grandmother, died over thirty years ago," she told me in the 1980s.

THE BAN OF 1883

Not surprisingly, a tribe under Dominant Society for a hundred years or more would become very culturally diluted, especially given that early U.S. Christianity was extremely zealous about destroying any and all ethnic groups that had dissimilar views. The fledgling federal government refused to restrain various unconstitutional religious actions undertaken by the Christian hierarchies. Missionaries lobbied the Grant Administration prior to 1883, in the 1870s, and such lobbying resulted in the unconstitutional Federal Indian Religion Ban promulgated through the Rules for Indian Courts after Grant left office.[8] Federal reservation Indian agents colluded with missionaries to root out Native beliefs. Agency documents show both the missionaries' tenacity in evangelizing and the free hand the government gave them. For example:

> *The Christianization of the adult Indians of this agency, with their pagan superstitions so deeply rooted, is but very slow, and, notwithstanding that some of them have been under missionary influences and religious instructions for several years past, yet it will require some additional years of patient missionary labor to convince the middle-aged and older persons of the absurdity of their early beliefs, or to bring them to accept the teachings of Christianity.*[9]

Given this kind of zealotry, condoned as it was by governmental powers, it is not surprising that American Indians were severely challenged in their efforts to maintain the value of "one among many." Like Wolf, who is skittish about relating with Human because of similarly zealous persecution, they were skeptical of what white society offered.

What happened to the Wacamas would have developed for the main body of Sioux had it not migrated or exited westward approximately four or five centuries ago (give or take a century or two)—before the influx of white settlers, at any rate. As a large tribe they would have had to undergo their own Trail of Tears, as did the Cherokee tribe, had they not left on their own. In fact, they would more than likely have been exterminated.

The less exposure there is to Dominant Society, the more cultural retention a tribe will maintain. This is not a difficult formula to understand. And it explains why the Sioux are one of the best North American tribes to study if someone wants to understand what Nature-based people believe in. Like the wolves the Sioux admire and emulate, they chose to migrate away from a looming threat initially and were the last to come in from their freedom on the Great Plains.

ONE ROOT, MANY BRANCHES

The Sioux, Iroquois, and Cherokee (the latter with a lighter complexion and rather Caucasian features) look dissimilar from most of the other North American tribes. The Mandan (whose main reservation is in North Dakota, far north along the Missouri) are almost as light as many Cherokee, with the height and heavy bones of northern Europeans, but the Mandan have more Indian features to go with their light skin. The Cherokee, on the other hand, have various European features, such as a receding hairline just above the brow, a monk's spot (premature balding) at the top of the skull, and (unlike the Mandan and most other Plains Indians) a tendency toward hair on the chest, back, and extremities. The Mandan have a "commonality" in their facial appearance, whereas just about every Cherokee I have met (at least those not enrolled from the Oklahoma reservation) seems to have had differing, unrelated, Caucasian-dominant features.

The Hunkpapa Sioux in central North and South Dakota are also large people in general. The Hunkpapa are darker than the Mandan and also comparatively hairless, with little or no facial hair. Most Siouan people have a heavy head of hair where it counts—up on top—and do not go bald, even in senior age. Their hair may thin, but I have yet to see a full-blooded Sioux who went bald (unless some sickness caused it).

The term "Sioux" was not an early name for the various related Native groups that eventually settled on the Great Plains. It was coined later, shortened from a hybrid ("Nadowessioux") that combined French and Chippewa elements and meant "lesser enemies." We Sioux were considered the "lesser enemies" from the south, while the Iroquois in the east were the "greater enemies" (along with the whites), who were driving the Chippewa (Anishanabe) out of their ancestral homes near the St. Lawrence Seaway.[10]

Although the term "Sioux" is a much more practical nomenclature than "Lakota" or "Dakota," especially for the reservation Indians themselves, many academics, both Indian and non-Indian, disapprove of the label. A sign on a tribal building wall back on my home reservation reads simply "Oglala Sioux Tribal Council." The Tribal Council stationery also reads "Oglala Sioux Tribal Council." On the adjoining reservation, about a hundred miles east, the signs announce "Rosebud Sioux Tribal Council." If it bothers an academic that we're incorrect, start with the Tribal Councils.

What these names reveal is an underlying "one among many" adaptability. Clearly, the strength of "one among many" doesn't disappear with a change in name. Any name can be a source of pride and respect if Native Americans have dignity and self-respect. We will not be undermined by the labels Dominant Society (or anyone else) gives us.

In any given summer there are usually some old-time Indians sitting around on the reservations discussing yesterday. Ask them what tribe they are from, and they will say Sioux. Ask them what particular band they are, and one will say, "I am an Oglala Sioux, and he"—pointing to a friend—"is a Sichangu Sioux from over there on the Rosebud." Ask them if they are Lakotas or Dakotas, and they will respond that they are Lakotas. One may comment, "The Dakotas are way east, but we are all Sioux." One among many. I hope that takes care of the academics.

The Sioux are believed to have tilled the prosperous corn lands of the Carolina Piedmont after they were driven out of or left the coastal areas.[11] The Cherokee, having discovered the more fertile and bountiful area southward, were no doubt glad to offer the Piedmont area to the Sioux, thereby gaining an appreciative ally, a strong buffer between them and the powerful Iroquois. The continent was huge and the populations were small. The people were wise in their use of available open areas. Although they had already lived in the region for thousands of years, they did not foolishly overpopulate. Overpopulation is an unforgiving and unforgivable mistake, as the European descendants are about to find out!

CEDING LAND VERSUS WAR

In the south, the Cherokee became the largest and most powerful tribe. I have speculated that the Sioux possibly relied on ceremony to warn them of the approaching danger of an oncoming Dominant Society. Were not the other tribes similarly warned in their ceremonies? This may sound highly preposterous after all. Please bear with me. The Eastern tribes held a commonality of spiritual beliefs that were based in and from the same Nature. I doubt that a benevolent Creator would have picked out one chosen tribe. "One among many," as observed in Nature, certainly doesn't favor one chosen species among the animal or plant kingdoms; rather, it favors all in that all are interconnected. There is no species that exists alone.

Maybe the Iroquois thought nothing could defeat them and ignored spiritual warnings. Maybe the Cherokee thought any invading force from the east could just as easily be appeased by a simple ceding of lands, which appeared to be almost limitless, given the penchant of sharing and generosity that possibly all northern tribes held as part of their cardinal virtues in commonality with the other tribes. This is mere theory, of course, in response to why the Sioux migrated rather suddenly and these two other major tribes remained, given the possibility that their ceremonies warned them as the Sioux were warned. Maybe this is a bit too much speculation, but it is interesting as it pertains to the events that followed. Did the Cherokee come under the conception that all two-leggeds (humans) were not materialistic and could be satisfied with an amount of land that would comfortably feed them? Whatever this oncoming force, they would be expected to be content with land offered to them. Hence the Cherokee would have no need to migrate away to the west as the Sioux had chose to do.

EXODUS WEST

The Sioux migrated down the Ohio River Valley and on to a once-blue Mississippi. An as-yet unidentified danger was approaching, and they were going to avoid it! The Kansa and Arkansa were among the migrating Sioux. They broke off eventually, when the tribe came to the confluence of the broad Missouri and Mississippi Rivers, and for the most part remained in that area (though some headed across the river and westward). The main Sioux group started upstream to the headwaters of the Mississippi. On the northward journey, other Siouan-speaking bands broke off. The Omaha and Mandan left to cross the big river and eventually headed up the Missouri. The Crow soon parted at the mouth of the Wisconsin River and headed northeastward toward Lake Superior.[12] Joe Medicine Crow, chief historian of the Crow Tribe, maintains this theory, declaring that his people wandered about, even to the shores of Lake Superior, before heading westward to settle in the Montana area.

MYSTIC WARRIORS OF THE PLAINS

What followed next in Sioux history clearly demonstrates an adaptive resilience distilled from living the value of "one among many." Initially the Sioux won their battles on their move westward and then northward into *Minneahtah*, which means "much water." ("Minnesota" is a corruption of this word.) The cold and deep snows led them to send scouts westward in search of a more hospitable clime. The Chippewa and their Cree allies, however, received guns from French traders, tipping battle success in favor of the Chippewa. In the meantime, Sioux scouts reported back of the discovery of the horse out on the Great Plains. With less access to firearms, the Sioux decided to head farther westward. Leaving Minneahtah was a blessing, however. With the discovery of the prolific *Tashuunka Wakan* ("big dog holy"), as Horse was known, the tribe began a glorious era and earned the title "Mystic Warriors of the Plains."¹³

Indigenous tribes were content to remain "one among many," but as distinct tribal entities. With the exception of the Iroquois Confederacy, most tribes did not form official unions or leagues with other tribes, preferring to be occasional allies as circumstances dictated. As the Sioux increased in numbers upon the Great Plains, their bands became larger and took the form of new tribes with separate chiefs. They were held together by a common language, along with common religious and spiritual ways. Hunkpapa, Oglala, Minicoujou, Yankton, and Sichangu (Brules) are examples of these tribes that made up the Sioux Nation. During the annual Sun Dance, these former bands, eventually designated as tribes, camped together on the Great Plains for an annual thanksgiving ceremony to their shared Higher Power, Wakan Tanka, the Great Spirit.¹⁴

DEFEATING THE U.S. CAVALRY

When the Sioux left Minnesota and went out onto the Plains, they concentrated on finding a safe place to live as "one among many." However, that "many" now included the U.S. Army. Given their new and hostile neighbors, the Sioux developed creative strategies to build strength and defend themselves in an effort to hold their own.

A favorite ploy they used against the Army was to utilize the strength of their horses, which were daily exercised and conditioned, in contrast to the cavalry's horses, which were enclosed within hastily built and confining stockades. A select group of Sioux riders would ride before the forts just out of rifle range and tantalize the troops inside. The Army would often respond by saddling up their horses and weighing them down with rations and ammunition. Out the gates the Army troops would charge, bugles blowing, the men mounted on poorly conditioned horses. The Indians would flee down a pre-designated route, leading the pursuers to a gully or draw where the main band of warriors would be concealed, waiting to erupt just when the Army horses were becoming winded. The Sioux would then hit the Army with spirited mounts after the cavalry horses were too winded to maneuver effectively.

Historians may argue otherwise, contradicting Sioux accounts, but how else could the Sioux capture so many weapons and an abundance of ammunition? They were well-armed when they defeated Colonel Custer at the Battle of the Little Big Horn.[15] Now where would the Sioux have obtained their weapons and ammunition, if not from the U.S. military? Maybe some Euro-centric-thinking historians just cannot admit that the Sioux actually took the arms from the U.S. Army. Maybe if we let them think that the guns somehow were traded from the Chinese or the Arabs, they would feel better!

CHIEF RED CLOUD

Displaying powerful and visionary leadership, Chief Red Cloud, concerned about the self-preservation of the Sioux tribe, forced the U.S. Army to agree to burn the forts it had established on the Bozeman Trail—a route passing through Montana and the Dakotas. Having won skirmish after skirmish in the area with the tribe's conditioned and effective mounts, Chief Red Cloud negotiated and signed the Treaty of 1868. It stated, in effect, that all of the land west of the Missouri River, continuing past the Black Hills, and between the Nebraska Sand Hills and the Cannonball River in present-day North Dakota, would belong to the Lakota/Dakota Nation for as long as the rivers flow, for as long as the grass grows, and as long as the Sioux dead lie buried. That is *forever*, in my estimation. Red Cloud envisioned that the Sioux people would make their existence within this territory.

Judging from their conduct to that point, I believe that the Sioux would have set an excellent environmental example if Dominant Society had honored the treaty commitment to which they bound themselves, and had the Sioux not been influenced by the missionaries' disregard for population control. It must be said, though, that Sioux families, as with most Plains tribes, had fewer children than European families did.[16]

Instead, the white man (Black Elk's Blue Man of deceit, greed, dishonesty, and untruth) lied and did not keep his word. The rest is standard Dominant Society history: gold was discovered in the Black Hills, settlers coveted choice agricultural lands, and the treaty was broken. Today, after hundreds of years of movement and adaptation, and generations after Red Cloud's efforts to secure a homeland, Sioux people live on the least productive lands in western South Dakota. The largest gold mine in North America operated in the Black Hills for almost a century and has finally shut down after depleting all the gold.

"One among many" applies not only to intertribal values, but also to the Sioux sense of spiritual leadership, which allows for unique and spiritually strong individuals to be "one" among the many for communicating with the Spirit World. The story of Black Elk and his vision described at the beginning of this chapter demonstrates this value and the power of spiritual leadership. Black Elk's enduring vision constitutes the powerful core of present-day Sioux Nature spirituality—a visionary teaching that brings to this present time the ancient values of Nature's Way.

Is Black Elk's vision mythology? Many will claim that it is. And yet all of what he predicted does exist. We can observe daily the dire effects he forecast, if we care to look for them. Black Elk's predictions of the Blue Man are being proven with each new day. The present environmental dilemmas and warnings are all fulfillment of those predictions.

As I said earlier, the Lakota/Dakota—the Sioux—were the last of the big tribes to come in from their natural freedom on the Great Plains. After Colonel Custer's cavalry was defeated in 1876, most of the Sioux tribes came into the federal reservations. Pursued by the U.S. Army, Chief Sitting Bull's Hunkpapas fled to Canada for several years. The U.S. government sent peace envoys for his return. Gradually, most of his people returned to the reservation on their own. Finally, five years after the Custer Battle, Chief Sitting Bull rode into Ft. Buford, North Dakota, with only 187 of his people left to surrender to the Army garrisoned there.[17] It took several generations for any degree of assimilation or "white man–izing" to have a significant effect. In reality, then, the Sioux have had little more than a mere century of contact with Dominant Society. The size of their large reservations has helped to give them some degree of privacy and cultural insulation. (The Hopi also have remained quite isolated from Dominant incursion, especially in comparison with tribes who have had many more decades with Dominant Society.) The Sioux have worked hard to retain their culture. After the U.S. government passed (unconstitutional) regulations forbidding Sioux religious ceremonies, the tenacious Sioux traditionals went out to hidden reaches of the sprawling reservation Badlands and conducted their age-old ceremonies, determined to maintain their connection with Nature.

> [A]ny Indian who shall engage in the sun dance, scalp dance or war dance, or any other similar feast, so-called, shall be deemed guilty of an offense, and upon conviction thereof shall be punished for the first offense by the withholding of his rations for not exceeding ten days or by imprisonment not exceeding ten days.[18]

While the Sioux could remain in touch with Nature, they could not regain the freedom to roam that had been their greatest joy. A nobility—a class of people who owned land while others did not—had not been allowed among the Sioux. Among these nonmaterialistic people, *everyone* had the freedom to roam in the wilderness; it was not a luxury, as it would be for the average European, but a given. The freedom to hunt or fish was likewise a common allowance. Now, though, with the encroachment of the white man and the overpopulation of the continent, it is the corrupt corporations that own our government, that misuse our lands, and that make once-common areas inaccessible to the public. Try to get to a favorite trout stream you once had easy access to. Each year more barriers seem to be erected, by corporations and private ownership, to bar public access to Nature's riches.

ORIGIN AND MYTH

"One among many" applies to the various origin theories and Sioux creation myths, as well. Not all Sioux support the migration-from-the-Carolinas theory. Charlotte Black Elk of the Pine Ridge Reservation (who claims to be a descendant of the Black Elk family but is not listed in the genealogy of a book written by family members and edited by J. Neihardt's daughter, Hilda Neihardt), believes that the Sioux evolved from Wind Cave in the Black Hills of South Dakota.[19] She contends that we originated in the Black Hills and then took a rather circuitous journey eastward, in time circling back to the Midwest. She has some support from Sioux people, especially those who are wise enough to have discovered that this attitude may sway the U.S. government to allow the return of the Black Hills to the tribe.

I hate to disagree with Charlotte Black Elk regarding her Black Hills origin theory, but I have difficulty with what appears to be mythology; I do not see historical grounding for her claim. It gets a little tougher when your tribe has a legal claim to a specific area. If we can convince Dominant Society to become more truthful in all their endeavors, I think we will stand a better chance of getting back at least some of our Black Hills than trying to convince the federal government we came out of a cave.

THE CONTRARIES RETURN

At this point in my writing, I felt my Iktomi friends looking over my shoulder. Finkley tapped my arm and said, rather combatively, "The Treaty of 1868—a treaty that, though broken, has never been legally renegotiated or rescinded—declared that the Black Hills belong to the Sioux. That treaty encompassed an area from the Nebraska Sand Hills to the Cannonball River in North Dakota, and westward from the Missouri to and past the Black Hills." Taking a fighter's stance, he said, "Don't you want the Black Hills rightfully returned to the Sioux?"

"Be honest, now," Finchley demanded, joining in the fray. "You *would* like to see the Black Hills returned to the Sioux; and if the white populace could be convinced you all came out of Wind Cave, you'd have some bonafide, gen-u-ine historical grounds. It would help get your treaty rightfully honored."

"If it comes to that, tell them you changed your mind about anything you said or wrote before," Finkley added. "Politicians do it all the time." Both Iktomi howled like a pair of coyotes.

Well, maybe we *did* come from Wind Cave. Alternatively, the Wacama tribe, which remained in North Carolina, has an origin myth that suggests that a comet or some other thing crashed into nearby Lake Waccamaw, and we came out of the rubble.[20] Many Sioux think we came from the Pleiades, a star group visible in late summer. Sure seems a long way to be coming from. But who knows?

THE HUMILITY OF NOT KNOWING

Most older traditional Sioux whom I have known—in particular, my teachers—consider the Great Spirit, Wakan Tanka, to be beyond the mind of men and women. If you ask a traditional Sioux who the Great Spirit or God is—who *exactly*—they will respond that they do not know. This is why I respect these people so highly: they are humble and honest. They are not overcome with the ego that I have seen so often displayed by the white man. When you ask the *wahshichu* (white man), "Who is God?" he brazenly and pompously tells you exactly who Creator is; then he demands that you share his belief and tells you that you will go to his hell if you do not follow his ways.

To a true traditional Indian, a question such as "Who is God?" is so deep that it is not just beyond *answering* by two-leggeds; it's even beyond *contemplation*. If the Great Spirit has made time and space, which are certainly incomprehensible (though we may grasp certain of their characteristics through science), then is not the Creator who made such imperceptible entities even more incomprehensible? How far out is space? When could time begin or end? No human can truthfully answer such queries. Therefore, why should we argue over the vast Power that created time and space?

"The Great Spirit is a Mystery" might be the best starting point for an exploration of North American indigenous thought.

FIGURE OUT YOUR OWN TRUTH

"Faith, faith!" the white man argues. "You Indians do not have faith in God."

"That is not altogether true," we argue back. "We have tremendous faith in our all-benevolent Creator, but we also realize that God has placed limitations before us. Creator exists and provides for us, yet is way beyond us. We have little problem with accepting that such an Ultimate Entity is indeed a Mystery."

In the "one among many" worldview, it is the duty of Human to figure out his or her own truth. Being "one among many" does not mean that we naturally accept the beliefs of the larger group.

Most indigenous definitions of the Supreme Being relate to the immediate creation upon which we are dependent. Some tribes refer to these "immediacies" as the Four Winds or Four Directions. The Sun and the Earth are also immediate; like the winds and the directions, they are observable and foundational. Although indefinable, Creator manifests much of its force, power, direction, and provision through these major creations. Creator can also manifest through lesser creations: for example, even a tiny cloud in an otherwise cloudless sky at an important ceremony, such as the Sun Dance, can manifest Creator, demonstrating to us that, yes, what we are doing is obviously pleasing or needed in order that we may live fully.

UNACCEPTABLE "TRUTHS" OF ORGANIZED RELIGION

Truth was imperative to Sioux interpretations of life and ways of relating. The Sioux were very careful to not invent what was not there. They were so pure in thought that they never invented a devil or demon (though most other religions feature such creatures), because they had never seen one. What you never see does not exist, according to the Sioux. They see their Creator, made visible in Creation all around them. But the devil?

It was extremely difficult for the Sioux to accept the Christian concept of Satan. When the Ban of 1883 was enacted—you may remember from the earlier discussion that it was intended to suppress indigenous beliefs—the government, in collusion with the missionaries, forced the Plains Indians to learn about and adopt the white man's religion—devil and all.

Since in the context of the day, civilizing and Christianizing meant the same thing, the reformers believed that to save the Indians they had to destroy their religion and culture."[21] I have mentioned the white man's devil before, but it is such a powerful superstition throughout the world that I believe it deserves repeated reflection. I have never seen this so-called Satan or any of his buddies ("demons," I believe his compatriots are called); and although millions of Christians are reluctant to admit it, they have never seen Satan or his henchmen either.

A television preacher named the Reverend Robert Tilson told his audience that Satan and his demons repeatedly appeared in his hotel room demanding that he stop his evangelical television show because it made them very unhappy. He used that ploy to appeal for more money to keep his show alive (and to add those golden beads—money—to his insatiable bead bag). Many people say that the devil is seen in the actions of others, but I have never been able to see one. I would be willing to bet that Tilson's claim was just another white man's lie, of which we Indians have heard so many.

It is common knowledge that Galileo Galilei (1564–1642) concluded, on the basis of his scientific research, that the sun did not rotate around the earth. That conclusion had serious ramifications: the Earth could no longer be envisioned as the center of the universe; therefore, God could no longer be regarded as directly involved in the day-to-day affairs of human beings. Galileo dared to question the ecclesiastical powers of his era, and he was promptly condemned to death as a heretic. He recanted, which saved his life, but his conception of the universe made sense and was thereafter (though gradually) adopted as correct.

It took the Roman Catholic Church a few more centuries to admit their error, however. In 1991 the Vatican finally officially admitted that Galileo had been right and the Church and the Bible had been wrong regarding the shape of the universe and the place of human beings and this world therein. With Galileo's starting discovery, the biblical view of the universe began a downward trend. False assumptions and unreasoned dictates have now been successfully challenged by leading scientists in the intervening centuries.[22]

Episcopal Bishop John Spong is a rare outspoken critic of the modern state of Christianity. He is especially critical of the Church's relationship with Nature, seeing the world in ways that resonate with the point of view of Nature's Way. Spong points out that in 1859 Charles Darwin published his *On the Origin of Species*. Prior to that time, the origin of human life had been understood in strictly religious terms. Darwin, contradicting the literal biblical text, suggested that the world was still evolving, still being created. His insights brought human and subhuman life much closer together, made them much more related, if you will. Since Darwin's time, we have seen many of the Church's other presumptions about humanity's origin go up in smoke as well.

Spong highlights the dilemma that Darwin's research posed for the Church. The Bible places humans just below the angels, but science had started to see humans as just above the animals. The Bible traces the origin of humanity back 10,000 years, but science has discovered evidence that modern humans evolved around 140,000 to 290,000 years ago. As Spong notes,

> The Christian Church resisted Darwin with vigor, but the ecclesiastical power of antiquity had already been broken, and the Church's ability to threaten Darwin with execution as a heretic no longer existed. Besides, truth can never be deterred just because it is inconvenient. Today, whether his critics like it or not, Charles Darwin's thought organizes the biological sciences of the Western world. His work has made possible such once-unimaginable things as organ transplants using organs derived from sub-human species. They work because Darwin was right. That strange thing called "creation science" is nothing more than ignorant rantings reflecting a frightened and dying religious mentality.[23]

GENUINE TRUTH CAN NEVER BE DETERRED

I find a strong connection to Nature's Way when I reflect on Bishop Spong's worthy phrase, "Truth can never be deterred just because it is inconvenient." A person's observations and discoveries in Nature's Way cannot deviate from the truth if the seeker holds to what is directly observed. The truth will speak out as Creator's truths within Nature. Those truths do not deviate unless intentionally altered. We can trust in pure observation, though all human pronouncements and declarations, laden with selfish ego, paternalism, and deceit, have proven untrustworthy.

I am sure I will be condemned by some for not believing in the white man's mythology, including his mythical devil, even though my ancestors did not believe in it either. But the zealots who condemn me have likewise never seen the devil. What gives them the right to condemn a person for not believing in something that cannot be observed? Wolf would not go back to his pack and report a lie. Therefore, why should I be expected to, just to please Dominant Society? Haven't we left the Dark Ages?

Learning the lesson of Wolf, we need to cultivate the value of "one among many"—one of the enduring values of Nature's Way that will work toward keeping us from the fatal, overconsuming path that the entire world has embarked upon. We cannot afford to alter or lose this basic, ancient, Creator-given lesson. We must work for the good of all, speaking out in truth and courage, as Black Elk and John Neihardt did, to protect our society and our planet, to which we owe a supreme duty (regardless of how "modern" we think we have become). We cannot afford to ignore the spiritual strength of "one among many," sorely lacking in Dominant Society (despite the message of nationalism and global internationalism generated by burgeoning threats of terror).

So the lesson of Wolf is ultimately a model of spiritual leadership. Like Wolf, we learn that each of us does better when we care for the good of the many. And we learn that we must pick our leaders, both spiritual and secular, based on that same value. We find that humility, not pride, is the easiest way to foster cooperation. We conclude that compromise and concession usually lead to better results than combat or confrontation; but when we must fight for our survival (rather than for our vanity or our limited self-interest), we fight like Wolf's pack—all who are able participate helping the common cause.

In a time of so many lawsuits over ownership of words and ideas and concepts, we may find value in the very important function of the scout in Wolf's pack. He goes out alone to discover the truth and reports back to the others for their benefit. Too many of us come from such a feeling of lack and poverty (whether real or imagined) that we are like scouts who find a valuable resource (such as prey for the pack) and keep it for ourselves, failing to report it to those who stayed behind.

The Six Powers of Black Elk's vision can help us to defeat the Blue Man's selfish destruction of Mother Earth, through the illumination of undistracted focus, the patience for cleansing and renewal, the peace of knowledge, the security of abundance, the limitless feeling of sky, and the connected calm of Earth. We cannot honor the idea of "one among many" and heal ourselves and the Earth if we are too distracted, too fatigued, too ignorant, too fearful of loss, too constrained, or too ungrounded.

Moving on, we turn in Chapter Five from a necessary focus on the outer world (which we observe like Eagle, heal like Bear, and manage like Wolf) to a focus on spirit. The lesson of following our inner direction is demonstrated by Orca, the Killer Whale.

DEVELOP INTUITION

Lesson of Orca

Orca has a mysterious power of communication that humans, despite all of their progress in science, have yet to fathom credibly. Often called Killer Whale, Orca knows the presence of its prey, and the prey's direction and speed in murky depths, long before the great ocean mammal is upon it.

Alaskan halibut boat captains tend to travel with a rifle to ward off large scavengers. Sea captains have told me that Orca seems somehow to know when a rifle is on board a fishing boat, and also whether a captain will use his rifle to keep the Orca pod from raiding the catch! The older bulls know the range of the rifle and keep the younger bulls out of danger. Ask a halibut fisherman from Alaska how smart Orca is. It can remove the large, flat fish from hooks and consume them then and there. All this takes place in the murky depths, of course, and yet Orca does not get hooked. Furthermore, it manages to pass this skill on to other members of the pod. Many people who have experienced swimming with dolphins, relatives of Orca, will readily attest to the mysterious intelligence these friendly creatures are gifted with.

Truly, Orca has a deep sense of communication that reaches into a higher realm of mystery than two-leggeds commonly attain. Orca is gifted with an intuition that puts it in contact with all of Nature around it. We humans have much less intuition, and what we do have seems mysterious and fearful to many of us—as if it were a huge undersea creature. Rather than fearing our intuition, we must work to develop it, to hone what we receive. Developing that intuition leads to immense gifts that can help us survive and thrive both individually and as a society. A society without intuitive initiatives doesn't grow, doesn't develop. It becomes conservative and fundamentalist, and tends to want to dominate and exploit Mother Earth instead of honoring her bounty and mystery.

I once "talked" to an orca, and as it blew various sounds from its air hole and splashed water with its flippers in response to my words, I had the feeling that I was communing with God. I talked to it in Sioux, introducing myself in broken Lakota, a Nature-based language:

"*Hau kola, hey hogan wakan, hau tanka ahtaah wakan hogan — miye Wanblee Wichasha, Oglala Lakota.*" (Hello, friend, oh holy fish; hello you big very holy fish; I am Eagle Man of the Oglala Lakota.)

That is how I started out. (I am not a Sioux linguist by any means, but since both of my parents spoke Indian around the house while I was growing up, I certainly could try to introduce myself.) I then pointed to the sky, to the flesh-eating whale, and back to my heart. I spread both hands upward in a half-circle, making an arch.

I was then saying to Orca that we both (that is, our respective tribes) believed in the Great Mystery or the Great Spirit—meaning we both shared a very common bond—we both believed in the same highest Entity. I ended by pointing to Orca and then to myself and saying, "We are meant to protect Mother Earth!"

With that statement, the orca made a huge splash and actually nodded its head.

CEREMONIES FOR DEVELOPING INTUITION

Ceremonies can help individuals to grow in their life's quest. Since we are not gifted like Orca or Dolphin as to the murky waters of life, I believe ceremony is our tool to hone our intuitive abilities—those abilities that enable us to be more sure of our perspective toward truth. Many ceremonies are universal across all North American tribes. I hope that these universal ceremonies can be rescued from any sense of ownership in order that all creeds and tribes might rightfully enjoy the blessing of our common ceremonies. It is my belief, however, that some ceremonies are tribal, and not meant for everyone.

Vision Quest is a ceremony that has been practiced by many tribes down through time—and not just the Native Americans, either. Vision Questing, or spending an isolated time out in Nature, is not owned by any Indian tribe. In fact, even the Christians claim that their Jesus fasted and prayed in solitary out in the wilderness. And Moses, I understand, went out alone to a mountain to commune with his concept of the Higher Power. I did the same on Bear Butte Mountain to fulfill my instructions from Chief Fools Crow through Chief Eagle Feather: "Go up on the mountain and fast and pray before the next Sun Dance"—these were my instructions.

I had a rather startling quest that time. A rattlesnake actually snapped off a portion of my peace pipe on a dark, stormy night—snapped it just below the bowl, where the pipe-maker had carved an ax blade. The top portion of the pipe was a bowl for peace, but the ax was a symbol for war (added to signify that I had been an actual combat warrior). The ax portion was snapped flush by the snake.

When I told my experience to Fools Crow, he raised nary an eyebrow; he calmly sent me to Chief Eagle Feather in a nearby reservation with the simple words, "*Wah ste aloh!*" (It is good!) I was a bit perplexed but assumed that he considered me more Chief Eagle Feather's student than his and did not want to interfere.

Chief Eagle Feather was slightly more informative when I described my vision to him. "You had a good Vision Quest, Nephew. Now
you get your things ready for the Sun Dance." I concluded that I should
not expect a holy person to give me a detailed explanation of my quest
(if there is such a thing). The quester's own observations are what is
most important.

A JESUIT PRIEST QUESTS FOR A VISION

Father William Stolzman was the chairperson of the Medicine Men and
Pastors' Meeting held at the Rosebud Reservation from 1973 to 1979.
This meeting—a long series of meetings, actually—sought spiritual discussion and an exchange of information between the spiritual leaders
and laypeople of the Sioux tribe, and the pastors, priests, and laypeople of
the white man's faith. The meetings were well attended for a reservation
function that met bimonthly, nine months out of the year. With Lakota
relatives present, often there were as many as forty people at a meeting.
My main mentor, Chief Eagle Feather, was a regular participant.

Unlike most priests, Father Stolzman—a missionary and educator on
various Sioux reservations—became very open-minded through contact
with the traditionals. He discovered natural ceremonies, observing and
participating, and described his own personal observations in his book
The Pipe and Christ. In talking of his Vision Quest in that book, Father
Stolzman described the dark rain clouds that threatened his solitary vigil
on the mountaintop as he faced the Four Directions and prayed:

> As I faced the West, the wind became more and more ferocious. The
> black flag in the West was long, and it whipped me and lashed me
> painfully. How hard and testing is the West! The wind became so
> strong that I seemed to lean 45 degrees into the wind to keep my bal-
> ance. Finally when I could no longer stand, I descended into the pit
> and sat facing the West. The wind roared, the flags slapped, and the

lightning flashed from the West overhead. Suddenly, "Yehhhhhhhh-hhh . . . ," the most blood-curdling eagle scream I have ever heard! It was a thousand times louder than any eagle cry I had ever heard before. The wind immediately stopped! The sudden silence was shaking. There was only the snapping and crackling of the lightning in the West . . . and the lingering memory of that frightening eagle's scream. I sat and shuddered. It was the Wakiyan, the Thunder Bird, controller of storms.

The lightning then moved to the South. Something was wrong. This was contrary to the way it should be. It should have turned toward the North! Only later did I understand that this was a sign of the companion of the West, the contrary one, Heyoka, the Clown. With the wind quiet, I returned outside to pray. As the lightning moved to the South, the wind began to come from that direction. With it came a fine mist. As it touched my face, I could not help but think of tears. I did not want the mist to come into the square, so I prayed, and even the mist stopped. (This was amazing, for at the medicine man's house a mile away, the people were anxiously praying for me. They were having a downpour, and it hailed several times. In fact, the entire region suffered the worst hail storm in years that night.) On the hill, however, there were only wind, lightning, and thunder.

I began to hear voices coming out of the floor at the southern edge of the pit. There were thousands of voices resembling the drone of a crowd. I bent over and cupped my ear in order to pick up some words to discover if they were speaking to me in Lakota or English. After a few minutes the voices stopped. These were the voices of the dead who journey south to the place called Tate Makoce, what White men call the "Happy Hunting Ground."

I remained for quite a while in the pit, praying and feeling very close to the earth, to which the bodies of the souls had returned. Then I decided to go outside. As I got up to leave, the earth gave a great heave one direction and then the other. I was bounced back and forth from

side to side in the pit—gently. It seemed as if Grandmother Earth was
showing her presence and love by rocking me back and forth in the
"arms" of the pit as a little child is rocked in the arms of its grand-
mother.[1]

The rest of Father Stolzman's story, though full of how Nature communicated with him during his Vision Quest, is most informative of
how the experience changed his life:

> *My prayers had been answered. In fact, every time I have gone to the*
> *spirits on the hill my prayers have been answered. Yet they are always*
> *answered in ways I have never expected. I have studied some psychol-*
> *ogy, and I know that a person can sometimes unknowingly program*
> *himself to see what he wants to see or symbolically hallucinate events*
> *for the past. Every time I go to the spirits I find their response to be a*
> *total surprise. I guess if there were no surprises, they would be giving*
> *me nothing new, and there would be no need for their coming. When I*
> *try to set up expectations for them, they refuse to come at all.[2]*

Father Stolzman's books are evidence of an openness that I never saw
in the many missionary priests I knew as a child. His participation in Native ceremonies helped to develop his intuition by attuning his senses to
Nature and helping him to take meaning from winds, eagle cries, lightning, and the experience of spending an awesome night out in the open
on a hilltop surrounded on all sides with thunderstorms and hail.

Before we leave Father Stolzman, I would like to recommend his
book for those readers who are not yet ready or able to completely em-
brace Nature's Way. His book is very informative regarding ceremony,
culture, values, and beliefs on both sides of the coin. Many people are
too laden with fear, from what I have seen, to step into Nature's Way;
others are not fearful but simply choose to blend Christianity and the
realm of Nature. Might be a smart move; they are covered on both bases.

My mother seemed to manage that approach, though my father preferred Nature's Way.

Participation in Vision Quest, Sweat Lodge, and Sun Dance recently affected one of my nephews. He has always been a respected and respectful person from my point of view, but I saw a profound integration of newfound confidence and pride when I conversed with him after he finished his Vision Quest and Sun Dance under the tutelage of a Sioux medicine man. I have another nephew who, though formerly a drinker, has not touched alcohol for years because of his many Sun Dances and related ceremonies. A grand-nephew had the same blessed reaction.

All these young men are now much better prepared for life. The ordinary quarrels and pettiness of daily living have no meaning to them; they have higher goals. This transformation has definitely honed their intuitive abilities. My nephews were not sitting and listening in some workshop or prayer gathering; they were out upon Mother Earth in all three ceremonies—Sweat Lodge, Vision Quest, and Sun Dance. Physically, they were immersed in a totally different medium than what Dominant Society experiences.

SACRED PLACES

At this point, if you are not tribally enrolled, I suggest strongly that you do *not* Vision Quest at Bear Butte Mountain in the Black Hills. Be polite: stay away from that mountain and from other places the Indian people deem sacred. Bear Butte gets very crowded in the spring and summer, with Indians going back to their once-banned religion. I used to Vision Quest on Bear Butte and was generally the only person up there at night, but now there is a tremendous upsurge in Native people returning to the old ways. There are plenty of other distant peaks and mountains and Badlands buttes, and all very isolated too. All over America, even in the east, mountaintops and hills remain vacant. Go there instead. Remember, this is a ceremony just between you and your concept of God (Creator). It is owned by no one person or tribe. While it is a universal ceremony, I believe the Native people should be given some allowance, since the Christian-dominated government wrongfully banned us from ceremonial participation for a long time. There is much to catch up on, especially for the young.

I do not want to trouble the reader with any mechanics of a Vision Quest. Some want to ask: What do I bring? How long should I stay? What will I see? But what is really important is for you to simply get up and go do it! At the rate this world's population is increasing, I would not wait too long. How long and where you go is your decision, unless you are fortunate enough to have a teacher in these matters.

In summary, I believe that Vision Quest is the most important ceremony you will ever do. All it involves is isolating yourself out in Mother Nature for a brief period of time. It will develop and promote your intuitive abilities, as long as you remain a "hollow bone." All the powerful holy men I have known honed their spiritual intuitive gifts with this ceremony. It is the first ceremony a Sun Dance leader will insist that participants perform prior to their first Sun Dance.

SWEAT LODGE

Sweat Lodge is also a universal ceremony; it dates back to the early Greeks. In 425 B.C.E., Herodotus wrote of the sweat bath customs of the Scythians, describing the *laconia*, or hot air baths. The Romans, who were notorious for copying everything Greek, expanded the hot air baths into small bath chambers that used heated water and steam. After the fall of Rome, the Arab world utilized steam baths, which were embraced by the prophet Mohammed around 600 C.E. In time, Turkish baths, with their succession of steam rooms, would come into being. In Russia, steam baths were constructed of wood and looked rather like houses, unlike the circular-lodge design of the American Indians. Yet the Russian steam baths served many purposes—social, medicinal, therapeutic, and ritual—not unlike the Native sweat lodges.

In his book *Sweat*, Mikkel Aaland states that sweat baths or sweat lodges are found in many countries around the planet and are utilized for spiritual and healing purposes:

> *Finnish women usually gave birth inside saunas in order to be in the presence of benevolent spirits. These spirits were thought to reduce the pains of childbirth and increase the chance of survival for both the mother and child. Islamic women went to the hamman, the middle eastern sweat bath, three times during many days of wedding ceremonies, attending the final rinsing bath on the eve of the marriage. Russian mourners would heat their sweat bath in order to warm their souls and . . . the souls of the deceased.*[3]

The Laps, Finns, and Celts utilized sweat lodges long before the advent of Christianity. Celts were deeply into all things spiritual. It would be highly doubtful that after a history of worldly travel and exploration they would ignore the spiritual and therapeutic benefits of sweat lodges.

This use of steam across time and borders attests to the fact that heat and steam feel good; but can the Sweat Lodge ceremony really hone one's intuition? I believe that *all* positive ceremony enhances that mysterious entry—the one that reaches out mystically to the murky waters beyond our vision. We become more like Orca, using some sense we don't understand to "see" where there is no light. Ask those who have been in Sweat Lodge and I believe you will find unison of agreement. Sweat Lodge cleanses and refreshes, whereas Vision Quest hones contemplation. Both are valuable to make one the shiny, hollow bone that Chief Fools Crow described—a "clean vessel" that allows one's medicine and intuitive powers to pass through less inhibited.

Among the Sioux, the sweat lodge itself is generally made of willow saplings, although I have observed holy men use other species of saplings. Willow is quite pliant, which allows it to bend without breaking as long as one cuts it for use in the spring or summer, and not in or toward winter.

The tools and materials you need to bring are these:

Tree saw or ordinary hand saw

Hatchet

Knife

Twine

Shovel

Some purists will insist that willow bark must be used instead of twine for tying. Perhaps they saw, somewhere on a reservation, a lodge tied together with the peeled bark of the willow. Willow bark may be hard to come by, especially when one has no access to willows. Just getting the saplings for the lodge can be a challenge. Neighbors who have aesthetic willow saplings gracing the edge of their duck-filled pond tend to object vehemently to the taking of eighteen to twenty-four of their pride and joy to build a small lodge!

Holy men and women do not charge for conducting a Sweat Lodge, other than the construction expenses, if there are any (which can be shared among all participants). If a holy person comes from a reservation and seems to be quite poor, however, that person should be compensated. His travel expenses should certainly be taken care of by those who brought him to speak and teach. If spiritual seekers visit a holy man or a holy woman on a reservation, they should take that person food (in quantity), or gifts such as blankets or clothing. They should *not* take baloney sandwiches or little rocks with ribbons tied to them! When a group does a Sweat Lodge among themselves, all should pitch in and help. Fortunately, there is very little expense in building a lodge or conducting the ceremony.

We learned in Black Elk's vision that the Four Directions or Four Winds are highly important entities provided for us by the Maker. These entities are often called upon or beseeched to in a Sweat Lodge when Native Americans conduct a lodge ceremony. The Celts also beseeched to the Four Directions.

In preparation the Sweat Lodge participants are smudged with sage or cedar. Then the Sweat Lodge begins, utilizing the Four Elements: fire, air, water, and Earth. The Four Directions are beseeched within the warm womb (the actual sweat lodge) of Mother Earth. Fire (*Wiyo*, the Sun) heats the stones; and water (*Wichoni Minni*, the life-giving rain), when poured onto the heated stones, produces steam. That added water is mixed with sweat—the waters of the participants—and with air. *Tate Topa*, the Four Winds, carry forth the mixture of steam to the four quarters of our planet. This carrying forth of a part of ourselves out to the Four Directions tells us we are participating in a universal ceremony.

A detailed description of the Sweat Lodge is found in my book *Mother Earth Spirituality*.[4] In summary, the ceremony goes like this. Stones are heated over a nearby fire. They are delivered into the lodge, one by one, after the participants have entered, and they are placed in a dishpan-sized central pit. A bucket of water with a dipper is placed within and set beside the lodge leader or water-pourer. At his or her discretion, more heated stones are called for as the ceremony progresses. (In summertime, fewer stones are needed to heat the lodge than in winter.) Once all is ready, the doorway flap is closed and the actual ceremony begins. Generally, songs or chants are sung to the beat of a drum; then individual prayers or beseechments are voiced. During this process, the participants sweat and are cleansed.

Picture the scene, if you will. Within the steaming lodge, participants are sitting on spring grass within the moist womb of Mother Earth. Everyone there is hoping to discover the depth of ceremony.

Most are clad in a T-shirt and a pair of swimming shorts. Often, though, women will wear light cotton dresses. The ground is cool even though the steam has begun to spread out from the first dippers of water splashed onto the glowing rocks in the pit at the center of the lodge.

The lodge leader calls out in the darkened interior, calling first on the West Power, the first power of Black Elk's vision. That calling begins the first so-called endurance, which is the introduction. It is the first of four endurances that will be beseeched to the Four Directions, which were the first four powers of Black Elk's vision. Mother Earth is present; participants are sitting upon her. Father Sky is present. The Sun's heat is within the glowing stones, bringing forth seekers' lifeblood, their sweat, to mix with the lifeblood of the world (as represented by the water within the bucket beside the lodge leader). All within the lodge are introduced to the onlooking Spirit World through the West Power. Each person calls out his or her name and a respectful greeting.

A simple beginner's song is then sung, most often accompanied by a drumbeat.

Wiyopeyata hehhhhhh, hehhhhh. [O *West Power.*]
Wee yohhh-peee-yahhh tahh hehhhhhh.
Wee yohhh-peee-yahhh tahh hehhhhhh.
Wee yoh-pee-yah tah hehhhhhh.

If the lodge participants are experienced, a more elaborate song might be sung. The following is an example of a Sioux song:

Wiyopeyata kiya etunwin na cekiya yo hey
Cekiya yo yo hena nitakuye yo hey.
Look to the West and pray to them,
Pray to them because those people are your relatives.

The first endurance, as we saw, is to introduce. The second endurance is to meditate. The third endurance is to beseech (in other words, to pray). The fourth endurance is to end the ceremony and to ask for healing and subsistence. Between each endurance, someone raises the flap and allow cooling air in. Sometimes the third endurance makes a ceremony lengthy, if it is a large sweat lodge with many prayers. If the oxygen within seems to be depleted during that third endurance, the flap can be raised after several participants end their beseechment.

Because beseechment should not be an endurance test (despite the Sweat Lodge label "endurance"), the lodge should not be made too hot, and plenty of air should be allowed in. I do not hold long-lasting lodge ceremonies. The few that I do anymore average ten to fifteen people. We do not generally go over much more than an hour. Even with the flap raised often, everyone seems to sweat profusely. I never bring in a huge stack of rocks either. In the wintertime I bring in more, but on a hot, sultry night I bring in but very few.

The final endurance asks for healing, growth, and abundance. Participants acknowledge themselves for being in the lodge, wherein they will gain spiritual confidence. They ask for healing of self or a loved one, ask for world peace, and promise Mother Earth that they will watch out for her, protect her, and do everything within their power to end the harmful dangers she and her inhabitants face. Lastly the participants move their hands forward toward the center of the lodge to touch the imaginary Tree of Life.

The lodge often ends on the statement "*Mitakuye Oyasin*." (We are all related.) Some interpret this phrase to mean "We are related to all things."

Every lodge leader does a Sweat Lodge somewhat differently. I learned from Chief Eagle Feather, so I do mine similar to his. I do not believe in nude lodges, although mixed lodges (both genders present) I have no objection to. Neither did my teacher, Chief Eagle Feather. Some

medicine people (which I am not) are loaded with rules; Fools Crow and
Eagle Feather were not. They had more important things to think about.
This ceremony is a universal ceremony as mentioned earlier. No one
owns it!

PEACE PIPE: BLESSING AND DILEMMA

A peace pipe was often used by the Sioux and other tribes as a beseechment instrument. Before a main ceremony such as a Sun Dance or a
Yuwipi (described in the next chapter), a holy man would bring forth
his pipe and place a portion of tobacco in the pipe as he beseeched each
direction. Turning to the West Power, he would hold forth his pipe and
then place a small portion of tobacco in the bowl. Some tobacco would
also be placed on the ground beneath him as a remembrance that all
things come from the Earth. The holy man would say words to each direction that he faced (always turning in a clockwise manner if he was a
Sioux). See the chapter titled "Peace Pipe Ceremony" in *Mother Earth
Spirituality* for a detailed elaboration.[5]

Beseechments vary by person and occasion. Sioux do not use rote or
memorized prayers as Christians do. Prayers are said from the heart,
composed for the ceremony at hand and shaped by the major reason behind that particular ceremony.

Many non-Indians today have peace pipes, as do many Indians who
know little of their culture or are not enrolled members of a tribe. Some
non-Indians insist that they are from a particular North American tribe,
declare that they are pipe-bearers, and conduct ceremonies from the
United States to Australia to Europe.

I know some good and sincere people who have peace pipes in their
possession and do a ceremony—mostly a private ceremony to the Four
Directions and the Six Powers. After over a decade of observance, I now
have to reverse a position I held earlier: while I used to think that the
peace pipe was for all, I now think it should be used only by tribal holy

men and holy women. Many well-meaning Indians claim that some on the outside do not know how to use their pipes properly. To avoid disharmony over an issue that is not critical, I will agree to restricting pipe use.

I always try to walk my talk, however, so I have given away my peace pipes, one of which I made myself and the other—a beautiful pipe—that I was given by Chief Fools Crow. Thus I am no longer a pipe-carrier. If I am going to ask non-Indians and non-traditional Indians to utilize their personal wotai stones instead of a pipe for their personal beseechment, then I should also do the same. Actually, I feel more comfortable utilizing my wotai. It was made directly by Creator and came to me in a rather dramatic way. Bear in mind that I am but a mere human. What do I know on this matter? What does anyone fully know? I am simply seeking some option that will bring harmony among all. We have too much else to do, environmentally, to allow quarreling to misdirect us.

A wotai (pronounced *woh-tie*), mentioned in a couple of anecdotes earlier, is a special stone that will come into a person's life if he or she simply asks for it. It is usually a smooth stone and typically runs from as small as nickel-size to a full handful. A wotai often enters into someone's life once that person starts upon Nature's Way. It might be found during a walk close to a mountain stream, for example, or during a stroll along a fast-flowing river. Several of my earlier writings illustrate how a wotai can come into a person's life. These wotai are usually picturesque, meaning that they contain images within. I have a wotai that is loaded with many images that were placed there by its Maker.

I honestly do not expect many on either side of the peace-pipe issue to change their view, but at least I have added my two cents worth. Maybe my view will strengthen the idea that a wotai stone is a more practical beseechment item for people who are not tribal pipe-carriers. It is quite a dilemma, really, in that I hate to see an interested non-Indian seeker turned away from any sort of participation. The majority of Dominant Society has ignored the wisdom and teachings of the North

American tribes. With the world now in jeopardy, facing planetary heating, ozone-layer thinning, resource depletion, and overpopulation, we need every non-Indian who walks down the Red Path to educate the majority of this land, for they can reach their own kind far more effectively than we who are tribal. I hate to see an argument involving the pipe alienate non-Indians, especially given the serious threats to humanity that lurk on our horizon, but I also realize that a wotai stone is a worthy option. Certainly no one has the authority to take away any religious article that another person deems sacred to his own personal quest, but the wotai stone is a viable alternative.

I have a friend, Deborah Chavez, who believes that she was spiritually called on to make a pipe, despite having no significant Indian heritage. Shortly after its completion, she took it to the Indian funeral of a young man who had committed suicide. The only person there with a peace pipe, she was called on by others to bring forth her pipe to send the departed on in ceremony. She was obviously *meant* to make that pipe and to be there at that funeral with it. She was the only contributing writer to my *Mother Earth Spirituality*, which tells the full story. Her own book is titled *Fallen Feather: A Spiritual Odyssey*.[6]

SUN DANCE

Most people will never experience this ceremony, because it is a tribal thanksgiving and most people are not of a tribe. Even among Natives it is a rarity: the majority of tribal members never become pledgers or Sun Dancers.

Nonetheless, it is important to know about the Sun Dance. That knowledge will help readers understand the spiritual depth of the old traditionals. Even a closed ceremony can give outsiders insight into the development of intuition when they hear or read the stories of those ceremonies.

There are many, many summer Sun Dances now held on the reservations in the Dakotas—especially on the Rosebud and Pine Ridge Reservations. When I was younger, there was but one Sioux tribal Sun Dance held at the Pine Ridge Reservation. This ceremony was banned by the government in the early 1880s, so for almost a century it was conducted only sporadically, held in secret out in lonely areas of the reservations by brave and stubborn holy people. It did not return in public form until the 1950s, after the old prophet Black Elk died. Chief Eagle Feather, the true Sun Dance Warrior, said he was going to bring back the Sun Dance. "Out in the open," Chief Fools Crow said, "I will pierce him." How a young half-breed boy that was only a mere dancer at the pow-wow the night before that famous event could be at that first modern-era public Sun Dance is indeed more than coincidence, but I was there and sitting beside my step-grandmother. It was a pitiful crowd, but it was out in the open, defiant—the beginning of the Great Return. Oddly, missionaries and government authorities paid us little attention. They were so used to winning that a couple of old holy men were considered harmless. The small crowd proved that, in their eyes.

Frank Fools Crow, who was Intercessor at that first public Sun Dance, was the Sun Dance Chief for the six Sun Dances that I eventually took part in, in the late sixties and early seventies. At my first Sun Dance as an adult, I participated but was not pierced (the fullest level of participation), since I had just returned from war; at the next four Sun Dances held at Pine Ridge, I was pierced; and at my last Sun Dance—one held way up at Green Grass on the Hunkpapa Reservation, where the sacred pipe resides—none of us dancers pierced. Chief Fools Crow and Chief Eagle Feather both officiated at that final ceremony.

In my time, only tribal Indians took part in the piercing ceremony, and I believe that all of the participants were Sioux—either Oglala, Sichangu, Hunkpapa, or Minnicoujou. Maybe a few of the other Sioux were also represented among the pledgers, but I would not know: in my limited capacity, I did not go about asking for credentials. My mother warned me, before my first dance, that I might not be allowed to participate, since I was only a half-Indian. A friend of mine, Sonny Larive—also a half-breed—had danced the year before, so I didn't quite believe my mother. I am sure she would have been relieved if I had been rejected by the elders, though, because the missionaries were pressuring her to forbid me to dance. They were fearful that we younger Sioux (especially me, as a returned combat warrior) would set an example that would encourage other youth to return to the old way. They were right! At my last piercing Sun Dance, the arena was vibrant with many young Sun Dance pledgers. Fools Crow had to have help from other holy men to pierce all of us. The once pitiful crowd almost two decades before had grown to a huge throng that swelled to the periphery of the arena.

Now it is a different world in regard to the Sun Dance. No longer is there one Sun Dance on one reservation, as in my time. A single Sun Dance could not possibly manage the thousands of pledgers who now come from many reservations and from off-reservation as well. Throughout Sioux country the ceremony has spread. I believe there are actually over a hundred summer Sun Dances a year in the Great Plains alone!

You can go to some Sioux reservations and see Sun Dances ranging from wide open (meaning non-Indians can participate as pledgers) to closed Sun Dances that require people to show a tribal enrollment card before they are admitted to participate or even watch. Some of these Sun Dances are so strict that a non-tribal spouse cannot be admitted with an enrolled tribal member. One of the most beautiful and respectful Sun Dances I have seen in years was such a closed Sun Dance, conducted by an honorable Oglala holy person, Rick Two Dogs, on the Pine Ridge Reservation. The term "closed" is often flexibly interpreted, though. People of Indian descent—whether full-blooded, one-half, one-fourth, one-eighth, or one-sixteenth—and all enrolled tribal members are finding themselves most welcome at many of the so-called closed Sun Dances. My nephew (one-fourth) and his son (one-eighth) just finished their first Sun Dance on the Pine Ridge Reservation, and they are pledged to dance at least four Sun Dances. There were over 100 participants (dancers/pledgers) at the Pine Ridge event.

However, I have heard too many negative reports regarding wide-open Sun Dances to support that practice. The most important negative point I have heard—and it is one I have observed personally as well—is the know-it-all attitude of a large number of young white men. Too many have declared themselves instant holy men after participating, and they have gone on to discover some tribe in their lineage that they are *sure* they are a member of. Worse, too many have quit learning and searching, having concluded that they now know everything that needs to be known in the realm of the spiritual. How a single Sun Dance can bring all of this about is indeed baffling!

The year before this book was published, the Sioux Keeper of the Pipe, Chief Arvol Looking Horse, issued a proclamation that only Sioux medicine men who speak the language should conduct Sun Dances, and only enrolled tribal members should pledge and participate. Surprisingly, many traditional holy men have taken a dissenting stand, believing that Native spirituality should not become exclusionary. They maintain that young non-Indians also need the medicine of the Sun Dance—especially those who have taken their pledges to dance at least four years.

Like some of my own relatives, many non-Indians want the strong medicine of the tribal ceremony to combat problems with drugs and alcohol or to keep former problems at bay. This is not the sole reason anyone participates, of course—but for many of the young it is an important factor. A few outspoken medicine men voiced strong rebuttals to the proclamation, advocating consideration for these non-Native pledgers to fulfill their pledges and for the ceremony not to be exclusionary; and they went ahead with their summer Sun Dance as planned. There are indeed many strong traditionals who conduct Sun Dances who feel this way.

It is a difficult situation. At a "closed" Sun Dance I attended recently, a good share of the "card-carrying" (registered and enrolled) Indians were one-fourth or one-eighth Native, and their children were even less. At one-eighth and even one-fourth, the Native lineage is hardly discernible. Among minorities in the United States, no race intermarries with other races as much as the Native American; hence the bloodline becomes thinner more rapidly. Those who advocate totally closed ceremonies must be reminded of this fact, since time most certainly moves on.

CHIEF FOOLS CROW'S SUN DANCE

The Sun Dance is an occasion for people to thank the Great Spirit, publicly and out in the open as a tribe. It is also a time for fulfilling Sun Dance vows—vows to be pierced if a favor or a request made in time of need has been granted. For example, a desperate hunter might take a vow that he would be pierced in the forthcoming Sun Dance if he were to find a winter deer to bring back to his hungry people. I personally took a vow to pierce in the Sun Dance if I came back alive from the war in Vietnam. No one forced me to take this vow, and the pain that I endured in the piercing was of my own choosing, much like that of a woman who gives birth to a baby. She chooses her own pain so that another might live. A Sioux woman can dance with the men in the Sun Dance, but she is not pierced, because she has given her pain already when she bore children. Such is the depth and recognition of woman in Sioux ceremonies.

The following description of the Sun Dance is based on what I viewed under Chief Eagle Feather's and Chief Fools Crow's direction. Though the meaning of the ceremony never changes, the details differ depending on who leads the dance. In recent years there have been many variations of the actual piercing, for example. However it is done, piercing is a personal and freely self-chosen sacrifice. No one is required to Sun Dance.

This is what the Sun Dances I participated in were like: Around the Sun Dance tree, placed earlier in the center of the tribal arena, the Sun Dancers would dance as singers gathered around a large drum to sing old tribal songs—songs that to my ears were hauntingly beautiful. For three days the dancers would fast and pray and dance around the tree, sleeping in a small tent at night not far from the arena.

On the morning of the fourth day, a bed of sage would be placed beneath the "Tree of Life." The dancers would be taken to this spot one by one and pierced in the chest by the Sun Dance Chief, the intercessor for the ceremony. A pair of small slits would be made in the man's skin with a sharp awl, and a wooden peg would be skewered through, passing in and under the skin. The end of a rope hanging from the top of the tree would be brought down and attached to the wooden peg by a buckskin thong. The dancer would rise after he was attached and would slowly dance backward, away from the tree's base, to the full extension of his rope. Other dancers would then be pierced and follow the same procedure.

After all were pierced, the piercing song would be sung and the dancers would dance inward toward the base of the tree to beseech strongly to the Great Spirit, who we believed was looking on. After the dancers touched the tree, they would go back, away from the center, to the end of their ropes again. Four times this beseechment would take place. The onlooking tribe would be in serious prayer all the while, with very little distraction. The tribe praying together in a concerted effort was considered to be far more powerful and beneficial than the drama of the Sun Dancers. This was the main focus of the Sun Dance: the tribe praying as a unit, praying together—an annual tribal Thanksgiving to Creator, Wakan Tanka.

The drama of the piercing assured an unbroken, undistracted spiritual focus. After the fourth beseechment, the dancers would be free to lean back and break themselves free by putting their weight upon their tether to the tree of life placed into Mother Earth. The rope was their spiritual umbilical cord. When the peg broke through, their Sun Dance vow would be fulfilled and the tribal Thanksgiving would be over.

THE LONE CLOUD SUN DANCE

At a Sun Dance I attended in the late 1960s, a lone cloud appeared far to the south on the final day as eight dancers waited to be pierced.

Chief Eagle Feather and I were the first to be pierced. As we prayed and watched the others, the large Sichangu Sioux next to me urged me to watch what was happening to the south. A distant, growing, solitary puff of white cloud seemed to be approaching across the vast western sky. The hot August Badlands air was still, yet that single cloud kept moving toward us.

I could feel a dull throb in my chest where the rope pulled on the peg that had been pierced through me. I held the rope up to lessen the pain. After a few minutes the throbbing changed to numbness and I eased my grip on the rope and let it hang freely. We watched each dancer lie on the bed of sage (face upward) at the base of the Sun Dance tree and be pierced by the intercessor. Chief Fools Crow would push his sharp awl in and through the chest skin and back out again, then insert a smooth wooden peg into the first cut and tunnel under the skin until he could push the tip back out. Then he would tie the pledger's rope to the peg with a leather thong.

Eagle Feather's voice broke into my concentration. "It's coming closer," he said in an awed tone. I looked south and saw the cloud, now appearing about half the size of a football field, still approaching slowly. I should have been in dead-earnest awe too, but I was so weak and tired from four days of fasting that, to be honest, I simply wanted the ceremony to be over. I had been pierced, as had most of the others, and all would be over in a matter of minutes.

Fools Crow came toward me after the last dancer was pierced. "Hau, Nephew," he greeted me. Bill Eagle Father called out. "That cloud is coming right at us!" The cloud was now closer still, approaching the edge of the campground full of teepees, tents, and trailers that surrounded the circular Sun Dance arena with its lone cottonwood tree. The drums were throbbing, seeming to accelerate their hypnotic crescendo—that pulsating, haunting tone that one hears only at a Sun Dance. Anyone who has ever Sun Danced will hear it for an eternity. It is so powerful that the pain in one's chest seems to be carried away with its soothing, magical tone.

Fools Crow took me by a sage gauntlet tied around my wrist and walked me inward toward the tree. All the other dancers came inward too, dancing a slow, shuffling gait to the heavy rhythm of the drums, blowing eagle-bone whistles. We touched the tree and blew our shrill whistles. The tree shrilled back!

We danced backward to the end of our ropes. The ropes tightened and our thongs held firm. The drums throbbed as if we were standing before a gigantic waterfall. Fools Crow signaled with a nod and we all danced back in toward the tree again, our eagle bones shrilly singing. Again the tree sang back! Four times in all we danced inward. After the fourth touching of the tree we danced slowly outward and then leaned back at the end of our ropes. The silent onlooking crowd sent up their prayers to Wakan Tanka.

The cloud was directly above as we touched the tree for the final time. It sent down a soothing, light rain on the dancers and the praying crowd, easing our discomfort when we leaned back against our ropes. Some Sun Dancers had visions as they leaned back against their bond; others simply prayed. Eventually all broke free and the ceremony was over.

For days we had been beseeching Creator, offering thanks and asking guidance. The cloud, with its blessing of light rain, felt like a greeting sent from Wakan Tanka, an acknowledgment of our offering. But was it? Was Creator watching over that particular ceremony, over the people gathered together? Did Creator send that lone, only cloud in the whole blue sky to acknowledge us?

A more important question is, Will Creator intervene someday and save our world, despite our foolish and irreverent course, which has led us to an overpopulated, overheated, resource-depleted state of affairs? At that Sun Dance with the lone cloud, we had been beseeching—formally calling, formally acknowledging—our Creator; and we felt that Creator acknowledged back. But modern materialists are not beseeching at all; they are not reaching out to contact God. They do not want God or any power to interfere with their disastrous taking of resources, and they could not care less about the generations unborn. I hardly think a Creator will rush to our rescue unless we change our attitude.

I look back now at Chief Fools Crow and Chief Eagle Feather. They were truly bull orcas for humanity. Their intuition, a mysterious power, was like that of the great stately beast of the sea—that beast that has no enemies. Their mysterious power could occasion wonders that no human could match. I firmly believe that their participation in the Vision Quest, Sweat Lodge, and Sun Dance highly enhanced their gift of intuition. Both holy men were advocates of the powers and confidence one could also derive from the wotai stone. Like the lone cloud that blessed us that day, both provided awesome encouragement that I had found a better path for myself—a path that would hone my intuition and bring me closer to the Ultimate Mystery.

With the help of mentors like Chief Fools Crow and Chief Eagle Feather, anyone who participates in spiritual ceremonies such as the Vision Quest, Sweat Lodge, and Sun Dance can learn (or at least appreciate) how Orca senses and interprets its realm and utilizes its endowed intuition or "power." Like Orcas, we can all learn to use our honed intuition to guide us in our realm.

The next step is to develop a bit beyond preparing for our earthly journey and giving thanks. Can we talk to Creator's spirit helpers as well? The answer is yes—and how we do that is the lesson of Owl.

SEEK TRUTH

Lesson of Owl

Many cultures have ascribed wisdom to Owl, that mysterious "eagle of the night." That wisdom can be credited, in part, to Owl's highly developed vision, which enables the big bird to hunt efficiently in darkness. Unlike humans, owls have forward-facing eye tubes, not eyeballs, so they must completely turn their heads to look in another direction. Like humans, however, owls have binocular vision, so they are able to see in three dimensions and judge distance. While they have extraordinary night vision, some see better than humans in bright light as well. Owls also have a highly developed hearing system. It involves a shape-shifting, radar-like facial disk that enables them to fine-tune sounds from above, from below, and from left and right.

With these two highly specialized senses, owls are able to detect the truth of a prey's existence, however hidden and deep in grass the creature is on the darkest night. Owls also have special feathers that cancel the sound of air rushing, so they are able to fly and dive at prey soundlessly. Although commonly nocturnal, owls are most active at dawn and dusk, the mysterious times when the world changes. They have few enemies and, like Orca, roam freely, whereas most animals have a limited territory.

Owls may "know" in a general way that prey exists, but Owl's truth is in its ability to open its senses and connect with the hidden. Owl reminds us of the qualities and strengths that can be developed and used in ceremony, with the guidance of the Great Spirit, to demonstrate connection with the hidden parts of Nature in the Spirit World.

Owl's special vision calls to mind those Sioux holy men who have used the spirit-calling Yuwipi (pronounced *yoo-wee-pee*) ceremony to discover hidden truths. (Historically, only men have led the Yuwipi ceremony.) Like Owl, these holy men are powerful and gifted in their ability to fine-tune their senses to see what is hidden from usual sight in the dark and in the Spirit World. Quiet in their demeanor and their ceremony, they are nonetheless powerful, "seeing" in the light and in the dark.

When a society stops honoring the guidance of the Great Spirit, especially in ceremony, its people become excessively selfish and manipulative toward each other and Mother Earth. When that happens, the necessary connection between Mother Earth and her creatures can be lost. We can renew that connection through ceremony—whether on a Vision Quest alone, or in a Sweat Lodge or Yuwipi with a small group, or in a thanksgiving ceremony with many. As we humbly honor and give thanks to the Higher Power, we can discover and strengthen our spiritual connections with the Great Spirit/Mystery/Nature. These connections may satisfy the many human hungers that drive the greed, obsession, and materialism of Dominant Society.

Ceremony has much to offer us, but it also demands much. Entering the higher realm of ceremony calls us to be owl-like, to focus our senses acutely so that we can connect with what ordinary senses cannot perceive.

YUWIPI

The often-misunderstood Yuwipi ceremony is a beseechment ritual that demands and hones participants' owl-like power to see and operate in realms at best unfamiliar, and at worst unacceptable, to Dominant Society. Yuwipi means "they bind him" or "they tie him up." (The ceremony known as *Lowanpi* is an identical beseechment and prayer service, except that it does not involve binding the holy man.) Being tied and bound is something the holy man chooses, should the matter(s) presented for healing or guidance be serious. That element of the ceremony is deeply symbolic of the constrictions of physical life and the blocks to healing and connection with Higher Power that humans in general, and those in attendance (including the holy man himself), carry in life.

Experientially, the constraining of the physical body helps empower the holy man's awareness as it moves into the Spirit World. The body, once bound, can no longer be a vehicle of separation; rather, it propels the holy man's awareness into the Spirit World and the Oneness of All. The Yuwipi ceremony is unique in its ability to enter that higher realm and, once there, to bring ancestors of the past into phenomenal, physical form. Because it is dependent upon the holy person's power, it is easily dismissed by white man in Dominant Society as non-rational or as manipulative—as "pulling the wool over our eyes." On the contrary, the holy person is the epitome of truthful and humble abilities.

In the Yuwipi, someone first ties the holy man's hands behind his back and then drapes a blanket over him. A special blanket is used for this purpose, embellished with designs. In addition, both Chief Eagle Feather and Chief Fools Crow had an eagle feather sewn to the top of their ceremonial blanket in such a way that the feather was positioned at the center of their head while they were standing.

Once blanketed, the holy man is tied seven times on the outside of the blanket, beginning with a noose at the neck and ending at the ankles. He lies face down within a rectangular area set off by 405 tobacco offerings strung together. The lights are turned out (or blown out, if kerosene lamps are used), and a calling song is sung to the beat of a drum. Soon, if there are no "detractors" present, the spirit helpers—those ancestors called up by the ceremony—enter with a flourish that is startling to new initiates. A "detractor" is someone whose priority is finding fault rather than being at one with the ceremony. At more than one ceremony I have attended, the holy man has detected the presence of a detractor (or several) who was told to leave, because the spirit helpers would not come in until that person (or persons) left the premises. In the past, detractors were often people sent as spies by the missionaries to report on those who attended.

Once the spirit helpers have arrived, each person's prayers are spoken in turn. Then a song follows, during which the holy man talks with the spirits. When the song is ended, he speaks a response to each and all of the prayers expressed earlier—a response based on what the spirits have said. Songs are then sung to the spirits to release the holy man, and then the spirits respond by untying him, as is evidenced when light is restored once again. As Father Stolzman described, the spirit helpers interact with participants during the Yuwipi:

> In the course of the meeting [ceremony], a person may be touched by a rattle, a paw, or a hand. One should not be surprised or afraid. The Indians call this a "healing." It is from "something spiritual" who is caring for that person, giving that person a blessing. One responds by saying, "Pilamiya, Tunkasila" (Thank you, Grandfather).[1]

Among the Sioux, the holy man demonstrates the ability to connect with the Spirit World not through statement—what is spoken aloud to impress others—but through quiet inner focus and humility in relation to the Great Mystery. The holy person is able to avoid distraction by the false frills of modern society. Fools Crow explains it this way: "While the power comes into and through us, it does not change the fact that we are human beings with human limitations. The Higher Powers have to work with us as we are, even though we improve as time passes and we become less of a burden to them."[2] A holy man such as Fools Crow or Bill Eagle Feather would never make a statement like "I will do a Yuwipi ceremony and my spirit guide Big Road or Grey Weasel will appear." Rather, they would simply state that a Yuwipi ceremony would take place and that they, as the holy man conducting, would try to help participants. It does not matter what the particular holy man's connections are or how his power can be explained rationally. A holy man's power is not dependent on "who he knows" in the Spirit World or on the exact process of his ceremony.

Neither Eagle Feather nor Chief Fools Crow considered Yuwipi to be a "secret" ceremony. They openly shared this powerful ceremony with all races. We find that the word "secret" is much more espoused by tribes that have lost their culture than by tribes that have kept their culture. Indians as individuals are divided, just as tribes are, into those who know their culture and those who know little or nothing about their culture, some of whom pretend to know so as to get needed attention or avoid embarrassment. The latter often claim such-and-such is too "secret" to talk about. They do this to compensate for their lack of tribal spiritual knowledge, in my opinion. Believe me, there are many Indians who know absolutely nothing of their culture. The conversion zeal of the Christians was remarkably thorough, their conversion methods backed by the unconstitutional federal bans mentioned in earlier chapters.

Some might believe that a spirit-calling ceremony ought to be explainable and should be conducted according to a set of rules. Many people get their ego needs met by trying to explain the Mystery and telling others the recipe for calling in the Spirit World. Both Fools Crow and Eagle Feather had tremendous spirit-calling power, yet neither was loaded down with "how-to" rules as some modern holy men seem to be. Yet for all the new rules that some know-it-alls give out, I have yet to see spiritual results like those of Fools Crow, Eagle Feather, and other traditionals. The need for excess rules in ceremony usually stems from ego's demand for control, just as it has (and does) in other unfortunate priesthoods of the past and present. If you are seeking to take the road of the intercessor or the holy person and want the spirits to work with you, then take heed: it is not a matter of doing ceremony "correctly" or ritualistically, or of learning the "right way" of saying certain words, but of personal spiritual and physical strength, truthfulness, openness, and surrender to the Great Mystery.

Too much focus on "correctness" and exact ritualism is distracting to one's main purpose—spiritual communication! People who rely too heavily on ritualism clog up their "clean hollow bone" and thus find difficulty bringing forth spirit helpers, who abhor distraction. Owl is a very cunning, effective hunter, because it not only sees in the darkness, but also adapts quickly when speeding through the darkness to catch a moving target. There is no correctness of ritual in Nature—only efficiency and results.

But as much as some of us admire and learn from Owl, many cultures view the eagle of the night with fear or distrust because of its nighttime activity, mysterious echoing hoots, and fixed, wide-eyed gaze. Owls have been portrayed for centuries as the helpers of evil magicians and demons. Religious fanatics and superstitious inventors forget that all creatures are designed by Ultimate Creator—the Grand Designer. They are falsifying what God has made.

Owls are not the only creatures whose strengths are a matter of suspicion. So too the Indians. It is, on the one hand, a matter of deep pride, contentment, and reassurance, especially to Lakota traditionals, to experience the power of the tribal spiritual way. Indeed, experience—active participation in various ceremonies—is the best way to gain deep spiritual knowledge regarding ceremony. On the other hand, it is very difficult for Dominant Society to believe that such ceremony can exist without some sort of "demonic" association, as whites have been programmed to believe for centuries. Dominant Society rationalism and skepticism have served to hide the Spirit World, and consequently have let the air out of ceremonial life. The white man's mind is often deadly toward experiences that are unexplainable (not to mention spiritual) in nature. Dominant Society religion is often derisively critical of the Yuwipi and other Native ceremonies because connecting with the Spirit World is considered to be the work of the devil.

Father William Stolzman explains, in *The Pipe and Christ*, what makes a spirit-based worldview distinctive:

> *Once a person enters into the realm of the spirits, things tend to penetrate one another, and it is often inappropriate or impossible to make standard material distinctions. . . . In the Lakota prayer meeting, there are many spirits, taku wakan kin, (the mysterious thing) but yet there is only one Great Spirit, Wakan Tanka. The spirits addressed are many, yet all prayers are addressed to one Grandfather. As a person enters into Lakota spirit ceremonies, one must take upon himself the Lakota religious worldview, in which the spiritual mystery of the "One and the many" is vibrantly alive and dynamically present. Their [the Lakota] worldview is holistic.*[3]

Father Stolzman, who as I noted in the previous chapter was a missionary and educator among the Sioux, is now a diocesan priest in Shakopee, Minnesota. He has stated that Sioux people, when doing spirit work, "are not analysts looking for the specific cause of a noise or spark" that occurs at times in some ceremonies—in particular, a Yuwipi ceremony; but "rather, they see themselves as relatives looking for a cure or an answer to their prayers":

> *They have a holistic view which brings together everything material and non-material, ordinary and wakan to work toward a particular beneficial result. A medicine man in his ceremonies is judged wakan primarily by the new beneficial results received by one's relatives. "By*

their fruits you shall know them." In many ways, the faith filled
Lakota is quite "indifferent" to the different phenomena that take place
in a ceremony. If they ultimately receive the healing or the goal desired,
all things, taku, involved are considered wonderful, mysterious, and
wakan.[4]

A bald eagle flew by over the Mississippi River right outside my
window years ago when I called Father Stolzman—Father Bill, as we
knew him—to discuss his writings. That was a good sign from the natural world, and Father Bill sounded pleased when I told him. Years later, I
called again to ask whether he still held the same views. He replied that
he believed as strongly as ever what he had written regarding his experiences with the Nature-based ceremonies out on the Sioux reservation.

FEAR OF THE UNSEEN

Many people are probably surprised that I can be so friendly with a former missionary, after all that I have said against the missionaries generally. The answer lies in his openness.

Father Bill wrote a powerful, open-minded book called *How to Take*
Part in Lakota Ceremonies, based on his personal experiences with Sioux
spirituality.[5] I recommend it highly. In it we see a man who obviously
respects Nature's Way and, like Owl, is capable of seeking and sensing
hidden truth. He is not trying to harm our way, as some of the Jesuit
missionaries were so blatantly doing. In fact, as mentioned, he has left
that rigid order to become a diocesan priest. Furthermore, he offers ver-
ification to the average white churchgoer of Native spiritual concepts
that they might find it hard to understand or believe. In fact, I strongly
suspect that any readers who know that a priest has taken part in and
written truthfully about the same ceremonies I mention will find my
writings to be more credible. Non-Indians who wish to explore Nature's
Way have many age-old, ingrained fears to overcome. I can understand

these fears, and the caution they engender. I once shared many of them. I have relatives in whom the white man's way is so ingrained that it may be too much for them to change, despite their Native blood. Change is never for the weak of heart!

Father Bill, though he had misgivings about Native spirituality, went on a Vision Quest to learn for himself what it was about. Suffice it to say, he believed in the inhabitants of the Spirit World in a stronger manner after his Vision Quest. "I am convinced that their coming is found not in me but outside of me," he said. "Spirits must be treated respectfully as persons. They are responsive to a person's faith and prayer."[6] He explained his change of heart:

> *It became clear to me that the dynamic force within the Lakota religion is found in the spirits, just as the real motivator within the Christian Church is the Holy Spirit. I quickly learned that to enter any Lakota ceremony and to walk the sacred red path, one had to believe in the Lakota spirits associated with the Pipe Ceremony. Because of my theological training and materialistic upbringing, I found it hard to believe that the Four Winds and Grandmother Earth were real spiritual beings. I wanted to believe but my past would not let me.*[7]

Because of the horrendous oppression of the past and the suppression of Indian religion, I am now a warrior and fight for what I believe in, but I cannot be a narrow-minded, overly zealous one. Father Bill is not a zealot who would drive a pickup truck into a Sun Dance ground and brazenly deny a people their ceremony, forcing them to replace it with his own, as did his counterpart, the narrow-minded, overly zealous Jesuit Paul Steinmetz. There is a tremendous difference between the two priests: Father Bill is a fellow seeker of truth, while Father Steinmetz thought he had a monopoly on truth.

I personally observed Father Steinmetz's intrusiveness on several occasions. Eventually, I had a confrontation with him. Once, when I was a newly returned Vietnam vet and a fledgling Sun Dancer, he tried forcibly to stop the ceremony. He shook his fist in my face when I curtailed his maneuvering and scheming, spoke my name in an angry tone, and yelled, "You must put 'Chrriisssist' in your Sun Dance!" It didn't happen, and he was eventually told by civil authorities to leave the Sun Dance arena because of disruption. From that day on, the power of the missionaries over my tribe was broken on my reservation.

That experience colored my feelings about missionaries, obviously. Still, no way would I ever attempt to denigrate or put obstacles in the truth-seeking spiritual path that Father Bill has chosen. Unlike Father Steinmetz and many others, Father Bill is respectful of our way in his writings. He has experienced what I write about, and by sharing that experience with Dominant Society, he helps the white man understand my writings.

Non-Indians are not the only people trying to sabotage Nature's Way. Nontraditional Indians have sometimes worked with non-Indians to show that a particular ceremony or holy person is a fraud. William K. Powers, an anthropology professor at Rutgers University, describes one such effort:

> Certain elements among the Teton have often tried to expose the Yuwipi men as frauds, usually without success. Horn Chips, now dead, can be considered one of those Yuwipi men who has greatly added to the cult's popularity. For one thing his spirits spoke in many voices, and all his prophecies are said to have been fulfilled. Some years ago, by order of the Agency Superintendent, who was in charge of Pine Ridge Reservation, Horn Chips meeting was held in a lighted room. Indian police were present and the police chief himself carefully tied and wrapped the Yuwipi man. Lights flashed on the ceiling, Horn Chips was untied when the flashing ceased. It is understandable that many Teton refer to him as the real Yuwipi man.[8]

The Chips family is still powerful to this day.

To observers, the Yuwipi experience is rather sensational. That some holy people have attained the power to reach into the Spirit World is not amazing to me, however, for it is obvious that they have found their truth to a very high degree and have earned their power by preparing themselves through related ceremonies, such as Sweat Lodges and isolated Vision Quests on mountaintops or lonely buttes. Like the owl, they have heightened their senses and empowered their skill for ceremony, enabling them to see into the normally hidden Spirit World. In ceremony, spirit helpers come forth and cause some rather startling phenomena, possibly to bolster the confidence and respect of some of the more dubious participants and also to keep a keen and alert interest going among those attending the ceremony.

FOOLS CROW'S AND EAGLE FEATHER'S YUWIPI CEREMONIES

I was once Chief Eagle Feather's helper for a crowded Yuwipi ceremony held in the basement of an abandoned church. Many Hunkpapa attended this long ceremony. The active spirit participation kept the crowd attentive. In another Yuwipi, Chief Fools Crow helped to find protection for me prior to my going to Vietnam. Over the course of the 110 combat missions I later flew, all the predictions in that ceremony came true. Fools Crow had a spirit helper named Big Road, who proclaimed, "You will see the enemy over 100 times and the bullets will bounce from your airplane. You will return and dance with a small boy beneath the Sun Dance tree . . . if you do certain things to show your appreciation." Because Big Road, speaking through Fools Crow, spoke in the Lakota language, my mother interpreted the Sioux prediction for me during the ceremony.

A Yuwipi by Chief Eagle Feather stands out vividly in my memory and demonstrates all that I have said about that type of ceremony so far.

This story is told in greater detail in *Mother Earth Spirituality*, but for the sake of the point I'm making here, some repetition of the details is pertinent.[9] Chief Eagle Feather went to the University of South Dakota to conduct a Yuwipi ceremony for five non-Indian students. The majority of the audience was made up of non-Indians, mostly professors. Undaunted, Eagle Feather conducted a truly powerful ceremony—one that, especially with such an audience, could hardly be deemed "secret."

At this ceremony in the late sixties, many people seen as "credible" from the white man's view attended—university professors with graduate degrees. (I guess a detractor would assume that they were maybe more "credible" than we ordinary folks.) This ceremony was conducted to assist non-Indian people in dire need of help: five students and their pilot/professor had crashed somewhere in the cold, remote, snow-covered Nebraska Sand Hills, and the wreckage (along with any potential survivors) could not be found.

The group had been returning from Denver to Sioux Falls, South Dakota, when they encountered a blizzard. The pilot probably developed vertigo in the whiteout, and it was presumed the plane had crashed on the windswept prairie and was covered by snow. An all-out search was begun as soon as the plane failed to land as scheduled—the National Guard was brought in to help—but it was too expensive to continue for long. When the search was called off, the University of South Dakota Indian Studies Department, where I worked, called on several Sioux holy men for help.

Bill Eagle Feather, one of the holy men enlisted, asked for a map. He specified that he wanted "the airplane kind of map, not an ordinary road map." On that map he drew a line from Denver to Sioux Falls, the plane's intended destination. Then he was ready for the Yuwipi.

Once Eagle Feather was covered and bound, we lowered the huge man face down on the rug. After the tobacco offerings were spread out and the lights turned off, the ceremony began.

The singer boomed out the calling song, and after a few minutes the spirit helpers entered in the form of blue-green lights. When the calling song to the spirits was over, the electrical-appearing lights exited through the wall. Eagle Feather called for the song of Chief Gall of the Hunkpapa. The singer sang out, and at the conclusion Grey Weasel, Eagle Feather's spirit helper, came forth.

A purring sound filled the room. The patter of small feet was accompanied by the excited chattering of a weasel. Eagle Feather began to talk in Sioux to the animal, and the visitor chattered and purred as the holy man spoke. They continued to converse for a long time, until finally the animal no longer chattered but only purred slowly.

Then Eagle Feather called for the same calling song again, and as the song began, the audience heard a woman singing at the top of a nearby wall. A glowing, ice-colored image appeared, superimposed on the wall, roughly the size of a human head. The woman sang briefly before the image disappeared. When her song finished, a loud crack came from the center of the floor and something slid toward the keeper of the pipe. I felt it stop at my feet.

Once the song ended, Eagle Feather called out, "Ho, Grey Weasel has made six predictions.

"One, the airplane crashed in a storm not far from a town that has two creeks with almost the same name. We should send an airplane out to look for it. A man and woman will fly that airplane.

"Two, the animals will point to where we should go.

"Three, if we fly where the animals point and head past the town and two creeks with the same name (South Loup and Middle Loup), we will fly over the plane, but it is pretty well covered with snow.

"Four, the plane sent out will have to land, but everyone will walk away from it. Do not worry, the pilots will be smiling as they look back.

"Five, in the next day or two some people who are not looking for the plane will be led to it by an animal.

"Six, only five will be found; one of the six will be missing. She landed away from the others, but she will not be too far away. Her face will be upon an ice-colored rock. She has a Chinese [pageboy] hairdo and wore big glasses. The animals will have been eating on all of them.

"Those are the six predictions. Now also, a rock that looks like ice has entered the room. It will have these signs I spoke of and one more prediction upon it. Ho, Nephew [meaning me]. Reach out in front of you and pick up the rock. Hold it until the final song. You are of the rock clan, and you should welcome your rock brother, not be afraid of it."

Before the final song and the return of the lights, Eagle Feather said, "The two who fly like the winged ones," meaning my companion and me (both pilots), would pass over the crashed plane by flying over the area and using the stone as a map. As it turned out, we followed the deer that seemed to be foretold on the stone and passed over the small town of Arnold, Nebraska. We figured out that the cloudy, unclear sign on the stone represented fog, because the clouds were beginning to cling to the ground. It was so foggy that we had to reverse course and land.

But the next day, close to where we had reversed the plane's course, two coyote hunters following the tracks of a coyote stumbled on the wreckage of the Cherokee Six airplane. The tail of the doomed plane was exposed by this time, the fog having caused the temperature to rise. The hunters reported the position, and soon rescue vehicles converged on the scene. All of Grey Weasel's predictions, communicated through Eagle Feather, proved true. All of the bodies were found in the plane, except for one; a girl with short hair was found several yards away from the fuselage.

Well, there you have a ceremony that preachers, popes, cardinals, and mullahs could never do. While other religions have their own ceremonies, most lack the spiritual clues to the Beyond that exist in a powerful Native ceremony. Nature's Way is truly the world's most powerful religion, if prediction and communication are the standards. The ceremonies of Nature's Way succeed because of the sheer truth and dedication of the intercessor and the sincerity of the audience—all of which makes a pleasing, inviting atmosphere for the spirits.

Owl, as we have seen, is specially gifted and unique. "Hollow bone" holy persons become like Owl by honing and developing all the lessons discussed earlier. The specifics of the ritual are not important: various tribes have a ceremony like the Yuwipi but call it by a different name, and I imagine that the old Celtic bards, with their sincerity and careful preparation, produced a similar ceremony.

Without harmony and undiluted truth, however, no communication with the Spirit World can happen. The spirits set high standards for honesty. It is nice to anticipate that the Spirit World we will all know someday is a truthful and sincere place where earthly lies and manipulation will not be condoned. Nothing but pure truth—that will be the mental atmosphere of the Beyond. Makes one wonder why we long to stay here!

"Life is but a mere shadow on the wall compared to the complete reality that lies beyond," as Plato noted.[10] As he suggested in his "Allegory of the Cave," what we experience and observe here on Earth will no doubt be reflected larger than life in the Beyond.

It is obvious, from this snowstorm Yuwipi, that spirits are able to go back in time and discern what took place earlier. "One of the six will be missing," Grey Weasel had predicted. "She landed away from the others."

What about the rock that helped my friend and me pilot in the right direction? I thought that rocks were millions of years old. This particular stone, which was similar to Black Hills quartzite minus the pink luster, held distinctive symbols that weren't mechanically inscribed but were relative to a recent happening. Yet the stone looked no different, really, than any other millions-of-years-old rock! The lines and images within the rock were not man-inscribed; they were natural! There must be a much different concept of time once we leave this world. It is evidence like this that makes the Indian accept Mystery. Some things, such as time and space, we admit are way beyond us.

BELITTLEMENT AND SUSPICION

Christian fundamentalist detractors aside, too many others have fallen victim to the white man's curse on truthful indigenous exploration. Too many white writers of the past corrupted their writings about Indians by interjecting their own prejudices and superiority over the Native culture. The white man's religion and social status were always so superior that he could not summon the courage to reflect praise, awe, or outright preference for anything outside his own culture. Therefore, the white writer always had to issue certain observations that belittled the Indian. Often the writer, in describing a Native ceremony, would make remarks that a reader could interpret as possibly meaning that the main participant—the holy person—was conjuring during the ceremony. Even if the ceremony described was supposedly "genuine," the writer might mention other ceremonies at which conjuring or manipulation was perceived to have taken place. The old whitewash of belittlement and suspicion was applied over and over again. Believe me, as a young Indian reader, I found that attitude insulting and denigrating.

There are a few good books out there—books written at a time when the real Native "old-timers" were still living. These books were written either by Indians or by white authors not overcome by the supposed superiority of Dominant Culture, humble and respectful Indian-culture writers such as John Neihardt, Ohiyesa, and J. Epes Brown, all writing at the turn of the twentieth century. A host of condescending writers (and university presses) have done hospitable indigenous people a great disservice with their volumes and insulted those Natives who generously shared with them new knowledge. Though that is true to a lesser degree today, things have not changed all that much.

RAISING SPARKS AT A BIBLE BELT UNIVERSITY

As I mentioned earlier, I think a superioristic or belittling attitude separates one from Nature's Way. The false superiority that many whites feel over us "ignorant" Indians has kept many well-meaning searchers from exploring, as Owl would, in the dark areas that most people cannot view. Perhaps many non-Indian authors write condescendingly in order to be published, especially by university presses, which have typically been bureaucratic and entrenched in Dominant Society's need to be right, definite, and superior—none of which will allow the spirit helpers to be seen. Perhaps it would raise the ire of a university press's funding source—the university's administrators and alumni—if the Indians' spirituality were respectfully (and more truthfully) recorded.

I'm remembering one university whose Indian students asked me to speak there. Two nervous professors met me at the airport and warned me not to talk about "Indian religion," as I was in the heart of the "Bible Belt" and would offend (they actually said "*might* offend") some in the audience, including Indians.

I sat on a chair about twenty paces from the podium as I was introduced by one of the professors. It was a rather dramatic moment: I felt like a bullfighter waiting for the first bull or, more familiarly, like a bull-rider ready to come out of the chute at a rodeo. A big Indian sitting in the front row winked encouragement to me. His name was Conrad Galley. As I listened with trepidation to my introduction, I thought about having flown 110 missions in Vietnam and, earlier, having been a young ground Marine in Korea. I knew that the college was a federal land-grant institution, not a private school.

Here I was in a *democracy*, I thought. I, who had volunteered for my combat tour and fulfilled it faithfully. And now, having been invited to speak at a large university, I was being told what I could and could not speak on. Some democracy!

The introducing professor concluded by saying, "Captain McGaa will speak on Sioux culture, history, and values." The big Indian gave a look of dismay, wondering, no doubt, what I was made of. The term "freedom of speech" rang in my ears as I walked to the podium; "democracy, Iroquois, freedom" chorused silently from a phantom audience in the packed auditorium. I surveyed the crowd, wondering why it was so full if I was expected to hurt a bunch of feelings. Personally, I stay home if I don't care about what someone is speaking on at a campus or community center.

Clutching the lectern for moral support, I took a deep breath. "I have decided to speak on Native culture, values, and . . ."—I paused—"and *spirituality*—or religion, as some of you are used to referring to it." I glared at the two professors, also sitting in the first row, then threw a sideways glance at the Indian. I received a strong reassurance from him. He reminded me of Will Sampson in the movie *One Flew over the Cuckoo's Nest*.

With another deep breath, I spoke from the heart: "And if you Bible-thumpers don't like it," I warned, "you can go to hell!"

"A *ho!* [It is so!]" the Indian yelled. (Later we would go off to dinner together. I still have the expensive Seiko watch he gave me as a token of appreciation.) At the end of my talk I received a standing ovation.

Like the mysterious creature of the night that Owl has become in some cultures, this book may be branded as scary or controversial by the simple- or perhaps less-open-minded, even though I have observed or experienced myself what I write about, or have listened to deeply spiritual holy people. I have sought truth in opening my senses to observation, listening, and experience and in connecting with the unknown and unexplainable. It is important that we, like Owl, observe truth that is obvious and seek truth in Mystery.

I have made up nothing of my own, nor have I tried to interject personal visions (of which I have had very few, despite being in a few Sun Dances and Vision Quests under the direction of Chiefs Fools Crow and Eagle Feather). I have not lied and will not lie about my experiences—

especially about the inner power some indigenous people have demonstrated during my journeys. Some people have cultivated that gift of inner power, and some have not.

DIRECT OBSERVATION VERSUS MYTH

The lone cloud arriving at the Sun Dance that I mentioned in the previous chapter was not a vision, nor was it mythology. It was real, seen by all who were there. I deliberately choose not to write from mythology, unlike so many non-Indian and Indian writers who apparently believe that a mythological approach offers convincing evidence of the deep power within Native spirituality. (I strongly suspect that, for many, this mythology is their only contact with Native culture, and their egos spur them on to convince the world that this is what Nature-based spirituality is about.) Owl asks us to find the truth hidden by false concepts (including mythology), piercing the darkness of negativity and fear.

In my opinion, the religious way of most whites is loaded with mythology; but Christians will never admit it, despite how they write about *our* culture, generating false concepts about true Nature-based spirituality. Already we observe their results: many indigenous North Americans now believe that the Christian devil and bad spirits—manmade, all—do exist and are incorporating them into their own tribal ideologies.

Thomas Mails, a minister now deceased, is a recent example of white writers who have had the opportunity to have close contact with major holy men. He brought out the depth of Chief Fools Crow in his biography, and I highly recommend it, yet Mails just could not write about the Sioux holy man without injecting that the venerable sage was indeed a Christian. In six annual Sun Dances and much personal contact, I never heard any proselytizing regarding any religion from either Chief Fools Crow or Chief Eagle Feather.

A host of writers use the same ploy regarding Nicholas Black Elk of *Black Elk Speaks*. Steinmetz and Steltenkamp (two Jesuit priests),

DeMallie, and Rice are the most notorious. They claim that Black Elk was a catechist without mentioning that he was dragged from an ongoing Native ceremony by a Jesuit, strangled until nearly suffocated, thrown in a wagon, and then exorcised at the reservation mission against his will by another Jesuit! What they cannot admit is that the old prophet returned to his old Native way (that is, Nature's Way) to tell his powerful vision. Black Elk had seen and experienced white religion, had heard white beliefs, but in the end found truth in his original way, especially when fewer restrictions were being imposed.

White writers just cannot stand to admit what is blatantly before them: the rejection of their religious system by thousands of North American Indians who are turning away now that the government ban against Native ceremonies and other unconstitutional restrictions have finally been lifted.

CANTON INDIAN INSANE ASYLUM

None of these writers mentioned above tell of the Canton Federal Indian Insane Asylum, wherin medicine men were banned, often for life, at the whim of an agency superintendent or by the agent's influence from reservation missionaries. Their primary theme is Black Elk's so-called conversion, slanted in favor of Christianity, of course. They fail to understand the fear that the medicine men must have had regarding the gruesome shadow of Canton. From what I have learned of Canton, I would not have done anything different than Black Elk did to keep from going there. It was a real horror chamber. I hope now these men can end their ceaseless introspection and overanalyzation of a great man.

RETURNING TO NATURE'S WAY

Why are Indians returning to Nature's Way? Because they prefer what the old holy persons preserved!

I have often been asked to speak across the nation and abroad, and on those trips I always talk with interested seekers. I have received many messages from those who have read my books. Through those conversations and letters, I have learned that indigenous people, and many others as well, are hungry for Nature's Way. They are not impressed with the organized religion that they have been exposed to. They are no longer afraid of what the missionaries held up as threats (hell and the like).

Take a serious look at the graduating class of any white high school—especially one in the suburbs. Seniors show very little interest in organized religion by the time they reach the end of their schooling. On the reservation, meanwhile, our youth are filling our Sun Dances. This has been my observation.

The world is moving beyond the controlling, contrived mumbo jumbo that makes up Dominant Religion, and growing numbers of intelligent minds can now see through it. It helps that Federal Insane Asylums for Disagreement are finally being shut down and abandoned. You think I'm kidding? How about the asylum at Canton, South Dakota, which for decades after the U.S. government first banned Sioux religious practices in 1881 incarcerated noncompliant Sioux religious adherents and, oddly, runaway youth from the federal Indian boarding schools? Several Sioux organizations are attempting to uncover documents proving that tribal members were incarcerated for refusing to abandon their religion. Since the federal government is supposed to make no law regarding the practice of religion, I can understand why bureaucrats are reluctant to release that information.

But suppressing the truth destroys the harmony of Nature. That is why Owl is calling us to look for truth that has been hidden behind layers of imposed fears, barriers, and constrictions. Nature's Way seems to stir the blood—maybe because we are but a generation or two away from the old culture, and with the Sioux that culture was never fully extinguished. More of us are also well aware of the fighting and the foolish hate that organized religions continue to practice on each other, and we want no part of that kind of thinking.

GOOD AND EVIL

Sometimes the antagonism of organized religion turns on Native practices. Many Christians accuse Indians of summoning evil spirits through the ceremonies of Nature's Way. Well, let us suppose, for discussion's sake, that Creator allowed some "bad spirits" to exist. Those spirits are certainly not going to come visiting here on Earth! Only the advanced of the Spirit World are allowed (or, more precisely, have the knowledge and connection) to return to help out humans who call for help via a Yuwipi or other ceremony. Big Road (Fools Crow's spirit helper) and Grey Weasel (Eagle Feather's helper) were both medicine men when they were here on this Earth, living their daily lives. Evidently, they found the key to communicate with the Spirit World from here. Then, once they entered the Great Beyond, they were advanced enough in spiritual skills to be able to return here briefly to respond to humanity's call.

Europeans and their descendants are so saturated with the dichotomous good-and-evil idea perpetuated by their organized priesthood that the majority will never be able to shed the concept—even though they will go through life never seeing an actual devil or "evil spirit." And we could not see such spirits even if we wanted to: they do not exist in Nature. For that reason, no one can have a successful spirit-calling by invoking "bad spirits."

But certainly evil exists in the world. We see ample proof of that. How can we explain its presence in Creation? Simple: knowledge is good and ignorance is bad. So-called bad people are really more ignorant, in my opinion, than bad. Ku Klux Klan members and the Taliban, for example, have acted out of ignorance, believing that certain ethnic groups or creeds are always wrong and always detrimental for society. These racists seek power over those whom they wish to oppress. Seeking power over another—or over the animal world, natural resources, and so on—is a form of ignorance as well. Such practices do not lead to the harmony and truth we find in Nature.

Harmony is always and obviously good in Nature's Way. Nonharmony among us and with Nature is always and obviously ignorant, wrong, false, destructive, harmful, life-threatening, species-destructive, polluting—even planetary-ending in the long run.

You can test for ignorance or knowledge. Colleges do it all the time.

HEAVEN AND HELL

I have stated several times that we should place as much on our Disk of Life (our knowledge-accumulating mind) as we can while we are here on our Earth Walk. This is what most believe they will take to the Spirit World—their memory. The bigoted Archie Bunkers of life (and the naive Edith Bunkers too) will go to the Beyond with basically blank disks, since they did not bother to add much to theirs while here in this world.

I believe that our "heaven" will be our memory (accumulated knowledge through observing, and the recognition of Nature's demonstrated harmonious values), though possibly there will be opportunities for further advancement after we arrive "there." The people who could not care less about observing while "here" will have their own portion of the Beyond to go to while "there." In the Spirit World, could we not be with our own kind? Freedom exists "here"; therefore, could it not also exist "there"?

Most certainly we would choose to spend eternity with our own "like minds," extremes of all sorts seeking out fellow-thinkers. Therefore, those who placed little knowledge or observation on their Disks of Life will congregate together, as will bad people who caused much harm to others. If truth reigns supreme, the latter will be removed from gentler souls and put where their victims can chastise them for eternity.

Creator has shown us, in the many examples of Mother Earth's provisions and in the physiological makeup of our own bodies, that the Great Mystery is indeed benevolent and caring. I find it most unreasonable that such a providing Mystery would also create a fiery burning hell for the eternal misery of us humans—a hell complete with pitch-forked demons whom we have had no indication of here on our life journey. They are as invisible as Sasquatch and the Abominable Yeti Snowman, whom so many fools insist exist. Having participated in spiritually truthful indigenous ceremonies, I am convinced more than ever that it is our track record and memories that will occasion either disappointment or reward in the Beyond World.

The above is not meant to be a dissertation on heaven and hell, but since the white man has always felt free to tell us Indians exactly what these two places will be like, why can't an Indian offer back a reasonable alternative? We Sioux base our supposition of the hereafter on the obvious concept that it is our mind (or memory) and not our pleasure-or-pain-experiencing body that moves on into the higher realm of the Spirit World. Our body will be back in some coffin—or better yet, in some crematorium urn, to free up six feet of Mother Earth. How will that dead body feel the jab of a theoretical pitchfork? Seems what I learned from the all-knowing white man was that it is only the soul (spirit) that moves on.

The spirit-calling ceremony offers many clues for us to wonder on— clues regarding the "atmosphere," "habitat," and "circumstances" of that Beyond Realm. Such ceremonies offer convincing evidence that a Beyond World exists—especially when predictions made in the course of the spirit-calling are proven true.

CLOSING THOUGHTS ON TRUTH

This chapter has focused on truth, the truth one uncovers with the spiritual perception Owl symbolizes. Perhaps the reason that Native spirituality comes closer to truth than other religions, as I believe it does, is that white people set themselves up as mini-gods, whereas indigenous people are quite the opposite. Sioux Indians, at least the traditionalists, are quite content to have their Creator remain the sole God and Highest Power, way above and beyond them. We Natives remain what we are and are quite content with that belief. When we look up at the great heavens above us and think of the billions of galaxies that lie unseen beyond the stars, we realize where and what we are in the vast scheme of things. Christians, on the other hand, look out at all that majesty and want to wear the mantle of godliness themselves—both now and in the Afterworld. Wanting all of the glory and none of the responsibility, they turn a blind eye to the failing health of the planet and to Nature's fast-vanishing resources.

Christianity has a man-God, the Koran has a biblical prophet who speaks divinely, and Judaism is waiting for its Messiah (who will, of course, be of Jewish blood and lineage only, not a Pygmy from Africa or an aborigine from Australia). Many sects within these religions offer extreme promises to "market" their belief systems—with the exception of Jewish folks, who are similar to many indigenous in that their Creator is a vast Mystery and they do not proselytize. I respect them and other religions and belief systems that do not proselytize. Do the folks who say, "No, thanks; I think I'd like to stick with my own beliefs," actually singe and burn when the biblical or koranic God appears in the sky?

The Koran offers the services of a number of virgins for their Jihad warriors. I wonder what the virgins think of that? And the Mormons promise a few extra wives in heaven, along with a kingdom in which, godlike, one gets to rule. (Or was that just the sales pitch of the particular band of Mormons who were sent out to our Sioux reservations to convert us?)

With all those virgins and extra wives, I have to wonder whether sex plays a role in the Spirit World. It is surprising how often afterlife sex appears in the religions of Dominant Society. It seems that the white man, like the fanatic Muslim, just has to bring sex into his afterworld. I honestly do not know what lies ahead (though sex without a body does not hold much appeal), so I'll refrain from making any promises on the subject, even though a favorable promise would probably increase the sales of this book.

Sex in the Spirit World is only one of a million things we wonder about. Like Owl, who calls out in the dark—searching, searching—we are searchers too, wanting to find and understand the truth. Sometimes that truth comes in unexpected forms and from unanticipated quarters; other times we sense just where to look.

Once truth is revealed, wherever it may be hiding, we are ready to act. The freedom to act on the wisdom we receive is what we will discuss next—the lesson of Tiger.

SEVEN

STRIVE FOR FREEDOM

Lesson of Tiger

What is an animal's or human's deepest desire? We will neglect food or shelter to acquire it. It is freedom.

The Bengal tiger is a prime example of freedom. Its spectacularly featured face reminds me of how graciously endowed this magnificent creature is. At ten feet, from nose to tip of tail, and five hundred pounds, it does not fear Human—or much else, for that matter.

Tiger covers a vast territory to secure its freedom from want. Jim Corbett, a government hunter for India, says that the range of one particular tiger he observed was thirty by fifty miles. That is fifteen hundred square miles—a considerable amount of freedom—and no doubt there are other tigers that roam over even more area. Corbett, the author of *Man Eaters of Kumaon*, had this to say about Tiger:

> I am convinced that all sportsmen—no matter whether their viewpoint has been the platform of a tree, the back of an elephant or their own feet—will agree with me, and that is, that a tiger is a large-hearted gentleman with boundless courage and that when he is exterminated—as

exterminated he will be unless public opinion rallies to his support—
India will be the poorer by having lost the finest of her fauna.[1]

Corbett defends Tiger from claims of aggression:

A tiger's function in the scheme of things is to help maintain the bal-
ance in nature and if, on rare occasions when driven by necessity, he
kills a human being or when his natural food has been ruthlessly ex-
terminated by man he kills two percent of the cattle he is alleged to
have killed, it is not fair that for these acts a whole species should be
branded as being cruel and bloodthirsty.[2]

Yet even a lowly ant seeks the same basic goals the big cat pursues.
There is nothing more sought after by a non-domesticated animal than
the freedom to roam. What about domesticated animals? They seem to
be more concerned about security. Their love for freedom has been bred
from them. The security they find behind fences is a sham: they live like
happy cows, all of them, eating their fill until they are led off to slaughter. Do you truly feel free, or have you accepted the stall you've been
placed in?

FREEDOM OF THE MIND

Humans have the same quest for freedom, especially the freedom of the
mind, but many have lost or foolishly given away their freedom in exchange for a false sense of security. For millennia, humans have given
over their freedom to manipulators of superstition. Large-scale excep-
tions, such as the old Sioux and the Celts, are rare. A person with true
freedom scares others, especially those who are in control, and is likely
to be subdued. Like tigers, for whom humans are not the natural prey,
people with true freedom are often seen as aggressors, even though the
most they really want is to defend themselves.

Most folks won't budge an inch from the beliefs instilled in them since childhood. The modern world's new forms of communication and knowledge-dissemination are making a strong impact, however. I see it, the great change, in our youth, many of whom downplay age-old superstitions and rigidity regarding religious beliefs. If anything can make a breakthrough to the lock-step hold of organized religion, it is knowledge of other points of view and the freedom to explore them.

In hopes of helping more of you to attain the freedom that Tiger demonstrates, I am going to take you on a little journey. In it, I will show you some of the truths about organized religion that Dominant Society doesn't want you to see. If, at the end of that journey, you should decide to remain in or find your spiritual home within an organized religion, then I will still have done my job, because you will be making the choice out of knowledge, not ignorance. And you will be truly free, like Tiger.

In human history, religion has restricted freedom more than any government or other institutional entity; therefore, a discussion of regaining our natural freedom needs to start there. We need to be allowed Tiger's freedom as we walk our own trails of proof and error. Only recently have we been allowed to take that walk. In many parts of this world today we still would not dare investigate religion, regardless of our motive.

I am not hoping to reach the overly zealous, those who think that their tribe or way is for their chosen people only. The otherwise fanatical are beyond my scope too. My appeal is to the open-minded, in whom knowledge has a hope of winning out. Those of a narrow-minded view will no doubt claim offense at this chapter, or object that I'm "picking on" one particular religion. This is not my intention. I am simply pointing out historical fact as to the track record of particular sects or churches—a track record that has seriously affected all of us today, and our environment as well. And I do not focus on Christianity alone; I also take issue with the harshness and imbalance of Islam.

You will hear me repeat that none of the organized religions are taking a stand for the environmental dilemma the entire world faces. That,
to me, is religion's most grievous sin. I believe that we must be reminded
of truthful religious history if we are to progress to a more concerned
lifestyle that has a better chance of saving this planet.

SPIRITUALITY OF TRADITIONAL
NATIVE AMERICANS

The Iroquois are credited with developing democratic governance in
North America long before the males-only version made its way out of
Greece. Tuned in to a spirituality that revered Creator's Nature, they
learned (or rather, discovered) both democracy and a respect for Mother
Earth from their constant association with Nature.

The Sioux were very much in step with the Iroquois, having witnessed both their natural spirituality and their straightforward democracy. Both tribes shared similar governing concepts and both practiced
secularization. No chief or leader, political or spiritual, would ever rise
up in either tribe and declare himself infallible and under God's explicit
direction.

The track record of any particular religion will truthfully show
whether or not it has been truly concerned about Creator's greatest gift
to Human—our living Earth! Most of the following material, though
true, will be unfamiliar to most North Americans (especially those of
European ancestry), if the conversations I have had with people are any
indication.

RESTRICTING FREEDOM BY INSPIRING FEAR

The restriction of freedom in Europe was the major reason so many immigrants began their trek to these shores. Those who fled from this op-

pression sought freedom from fear. North American spirituality never had the human sacrifices, which are attributed to the Christian Inquisition or the alleged Central and South American Aztec, Incan, and Mayan sacrifices. Within the same time span of the medieval Christians, the major Central and South American tribes similarly had an organized religion, a priesthood, and a class system controlled by a nobility that supported the priesthood. In most all civilizations, this has been the primary modus operandi for fear and control. Like the Inqusition, the Aztec and Inca priesthood is claimed by Charles Van Doren and many historians to have conducted human sacrifices to enhance or perpetuate their power. Is this another Christian ploy to demean Indians and hence justify their conversions? There is evidence that indeed the Central and South Amercan priesthood did commit some sacrificial atrocities found mainly on mountain peaks to this day but no hard evidence exists to the extent which the Aztecs are blamed.

Charles Van Doren's book, A *History of Knowledge*, claims that sacrifice of living beings existed in the most ancient religions. Van Doren chose the example of the Aztecs and the Incas to illustrate, in gruesome detail, the practice of human sacrifice within a religion:

> *Human sacrifice was practiced by both these unregretted civilizations of the recent past [Aztec and Inca]. Among the Aztec the toll of sacrifice stuns the mind. In the last years before the Spanish conquest, a thousand of the finest children and young people were offered up each week. . . . It is no wonder that all the enemies of the Aztecs rushed to become the allies of the conquering Spaniards and helped overthrow that brutal regime. Not that doing so helped these fervent allies. They were also enslaved by the victorious conquistadors.*[3]

I quoted Van Doren in an earlier work, Native Wisdom, but have recently discovered new material that seriously questions his accusations regarding the Aztecs and human sacrifice. Countering articles (some are book excerpts) can be found at http://www.mexika.org/Heritage.html. Readers can study this site and decide for themselves.[4]

Van Doren maintains that following the example of Abraham and his son, the Jews were the first to decide that human sacrifice was wrong, that God did not desire it. The Christians, following the Jewish tradition, never practiced human sacrifice, according to Van Doren. He studiously omits from his book (which is subtitled *The Pivotal Events, People, and Achievements of World History*) all details of the Great Inquisition in Europe, with its thousands (or possibly millions) of victims.

Van Doren will not admit that someone being burned at the stake by a priest-led, pope-inspired Inquisition is human sacrifice. His very title, which innocuously refers to "pivotal events," denies the influence that religious fear held on the populace for centuries upon centuries. *Everything* was controlled by Rome in the Dark Ages and during the three following Inquisitions. The Christian Church's denial that no human sacrifice took place during the Inquisitions is sheer lunacy. The directions for human death came directly out of the hierarchy of priests—men who were as carried away with their self-righteousness as were the Nazis, the Croatian Ustashe, and the Muslim Taliban. They had no room for Mystery and presumed to think for God.

True indigenous holy people, despite their ability to contact the Spirit World and gain otherworldly input, never dictated dogma. Such thoughts were beyond them. Understanding that Creator and life are Mystery, they did not presume to have the *only* path to truth. Thus despite all the "power" they had in ceremony, they did not demand that other people follow their way. Mystery was too vast and too obvious for an intelligent human to dictate his or her unproven so-called knowledge. The holy men I have come to know differ extremely from what I have seen of the white man's pushy, all-knowing religious leaders; and they stand in stark contrast to the horrid hierarchy of tormenters who stain the distant past, the recent past, and even, in some blighted regions, the present.

NATURE AS FINAL RECOURSE

Nature is the final recourse in the minds of most North American Indians I have had experience with. What Nature avoids, the northern Indians will also generally avoid. What Nature's animal world does to bring harmony, balance, and peace to the myriad species is generally regarded as a teaching tool among the Iroquois, Sioux, and other northern tribes—especially those that beseech with the help of the medicine wheel. Following Nature's guidance, the Sioux and Iroquois have avoided sacrifice in any form.

I asked Chief Eagle Feather about this issue once when he came to visit and do Sweat Lodge ceremonies for some metropolitan Indians. The great Sioux holy man had held meetings with medicine men of other tribes and thus had a broad knowledge of other tribes' practices.

I remember Eagle Feather's response: "Indians might hold a buffalo skull up to the Great Spirit in thankfulness after butchering out a kill, but the whole animal would be used by the people after a hunt.

"White people, on the other hand, would get some goat or lamb and kill it and offer it to their God Almighty. We all learned that from the priests. Such a waste of the animal, and for what purpose? God is not going to come down and eat the animal. We knew that.

"To waste a gift from Creator did not make much sense to the Sioux, who took their lead from Nature. The wolves and coyotes never would do such a thing, killing an animal and leaving it. To sacrifice a *human* would be even more unthinkable. Anyone who did such a thing would have to be under the influence of some crazy priest or some *witko-ko* [deranged] two-legged."

Animals just do not sacrifice their own; it does not happen. And as I have noted before, the Sioux believe that if a practice is not found in Nature, it is not something Creator would want anyone, including the Wamakaskan (the animal world), to have anything to do with.

Bill Eagle Feather never mentioned the Aztecs, Mayans, or Incas to me, so I think he was unaware of their history. He did explain fully, in my mind, the example of the animals and how they reflect Nature's Way. Once again, I learned a new teaching from the wizened old holy man.

ORIGINAL SIN?

The northern Native Americans considered themselves born free. They resisted slavery, and few kept slaves (though some held captives for brief periods before freeing them again). In their religious conceptualization, they could not conceive of being born already tainted by some imaginary sin, which is what the missionaries attempted to convince them of. They would have appreciated the words of Bishop John Spong: "We human beings do not live in sin. We are not born in sin. We do not need to have the stain of our original sin washed away in baptism. We are not fallen creatures who will lose salvation if we are not baptized."[5] I wish my catechism teachers had told me that back when I had to go to catechism classes! That perspective would have appealed to my questioning mind.

When I consider the evolution of Human as explained by science and backed up by scientific measurement, I have to presume that original sin does not exist. Modern science seems to be a more plausible authority regarding the evolution of bipedals than the Bible, with its six creation days and so-called first parents. Science shows me much evidence; the Bible and the Koran show me nothing! Bishop Spong also questions the biblical account: "How can there be a fall into sin if there has never been a perfection from which to fall?"[6]

I have often wondered that too. Chief Eagle Feather's thoughts on the subject, when I asked for his opinion, were simple: "A Great Mystery, a Creator, would not make such a thing—this sin. Where is it? What does it mean?" Looking reflective, he added, "Now here is a teaching, Nephew. The white man will back himself in a hole someday when people start to question these things he cannot explain."

If I had to worry about original sin, then a priest, medicine man, mullah, or some such person would have considerable control over me, especially if I had to go to such clergy to gain relief from sin's potential harm. If I were threatened by something like a punishing hell over original sin, I could easily fall victim to the dictates of religious leaders. I would lose my freedom, and they would own me.

Fortunately, I *do not* have to worry about original sin. Creator has allowed us free will—as free as that of the wide-ranging tiger—and given us a free-thinking mind to insulate us from the dangerous dictates of zealous soothsayers who seek control. It makes me wonder whether false soothsaying (spreading the doctrine of original sin and the like) was invented just to control others! Tigers have no one to control their actions, yet they live in accord with Nature's desires.

HIDING RELIGIOUS MISCONDUCT

A Catholic cardinal's picture was highlighted on the cover of a major news magazine for his deception and ability to cover up heinous parish crimes for years. That cardinal, Bernard Law of Boston, allowed himself to be distracted from truth for several decades. He knew he had a notorious pedophile priest in his parishes, yet he never had the criminal defrocked and removed from young, innocent boys. Scores of victims may have suffered at the hands of this particular pedophile priest and also at the hands of others in his archdiocese. According to *Time* magazine, "It has been revealed that more than 70 priests in the archdiocese of Boston—out of a total of less than 700—have been accused of the sexual abuse of children. That's 1 in 10."[7]

Obviously the cardinal wanted to hide what would embarrass his performance in a large diocese, apparently believing that the source of his troubles would somehow evaporate harmlessly. He did not seem to care about the priests' victims or future victims. What was important was hiding the offense, and hence saving the cardinal's image and position. Real truth was not his primary goal. Real truth has come back to haunt the Church, however, in this day and age when unnatural dictates are no longer enough to sway young men to take the unnatural vow of lifetime celibacy. It is a policy completely contrary to Nature's Way.

As *Time* magazine acknowledged,

The most devout and trusting have often been the most victimized. "After he molested me, he would bless me," a former altar boy, abused in the Los Angeles diocese, recently told the Los Angeles Times. *"It's very confusing. I was in the center of my mother's life—the church—and she thought I was doing constructive things by being with the priest. After we did these things, he'd put his hand on my head and make the sign of the cross."*[8]

We learned a lesson the hard way in that Catholic scandal: never give up your freedom to a human being, regardless of how much closer to the Creator he claims or appears to be!

RELIGIOUS ABUSE OF NATIVE YOUTH

We Native Americans well know what restriction of our freedom means. The religious boarding schools many of us were sent to severely harmed us. These schools were just as bad as the federal institutions on our reservations. A large lawsuit is finally underway for victims who suffered terribly from such treatment as starvation, isolation, the shaving of heads, sodomy, and shackling.[9]

I was fortunate. When World War II came, the entire northern end of the reservation where our ranch was located was made into a military machine-gun and bombing range. Forced to get out quickly, we moved off the reservation and my father took one of the many jobs that were available at the new Air Corps base at the edge of the Black Hills. Unlike my eleven brothers and sisters, who all attended boarding school, I went to public school and remained with my parents. One brother, William D., was fondled by a priest; a nephew of mine was abused worse. When William reached age sixteen, he severely beat the offending priest and was expelled from mission school. He joined the Navy and has hated things Catholic ever since.

THE GREAT INQUISITION

I received an A in church history from a scholarly Catholic university. I mention this only to establish that I was not a disinterested student. I learned nothing about the Great Inquisition during my university career, however, although it was a major force of the past and reigned for centuries.

Very little has been written about the truth of the Inquisition, despite its influence on European history, thought, and fear. Such is the power of organized religion to suppress the truth. If you do not believe me, go to your local library and see how much you can find regarding the detailed practices of the Inquisition.

James Haught, author of *Holy Horrors* (one of the few honest explications of this subject), describes the terror of the Great Inquisition, which lasted over half of a millennium. As far back as the thirteenth century, the popes allowed torture. As the Church became increasingly paranoid regarding heresy, people were put to death—or worse, tortured inhumanely and *then* killed—on the slightest whim of a false accuser. Someone accused of heresy in the Dark Ages would be locked in a cell without ever knowing who had initiated the accusation. And if a prisoner didn't confess quickly, unspeakable cruelties began. "So that the torturers would not be disturbed by the shrieking of the victim, his mouth was stuffed with cloth. Three and four hour torture sessions were nothing unusual," says Haught.[10] Often the torture instruments were sprinkled with holy water, which might have eased the conscience of the torturer but would have done little to ease the pain of the victim. "A papal statute of 1231 decreed burning as the standard penalty. The actual executions were performed by civil officers, not priests, as a way of preserving the church's sanctity."[11]

To preserve *sanctity*? In the Indian view, when someone designs, authorizes, and decrees an action, he or she sets whatever results into active fulfillment; that person is responsible, regardless of who actually carries out the plan and tortures, executes, or murders the victim. Stating that "sanctity" is preserved by a dab of holy water is a hellacious, outright lie—and definitely at odds with how indigenous folk would interpret the word.

When a church lies and gets away with it for centuries, dishonesty can easily become a trait for its followers. Lord Acton, himself a Catholic, wrote in the late 1800s, "The principle of the Inquisition was murderous. . . . The popes were not only murderers in the great style, but they also made murder a legal basis of the Christian Church and a condition of salvation."[12]

In the late fifteenth century, two Dominican inquisitors, James Sprenger and Heinrich Kramer, published their infamous *Malleus Maleficarum* ("Witches Hammer"), outlining magical acts performed by witches and wizards in cooperation with the devil, phantoms, and demons. For centuries this book was the official manual used by inquisitors, sending innocent victims, mostly women, to experience heinous (often sexual) torture and agonizing death. It became a bestseller in Europe and for three hundred years was the model for professional witch-hunters.[13]

Because of the tyranny of lies that pervaded thought and belief at this time, human freedom was at a low ebb. Witch hunts reached into every corner of Europe—even to Protestant England, Scotland, and the Massachusetts Bay Colony. The victims were mostly old women, but some were young women and a few were men. "Many in Continental Europe were simply citizens whose names were shrieked out by torture victims when commanded to identify fellow witches."[14]

It is no wonder that so many Christians have a fear of their religion or their concept of God. Some deep part of the psyche of all descendants of that madness would surely carry over some of that fear, implanted in a horrible age of suppressing ignorance so grievous that it lasted down through generations.

In the study of history, everyone should be allowed to search freely for the truth. No one should attempt to curtail freedom by coloring the past because of a cultural or ethnic mindset or a particular religious persuasion. Certainly, we should never let our ego color our judgment. Unfortunately, Human is weak, and excess pride can make the mind weaker yet, allowing untruth to seep in. Ego limits one's freedom to use gifted reasoning, for it not only allows but encourages untruth—no, it *forces* untruth. *Real* truth can never be forced.

Limiting the truth is one of the most serious errors we can make. I would rather enter the Spirit World without that harmful handicap upon my character, my true self. And I can; I have that choice. I am my own creation, after the Great Spirit allowed me my life. Likewise, you are your own creation after your birth. If humanity would acknowledge that fact, we might be able to move forward, as a species, toward ultimate knowledge. What other goal as worthy is there?

Any desire to press onward to true knowledge must begin in this world; we cannot wait for this particular "cleansing" to happen in the Spirit World. Pure reasoning must overwhelm our ego-distorted imagery, because the latter will not stand up in the Spirit World—at least not if Creator is all truth, which Creation certainly suggests. Why be held back from advancement in the Spirit World (if there is one)? It is our choice.

As we saw earlier, Chief Fools Crow said we should all make ourselves into hollow, clean "bones"—tubes through which Creator's healing
and knowledge may pass. A pure, shiny bone without inhibiting obstacles is the ultimate in one's advancement toward the spiritual. We need
to work out clutter or blockage in our body, our mind, our emotions,
and our spirit so that nothing impedes our spiritual growth and advancement.

THE CHURCH DURING WORLD WAR II

Not only did the Church attempt to rein in its own followers through
the Inquisition, but during that time—and more dramatically, during
World War II—the Church attempted to gain a monopoly on religion.
The Jews were the major target.

In *Constantine's Sword: The Church and the Jews*, James Carroll, a
Christian and a former priest (like Father Stolzman), gives us an
overview of the Church's position on Jews, from centuries back and on
into World War II.[15] The book's main subject is the Church's refusal,
down through the centuries, to see the Jews any way except through the
clouded lens of religious hatred—a refusal that culminated in the outright murder of millions of people in World War II.

Hitler's Pope: The Secret History of Pius XII, by John Cornwell, fits like a
glove with Carroll's work.[16] Cornwell started out to write a sympathetic
papal work when he was allowed to look at Vatican archives, but the
foul truth of what he discovered came through. Expecting to find material that exonerated Pope Pius Pacelli, Cornwell found indicting material
that left him in a state of moral shock. Pope Pius XII, the papers revealed,
had showed obvious prejudice against Jews. What's more, through his
diplomatic work with the Germans in the 1930s, he betrayed Catholic
political associations that might have made a difference challenging
Hitler—even foiling the Final Solution.

The freedom of thought and inquiry that John Cornwell demonstrates brings us all to the discovery of hidden truth. Like Tiger, he pursues knowledge in freedom, helping us to preserve truth. From his pursuit of truth we are better informed about Catholic collusion with Nazi Germany. People now have reason to be alarmed about Pius XII's career, negotiations, actions, and inactions, and to question not only his apparent obsession with absolute papal authority and moral betrayal, but his proposed elevation to sainthood.

The elevation to sainthood is rather trivial, I know, in comparison to the other matters. The following example is of far more concern.

"UNDER HIS VERY WINDOWS"

Susan Zucotti sets the scene for us: "In October 1943, the Germans occupied Rome. 4000 Jews were herded out of their Ghetto right next to the Vatican. Gunfire broke the early morning. The Jews were taken to a temporary jail in the Italian Military College. Yet from the Vatican, no voice was raised in public support of the Jews." All this happened within earshot of Pope Pius XII—"under his very windows," to quote the apt title of Zucotti's book.

Two days later, the prisoners were put on trucks, taken to the railroad station, and loaded into boxcars. Again no voice was raised in protest. The arrested Jews were gone, and no one cared. Five days later this entry appears in the meticulously kept log at Auschwitz: "Transport, Jews from Rome. After the selection 149 men registered with numbers 158451–158639 and 47 women registered with numbers 66172–66218 have been admitted to the detention camp. The rest have been gassed."[17]

TIGER-BRAVE EXCEPTIONS

A pitifully small but brave group of German Jehovah's Witnesses spoke out against the injustices of Nazism but were then, in turn, incarcerated and made to sew a purple triangle patch on their clothing. It is a pity

that most people in this land are unaware of the courageous stand the
Jehovah's Witnesses took on behalf of the Jews. They acted on their beliefs in the thirties, and they paid dearly for their truth. By 1939, six
thousand of them had been imprisoned, and thousands more had been
sent to concentration camps. By the end of the war, two thousand imprisoned Jehovah's Witnesses had died, over 250 by execution.[18]

The Jehovah's Witnesses were not the only religious dissidents, of
course. Many other German Christians (and believers in countries
across Europe) joined in the fight against Nazism. The Vatican recently
released documents showing that many thousands of Jews were rescued
during the war by various officials of the Catholic Church. In making
these documents public, John Paul II praised the Roman priests,
monks, and nuns who opened "the doors of our religious houses, of our
churches, of the Roman seminary, of buildings belonging to the Holy
See and of Vatican City itself . . . to offer refuge and safety to so many
Jews of Rome being hunted by their persecutors."[19] The pope made no
mention of his predecessor, but defenders of Pius XII credit him with
having directly sponsored this multitude of acts of individual heroism.
According to Pope John Paul II, "The 1988 Vatican document, 'We Remember: A Reflection on the Shoah,' honors Pius for what he did 'personally or through his representatives to save hundreds of thousands of
Jewish lives.' Acts of rescue performed in secret by the lower clergy and
Catholic laity are defined as acts of the pope, although no records directly tying such heroism to Pope Pius XII have ever been uncovered."[20]

RACE AND ALBINO SQUIRRELS

As we know, religion is not the only basis on which people are judged
and have their natural freedoms removed. To become truly free, humanity must shed all prejudices, including those about other races.

Over here in America, it seems that the blacks have borne the
major blows of persecution. Yes, and Indians too. Blacks in the south

still go to their churches and the whites to theirs, though it is approaching fifty years since Martin Luther King Jr. made his march. Does this tell us that a predominantly Christian nation must have someone to persecute, other than their own? Is the urge to persecute an inherent trait? I hope not.

Blacks, Jews, and Indian people (especially the Sioux) are survivors and have learned to live without. That is one of *their* inherent traits. And it will be an important trait in the future, given what is coming from Nature's realm. Nature will not spare any particular group of humans; we will all suffer unless we wake up. Maybe the persecuted will be those who will survive, since they have had ongoing practice of going without. Persecution and prejudice do severely curtail one's freedom.

It was inconceivable for the North American Indians, when they first met the white man, to base hatred purely on race. They were receptive to the Pilgrims in their first meetings. Then later, during the nineteenth century, they took in and protected runaway black slaves to such an extent that many southern Indian tribes now reveal elements of black heritage.

Nature is not prejudiced. I see proof of that in my own backyard. Maybe the common tree squirrels that abound there cannot perceive color; maybe they can. In any case, the lone albino squirrel is never isolated or shunned. It chases and plays with the normal-colored squirrels and gets equally chased in return. Buffaloes are the same, accepting the rare white buffalo as an equal and treating it no differently than the rest.

RED, YELLOW, BLACK, AND WHITE

Red, yellow, black, and white are our traditional colors and the colors of the four races of Human, and all are related. *Mitakuye Oyasin* ("We are all related") is one of our tribe's most important statements. We maintain freedom by living in openness with one another. We do not relate by hating and deciding what others can think. Imagine! No encyclicals, no canon law, no concordats, and no Vatican Councils, and yet we were able to walk down to our own shores and help keep the Pilgrims alive even after they stole from us. Like the Jews of today, we do not proselytize. How would we convert you? Pour wild rice over your head? After reading and learning from Haught, Carroll, Zucotti, and Cornwell, I am under the impression that proselytizing is a highly lethal business—not in harmony with Creator's Nature!

Actually, we would have quite a bit of bad publicity to get over before we would have a chance of proselytizing. We Native Americans and other indigenous peoples have been demeaned with terms such as "heathen" and "pagan" (apologies to my respected Druid brothers and their friends!) so much over the past couple hundred years that many people assume those labels are accurate.

THE CONTRARIES CHIME IN

Finchley and Finkley peeked their heads back into my office just when I was at the apex of some serious contemplation.

Finkley pointed a finger in my direction and said, "You pagan heathen blokes are named in the pope's Vatican apology called 'We Remember.'"[21]

I managed to keep my silence and let him continue. I thought to myself: *A Vatican apology? Hmmm. Interesting. Maybe these contraries can be helpful after all.*

Finkley continued, "In 1998, Pope John Paul II issued a paper that contends that the Holocaust was the product not of Christianity but of a 'neo-pagan' regime that had renounced the faith." He pointed at me. "You Indians are called pagans, are you not?"

I shook my head sternly (though he was right, of course) and argued that he was stretching his information somewhat. He knows I bristle when my spirituality is referred to as pagan or heathen.

Finchley chimed in on my behalf: "How in the world could the Church blame a group so small that it barely existed—German pagans being only a percentage of the non-Christians and non-Jews—for killing six million people or more?"

Finchley is a mischief-maker, but he does have scholarly credentials.

Except for the Jewish population, the people in Germany in the 1930s and 1940s were basically all Christian. In fact, according to James Carroll, "a mere 3.5 per cent of the German population described themselves as Gottglaubige (neo-pagan) as late as 1944. Now how did the pope figure out, half a century after the fact, that it was those very few pagans who killed the six million Jews?"[22]

Finkley was hung up on the numbers thing. He asked, "How many Jews did Hitler kill himself?"

"As Finchley just said, it was around six million he was responsible for," I replied.

Finkley bristled. "I mean *physically*," he clarified. "The actual act of dispatching or killing the victim. You know, it must have taken considerable manpower to kill six million people. It would have been impossible for the Nazis to do it all by themselves—every last party member—even with Hitler's personal help. So how does the pope think this little band of neo-pagans would have pulled it off?"

Finchley said, "Well, *someone* did it. It is a good thing there were not many Sioux living in Germany then. If there had been, they would have been the scapegoats, along with the blacks."

"Well wait a minute," said Finkley. "It *was* the Sioux. That is what the Vatican's paper claimed—that it was pagans who killed the Jews." The two of them got quite a chuckle out of that.

I got to thinking again, still trying to puzzle this out for real. "So all of a sudden an entirely Christian nation—well, almost entirely, except for the Jews and a few others—suddenly changes and becomes pagan? What does that say for the religious training of the churches? Seems pretty weak to me, if it was true, but I don't believe it."

Finchley snorted, "You are now learning the art of blaming others for something you or your people have done."

"The pagan Nazis get the blame, and it is kind of muddled after that on who carried out their orders," Finkley offered. "You Sioux blokes should blame the Cherokee for wiping out Custer. Maybe you can get your Black Hills back!"

"That is preposterous, Finkley. No one is *that* gullible," I chastised.

Both contraries laughed again, and said in unison, like a pair of cawing crows: "It works! Everyone now believes the Nazis became suddenly pagan, and the wartime pope is going to become a saint—like he had nothing to do with any of it!"

Contraries, I thought. Sometimes they do make some sense.

THE MUSLIM WORLD

In areas of the world where Islam dominates, the people exercise no greater freedom of thought than in the largely Christian areas. If we examine a map of Turkmenistan, Tajikistan, Kazakhstan, Kyrgyzstan, Uzbekistan, and Afghanistan, we are looking at some of the remotest countries in the world. The comparison between these countries and Western nations with regard to standard of living is stark. In the United States, for instance, the gross domestic product (GDP) per American in 2002 was $36,300. In some of the remote Muslim countries, the per-capita GDP is as low as $2,400 (Uzbekistan), $1,400 (Tajikistan), or even $800 (Afghanistan, even before the devastating effects of the war against the Taliban). Literacy for Afghans is at 32 percent for men and less than 15 percent for women. Life expectancy is forty-six years. Pakistan, a much larger nation bordering Afghanistan, has a literacy rate of only 43 percent and a GDP of $2,000.[23]

Muslim society in centuries past was a pioneer in democracy, economic development, and science. Under caliphates, the Islamic world rose to greatness. Muslim armies sacked Rome, that giant of civilization! Then, at about the time of the discovery of the New World (the Americas), the crescent moon went into eclipse, shadowed by an excess of religious fanaticism. As a result, the Islamic world today looks much as it did hundreds of years ago. Civil society, offering protective laws unrelated to any form of religious jurisprudence, never had a chance to develop in the harsh religious climate of Islam. One wonders whether such a zealous religion—one that left its inheritors in the Middle Ages—will be able to survive the truth that the age of communication is spreading throughout the world. Is fanaticism that powerful?

There are two main views as to what has happened to Islam. Fundamentalists claim that a falling away from "pure Islamic religion" brought the downfall. The fundamentalist mullahs are confident they possess the infallible truth—namely, that one is either Muslim or infidel. Modernists and reformers, on the other hand, hold the Muslim clergy responsible for stifling the once-great Islamic movements in science, commerce, and fundamental human rights. The woman has no rights in Islam, but the man is not exactly awash in freedom either. What rights overall does the Arab man hold, other than not having to wear a masculine version of a concealing burka?

Whatever the original cause, it is unquestioned that religious fanatics have stifled freedom of thought and religious expression and have encouraged the degradation and debasement of women. Hopefully the moderate Muslims throughout the region will be able to curtail those who would stifle basic freedoms. Turkey is an example of a moderate Muslim state that practices secularization and that allows women to dress in Western garb and enjoy basic freedoms.[24]

The Taliban in Afghanistan and the political mullahs of Iran are observable examples of religious nationalism led by fanatic clergymen. Freedom is so essential to an emerging society that the Islamic world will never rise up to a sense of greatness again until it manages to rein in these fanatic mullahs. It is as if the United States were to allow right-wing religious fanatics to dictate policy and lifestyle for all American

citizens. Extreme religion and true democracy simply do not mix fruit-
fully. Curtailment of freedom inhibits productivity and progress; and
when the curtailment is on a national scale, so is the lack of progress.

There is no "infallible truth" when that truth is propagated by humans, for *all* humans have proven fallible. Creator does not make infallible humans. Have you met such a one in your travels? I think not. The
observable fact continues to be our only true beacon: we learn from Nature who Creator is and what Creator wants from us. The Mystery that
is God is unresolved now, despite the conviction of Islam and Christianity; and it will most likely remain so. All we humans can do is carry
on with our lives in harmony, appreciating that somehow we have
discovered the great gift of democracy. We need to cultivate spiritual
wealth, replacing fanaticism with appreciation of our planetary gifts, respecting Creator as mysterious yet benevolent, striving to alter practices
harmful to Mother Earth and all our animal relatives, and respecting the
visions of others.

The absence of such efforts means spiritual impoverishment. This is
the dismal poverty of one-way-only fanatics who have allowed themselves to be so misled that they forsake their wondrous, rewarding,
God-given gift of intelligence. Giving away your sacred mind to allow
someone to brainwash you into flying into tall buildings—now *that is*
spiritual poverty!

A secularized society with a separation of church and state within a
democracy has proven itself worth fighting for, even if fighting means
going to war with those who disagree so strongly that they attempt to destroy us. (Of course, threatening a secularized society that has a wealth of
modern technology is a fairly stupid thing for a small, relatively primitive
society to do—a society whose religious leaders have kept people in not
only spiritual but also technological poverty.) A spiritual person within a
comfortable, democratic, secularized society is generally tolerant, but
when forced to the wall can be a formidable warrior.

Westerners have a different theory about what went wrong in Islamic territory than do the natives of that region. Bernard Lewis, Cleveland E. Dodge Professor of Near Eastern Studies Emeritus at Princeton University, sums up the Mideast situation with a practical, sweeping observation:

> *To a Western observer, schooled in the theory and practice of Western freedom, it is precisely the lack of freedom—freedom of the mind from constraint and indoctrination, to question and inquire and speak; freedom of the economy from corrupt and pervasive mismanagement; freedom of women from male oppression; freedom of citizens from tyranny—that underlies so many of the troubles of the Muslim world. But the road to democracy, as the Western experience amply demonstrates, is long and hard, full of pitfalls and obstacles.*[25]

Still, democracy is the Mideast's best chance. Organized religion, with Islamic mullahs at the helm, simply cannot restore an imagined Muslim supremacy. The Iranians or Afghans blaming an abandonment of divine heritage for the source of their present-day situation is akin to the Japanese believing that the divinity of their emperor would have been able to conjure a "Divine Wind" to blow back the American Fleet before it invaded and subdued Japan. It didn't happen. General MacArthur forced the emperor to appear on public radio and tell his subjects he was not all that divine. A few Japanese leaped off cliffs at that news, but eventually the populace settled down and became a democratic government, complete with women's suffrage. Secularization, democracy, and equality of women shot Japan to world-power status. Had they fallen victim to the sole control of their Shinto priests and a ruling "divine" emperor, I doubt that their economic status and subsequent standard of living would be as high as they are today.

WHEN FREEDOM FLOURISHES

When freedom is allowed to flourish, it benefits not only the individual but also the tribe, the society. Indeed, planetary survival is the reward when people as a whole see and rebel against harmful practices that benefit a corporate few but harm many in the long run. Deprive or curtail freedom and you penalize the wellbeing of the whole. Creator obviously wanted us to enjoy and appreciate all of the inventions and ongoing technology we have "discovered"; otherwise, I doubt that the benevolent Creator would have allowed them to exist or come into being in the first place.

We can see and feel freedom, probably more so if it has been taken away from us. Freedom has been shown to us by Creator. We cannot say the same about the religious concepts of any humans—be they mullahs, popes, bishops, rabbis, monks, or television preachers with a worldwide audience. What humans state as an absolute is not visible or provable. Furthermore, we have heard many such absolutes over the centuries, most of which bear little fruit. One person will state that his way is the only way, while another will make an equally preposterous, countering claim. But freedom—that is something we can all see and understand.

MODERN TECHNOLOGY AS FREEDOM'S TOOL

I believe there is a reason that we have such advanced technology—technology that, among other things, greatly expands our knowledge-seeking ability. It is not *our* technology; that is for sure. Everything that we think we have invented is something that the Great Mystery has simply allowed us.

At any rate, this new technology and its related tools are an absolute wonderment, especially for one such as me, who once thought of threshing machines and two-bottom plows as high technology. We now have an added freedom: the freedom to communicate worldwide. Hopefully that freedom will also become a safeguard, preventing any attempt by organized religions or their related agencies to move us back into a stagnant past by fostering fear and control. The hatred and blame of the Muslim world are not going to win anything for any society, whereas the various freedoms many people in the West now enjoy are our main hope for fulfilling progress as we and the rest of the unburdened-by-fanatics world moves on. Communication will continue to aid democracies in their efforts to remain truthfully informed. An informed society will continue to fight for and maintain beneficial freedoms. It is foolish—in fact, suicidal—for anyone to think otherwise. No holy war will make us "unbelievers" let our freedoms go.

What does all this mean? If there exists a Creator, a Supreme Being, or a Higher Power, it must appear to that being that we humans are playing a game with our various religions, each declaring a monopoly on truth and all contradicting each other. Actually, the only "real truth" is what we can directly observe!

If I am promoting the sacredness of Nature as a daily event—that same Nature wherein truth lies—then it could be said that I am promoting a more "religious" society. That does not mean, though, that I am promoting religion per se. A Nature-based spirituality cannot encompass a conventional religious hierarchy, which feeds on a growing membership. Such a hierarchy assumes and honors human dictates. Nature is far too vast to be influenced by human dictates. She reacts according to Creator's endowed truths only. Likewise, religion depends on human statements, but true spirituality is guided by Creator's created Nature only!

Nature's Way needs no formal membership. What it needs is support. The attitude of the entire population needs to change, becoming more environmentally receptive. Technology can help us reach that goal. As specialized scientists make discoveries in their specific fields, that information can be passed on from person to person. We need actual data and observed results, not hierarchical, controlling "ideology."

Nature's Way has no ideology, as such, for Nature's major function is to be directly observed. There is far less room for human misinterpretation when *all* people see (sometimes repeatedly) what *one* sees. Nature's Way is not an invented, human-designed attitude; it is a proven model from the past that has demonstrated centuries of compatibility with and for the Earth. Organized religion has demonstrated just the opposite, and now all its problems are coming to a head. The unfolding of time is beginning to reveal the conditions that organized religion, in all its many forms, has unleashed. These ongoing conditions prove how very correct the old "Earth spirituality" was, and how necessary it is that we all return to it if we want the human race to continue. It is as simple and factual as that!

FREEDOM: THE NATURAL INSTINCT

How many wars will it take, one wonders, to ensure freedom for all, as Nature's Way dictates? If the fanatics win any future war, it will bring world doom. The Dark Ages will surely return, as they have already in certain corners of the world. What amount of resources does the secular world possess to combat fanaticism? Not an unlimited amount, certainly. But we as individuals have the most powerful resource of all: intelligence.

We must hope that as human beings become more knowledgeable, they will also become wiser, developing the confidence to reason through the differences between myth and truth. Secularization, in combination with true democracy, can then ensure the ultimate protection against the doom of fanaticism. Religious fanaticism dooms itself because of its severe restrictions on freedom. Secularism, on the other hand, provides great freedom, because it acknowledges that Creator, that vast Mystery, is neutral to our wars and errors. We have to figure out our dilemma for ourselves—we have the *freedom* to do that. Creator will not rush to our rescue if we wait too long to act.

Fortunately for us, Creator put into all humans a strong instinctive desire for freedom—the same desire that drives Tiger. While we would all like to see Creator intervene—we enjoy fairytales, after all—historical evidence warns us not to count on it. Instead, we need to rely on our drive for freedom. When the dilemma of planetary survival finally comes home to us, our love of freedom will motivate us to act quickly and effectively to preserve our Mother Earth. We can only hope that will happen before it is too late.

Humanity, in deviating from real truth, abandoned early on the values and practices of the Earth-respecting Old Europeans, Celts, and Native Americans. We gave up our freedom to observe directly from Nature, not realizing that it was as much *obligation* as *right*. Surely the world would be in a less threatened environmental situation had those early Nature-loving societies flourished longer.

The range of Tiger's freedom has been severely curtailed. One can say the same for humanity, as a group. How about you, as an individual? If you have allowed your instinct for freedom to become "domesticated," if you are like those comfortable cows awaiting slaughter, then you know what I mean.

In the future, those who survive will have no choice but to be in harmony with Nature. Being one with Nature will be her primary teaching. But we cannot have such harmony without the freedom to seek and know truth. Imagine that some planet out in space, an orb like Earth with inhabitants like us, were to someday die, burned out by its inhabitants' many excesses. If a few survivors could manage to launch themselves toward safety on Earth, what do you think those people would tell us? I am sure they would have many dire warnings: live in harmony, preserve freedom and seek truth, conserve your resources, and don't overpopulate.

Because we have not yet heeded those warnings, our planet is failing fast. The remaining four chapters will take us to the environmental worldview, where we will consider the most serious of all our calamities, dilemmas, and impending disasters.

HEAT

Lesson of Cottonwood Tree

In Black Elk's vision of future threats to Mother Earth, he told of the appearance of four horses: one yellow, one black, one red, and one white. Like the biblical Four Horses of the Apocalypse, they represented specific ways that the Blue Man (self-interested humanity) would destroy life on Earth. If you have learned the lessons of the seven animals that preceded this point, you now have, as Black Elk did in his vision, the weapons you need to take on Dominant Society and turn back the Blue Man's four horses. We will take a look at each of the four threats to Mother Earth in turn. The first horse's name is Heat.

The first of the horses in Black Elk's vision, a yellowish bay, was meant to bring bounty—the natural, life-giving warmth of fire and the sun—but it is clear that Earth's atmosphere is now being unnaturally heated by the overuse of carbon-based fossil fuels, industrial pollution, and deforestation. Since that vision over a century ago, we have "adjusted to the temperature of the water." We have learned to adjust to less arable land, more droughts, warmer temperatures, coastal flooding, and a lot of the other consequences of global warming.

I think of the cottonwood tree when I consider humanity's reaction to worldwide rising temperatures. The stately cottonwood is the tree most often selected as the annual Sun Dance tree. Its inner core, when cut crosswise, reveals the shape of a heart. The Sioux say the Great Spirit gave it a heart, and for that reason they revere and respect it. The cottonwood symbolizes endurance, because it can survive with its roots deep in a flowing stream or grow for a century on the arid plains where water is scant. It survives the hot summer winds because it is supple and adapts. This tenacious attitude helps it to survive.

When I was looking for a house once in a comfortable suburb, I found what appeared to be a quiet, secure place, ideal for writing a book or two. In the backyard was a huge cottonwood that had four immense trunks, like four separate trees, emerging out of the large central trunk, which measured six feet in diameter. I would certainly have all the morning shade I desired, I thought to myself, determined to move in. Well, I live in that house still, and when a storm came recently, I saw how cottonwoods can bend. It was a violent storm, and most residents took refuge down in their basements. That tree bent so much as the wind increased that it actually touched the neighbor's garage with its branches. When it snapped back, two branches as large as some trees speared down into the lawn.

Fortunately, nothing was damaged other than the lawn, but the experience demonstrates the danger that arises when something bends too far: it can snap back suddenly and with great force.

Our ability to adapt to global warming and other environmental crises is a strength in some ways, but we are likely, like the cottonwood tree after the windstorm, to bend so far that we snap back and can bend no further. We cannot continue to neglect our partnership with the Earth. The longer we wait to deal with heat-related threats to Mother Earth, the harder they will be to remedy.

In most of the nations on Earth that have the capability of turning the tide, we are accustomed to relying on our leaders, both secular and religious, to sound the alarm about all matters of concern and institute a plan to restore balance. But most Dominant Society religious leaders have either been silent regarding this particular alarm or blatantly denied the steadily increasing dilemma. Those who acknowledge it maintain that God will appear in the skies to save us—well, *them*—from any trial or tribulation.

The Sioux spoke of living one's lifestyle with a concept that the "generations unborn" were always to receive serious consideration regarding the daily use of Mother Earth. Very little of such corresponding thoughts or practices do I hear voiced in the pulpits of Dominant Society; if generational concern is voiced, it has not been a common virtue.

Rather than making tough future-minded decisions and lifestyle changes, we seem to prefer painless "quick fixes" to our myopic problems. We allow ourselves to be seduced by mistruths from the world's economic interests. All too readily we believe President George W. Bush and his environmental advisors when they tell us that although the Earth's warming trend has clearly been established, the causes have not, and that our responses should be delayed until we are sure. We listen to whatever politician minimizes concern and assures us that everything is really okay.

And yet we are neglecting our responsibility when we choose not to see or to heed the warnings. Nobel laureate Elie Wiesel has stated on many occasions that indifference is worse than evil. Perhaps our individual and collective neglect of our responsibility to Earth stems from indifference—an indifference that has allowed corporations and global economic interests to routinely perpetuate the causes of the environmental crises surrounding us, an indifference that keeps us from growing in personal and collective strength to envision and empower something better. Indifference does not elicit a *response*; it is an *end*.

Indifference is not the only problem, however. Today's ecological crises are also due to the historical complicity of religious institutions, governments, and individuals who believe in exerting power over Nature and see Earth as a source of unending riches to exploit. That attitude has led to the separation of the sacred from Nature and the consequent desecration of Mother Earth. We can see that perspective's roots in historical events and biblical stories from more than 2,400 years ago.

THE HISTORY OF DESECRATING MOTHER EARTH

If the story of Eve and the serpent's banishment represents rejection of women and Nature as sacred, then the rise of the "mechanized view" of Nature represents the death of Nature in Dominant Society. Carolyn Merchant, author of *The Death of Nature: Women, Ecology, and the Scientific Revolution*, writes: "Between the sixteenth and seventeenth centuries the image of an organic cosmos with a living female earth at its center gave way to a mechanistic world view in which nature was reconstructed as dead and passive, to be dominated and controlled by humans."[1]

The actual shift may have taken place in the sixteenth century, but its genesis began much earlier. In the thirteenth century the Christian theologian Thomas Aquinas popularized a theology that combined Aristotle's purely intelligent Unmoved Mover with the Bible's dynamic, purposeful Creator and resulted in a distant, passionless Ruler of Creation.[2] Nature was assumed to be static, with all its species created in their present forms—a completed world with no newness except as God might act within it or as each life's God-given potentialities unfolded. "One might say," notes theologian Ian Barbour, "that the basic image of nature was that of a Kingdom—a fixed, hierarchical, ordered society under a sovereign Lord."[3] The mechanized view does not allow an interdependent and responsive relationship with Nature, for once Creation was done, it needed only caretaking. The nurturing Mother Earth, earlier viewed as sensitive, alive, and responsive to human action, came to be regarded as inanimate, passive, and merely functional.[4]

According to Merchant, as women and Nature have been linked throughout history, so has their devaluation, which came to the fore within the mechanized worldview. Symbolized as a passive female,

Nature could be used as a commodity and manipulated as a resource.[5] She could be "tamed and subdued," her "primary function" being "to comfort, nurture, and provide for the well being of the male."[6] Furthermore, notes Merchant, any action once regarded as a violation or desecration of Nature could now be sanctioned according to the potentialities that might unfold or the gain that might accrue to the perpetrator:

> The image of the earth as a living organism and nurturing mother had served as a cultural constraint restricting the actions of human beings. One does not readily slay a mother, dig into her entrails for gold, or mutilate her body. As long as the earth was considered to be alive and sensitive, it could be considered a breach of human ethical behavior to carry out destructive acts against it.[7]

By the sixteenth century this destructive attitude was firmly embedded in Western culture. The "mechanized" view of Nature had found its unwitting ally in the Christian Church, and Mother Earth has never recovered. Separating the sacred from Nature allowed the Scientific Revolution to flourish and gave free range to the Industrial Revolution, which was built on the back of the mechanized view of Nature. Class/race barriers were also encouraged by such change.

The world has benefited immensely from the inventions and ingenuity of this period, but the unbalanced and limited view of Nature eventually led to excesses that would be felt worldwide. Adaptability was learned, but it didn't have heart. Centuries later, even the Sioux who lived on the North American Great Plains would be impacted by this separation of Nature and God. When the mechanized view of Nature leaped the Atlantic Ocean and reached the American shores, it unfortunately worked like a well-oiled machine to take advantage of and overrun at an incredible pace most of the North American continent.

The concept of "Manifest Destiny" conspired to give early Americans a religious rationalization for taking land and disintegrating the

Nature-based ecologies that the indigenous tribes had developed. In religious language and hyperbole that seemed to foreshadow the German Nationalist movement in Europe during the 1930s, John L. O'Sullivan articulated the credo of America's "Manifest Destiny" in 1845 in his *United States Magazine and Democratic Review*:

> We are the nation of human progress, and who will, what can, set limits to our onward march? Providence is with us, and no earthly power can. The far-reaching, the boundless future will be the era of American greatness. In its magnificent domain of space and time, the nation of many nations is destined to manifest to mankind the excellence of divine principle; to establish on earth the noblest temple ever dedicated to the worship of the Most High—the Sacred and the True. All this will be our future history, to establish on earth the moral dignity and salvation of man—the immutable truth and beneficence of God.[8]

Congressmen quickly incorporated the concept of Manifest Destiny into their debates over annexing territory. It was used by U.S. expansionists to justify wars with Mexico, the taking of native lands, and the continued expansion of U.S. boundaries westward to the Pacific and beyond.

The ecological crises we face today are consequences of this "mechanized view of Nature" and Manifest Destiny, both of which characterized Nature as holding whatever a greedy industrial society needed. Mother Earth was perceived as simply there for the taking, waiting to give away her unlimited riches, like a ripe plum waiting to be plucked. This set the stage for simply taking whatever was wanted while losing touch with what was actually needed. It was not a healthy and honorable exchange, a balanced dynamic of Earth giving, humans receiving and then giving back again to Earth. It was take, and take, and take even more. Indeed, it was rape, and most of humankind has been continuing to ignore what Earth needs from us in a most egregious sense of unfounded entitlement, control, and domination. We have pillaged her riches without honor, respect, or even a simple offering of gratitude. To make things worse, we have left her in waste, poisoning her and suffocating her with barely a second thought.

THE SPIDER'S WEB

While Nature's Way seeks to recover a view of Nature as "sacred," as the Sioux for millennia have envisioned it, there are important differences between the Indian perspective and the early Western image of Earth as simply a living organism. The Native view of Nature as an organism is similar, but Indians have never understood her as passive. Mother Earth is not only alive and active, but also receptive and responsive. Creator itself is seen in Nature as an active and responsive presence. It is like a spider's web that vibrates in response to activity upon it.

Just as modern feminists have revolted against the image of passive and powerless women in their journey to equality, I would agree with authors Carolyn Merchant and Riane Eisler that Mother Earth is not dead and passive but alive and receptive, that all of Creation is interrelated, and that all creatures share mutual responsiblity for Earth. To an Indian, Nature is experienced as interactive, mutually powerful, and interdependent.

Earth is a living planet, and we are not separate from it. Our mutual health and well-being depend on our care for Earth. We cannot go back to some "Eden" in the past; we must look forward toward a new global understanding of our mutual responsibility for our Mother Earth.

Author John Gribbin reminds us of our interconnectedness with the Earth and the all-or-nothing choice before us:

> If we try to overcome our natural human chauvinism, we can see that the important thing about life on earth is all of life on earth—the fact that there is any life here at all. There is a web of life, in which we de-

pend on plants that convert carbon dioxide into oxygen and provide
our food, plants depend on bacteria that "fix" the nitrogen from the air
and deposit it in the soil in a natural process of fertilization, and so on.
As far as we know there is no life at all on our nearest neighbor planets,
Venus and Mars, while the earth swarms with life; it seems that you
cannot have a little bit of life on a planet, but that life is an all-or-nothing
affair, which infects a planet completely or does not take a grip at all.
This [is a] new perspective, on the earth as a living planet rather than
merely an abode of life.[9]

THE GREENHOUSE EFFECT

So the horse called Heat has appeared. What does this mean for the living organism we call Mother Earth?

Less glacial ice, for one thing. Andrew Revkin, of the *New York Times*, reports that "the icecap atop Mount Kilimanjaro, which for thousands of years has floated like a cool beacon over the shimmering plain of Tanzania, is retreating at such a pace that it will disappear in less than 15 years, according to new studies."[10] The vanishing of the seemingly perpetual snows of Kilimanjaro that inspired Ernest Hemingway is repeating itself in similar trends on ice-capped peaks throughout the Andes, Glacier National Park in Montana, the Swiss Alps, and Mount Everest in the Himalayas, and stands as one of the clearest signs of global warming. Mount Kilimanjaro has lost over 80 percent of its icecap since it was first surveyed in 1912. In the Peruvian Andes, the biggest glacier was retreating by fourteen feet a year twenty years ago, but today it is retreating by ninety-nine feet a year. Scientists are now estimating that by 2025, glaciers worldwide will have lost 90 percent of the volume of ice that was there a century ago.[11]

So why are the glaciers receding? Lewis Thomas, a writer in the field of biology, describes the Earth's atmosphere as "the world's biggest [cell] membrane."[12] As long as there has been life, as we know it, the so-called greenhouse effect has kept our planet at the right temperature for life to flourish. A natural process of our Earth's ecosystem, the greenhouse effect is the warming of the Earth's surface from heat trapped in the atmosphere. It is like what happens in a greenhouse: the enormous energy coming from the sun passes through the glass panels, and the greenhouse then traps the heat. Anyone who has been in a greenhouse on a bright, sunny day can attest that the heat and humidity build up.

The land and oceans normally absorb about one-half of the solar energy that reaches the Earth's surface. The other half is radiated back into the atmosphere. This energy is able to pass through the atmosphere unimpeded by the major gases (nitrogen and oxygen), but it is absorbed by the trace gases (water vapor, carbon dioxide, methane, and nitrous oxide). The effect is much like that of a blanket. These trace gases trap and convert the radiated energy into heat, which eventually warms the planet's surface. Without the greenhouse effect, the Earth's surface would be a frigid sixty degrees colder, and life as we know it probably would not exist.[13]

In other words, the greenhouse effect that we are hearing more and more about these days is a *good* thing. It is an entirely natural phenomenon, a self-regulating system that preserves the delicate balance of life on our living planet. As long as there is equilibrium between the amount of carbon dioxide entering the atmosphere (largely through decay) and the amount that forests and plants consume from the atmosphere (through the photosynthesis by which they convert carbon dioxide into food and oxygen), it will remain in balance. The problem is that humans are throwing that delicate equilibrium out of kilter. When greenhouse gases—those trace gases that impede the release of the sun's energy—are released into the atmosphere through human activities (such as the burning of fossil fuels such as coal, oil, and petroleum), an imbalance is created that affects the amount of carbon dioxide in the atmosphere, which ultimately affects the plants and forests that are creating oxygen, and in fact becomes a threat to the existence of our entire ecosystem.

Water vapor is the most common and dominant greenhouse gas in the atmosphere, but very little of it is the *direct* result of human activities. However, by releasing *other* gases, humans trigger the production of the major culprit. Ross Gelbspan, in his book *The Heat Is On: The Climate Crisis, the Cover-Up, the Prescription*, explains:

> *The recent buildup of carbon dioxide in the atmosphere traps in heat that otherwise would be reflected back into space. The resulting warmth expands ocean water, causing the sea level to rise—just as the level of water heated on a stove rises in its pan. The heating also accelerates the process of evaporation, even as it expands the air to be able to hold more water. The resulting airborne water vapor in turn traps more heat, perpetuating the cycle. The more heat that is trapped, the more intense the greenhouse effect.*[14]

Like a membrane that protects a cell, the atmosphere surrounds and protects the Earth. But each year we are filling the lower twelve miles of the atmosphere with over seven billion tons of heat-trapping carbon dioxide and soot from the burning of fossil fuels and industrial pollution.[15] Economic activities and agricultural practices that depend on the burning of carbon-based fossil fuels, and others that result in the destruction of forests and wetlands, are accelerating the release of carbon dioxide, methane, and nitrous oxide into the biosphere at levels critical to the planet's health. That pollution is taxing the ability of the forests and oceans to absorb carbon dioxide to the point that these ecosystems themselves are being destroyed. For hundreds of years, the Western hemisphere has depended on carbon-based fossil fuels to keep its various economies growing. But now, in the last few decades, coal and oil have turned into humanity's greatest unintended weapon of mass destruction. The membrane that surrounds the Earth to protect her is itself being turned into a threat.

A group known as the Intergovernmental Panel on Climate Change (IPCC) was formed in 1988 by the United Nations and the World Meteorological Organization. It consists of over 2,500 of the world's leading climate scientists, economists, and risk-analysis experts from over 100 countries. Its purpose is to independently examine current scientific findings and determine what the information tells us about the global climate and the impact of human actions on it. In 1995, the panel concluded that there is a "discernible human influence on global climate."[16]

According to the panel, historical records of the past 100 years reveal some established trends. For instance, the surface temperature of the globe has increased about one degree Fahrenheit overall, with nighttime minimums increasing more than daytime maximums. Since 1980 we have seen the ten hottest years in recorded history, with 1997 and 1998 the hottest. Sea level has risen between four and ten inches because of both thermal expansion of the oceans and the alarming rate of melted runoff from the Earth's icecaps and glaciers. The annual air temperature of Antarctica has increased steadily since the 1950s and is now five to nine degrees warmer in the wintertime. The unrelenting warm phase of El Niño, from 1990 to mid-1995, was exceptional in the 120-year record of the phenomenon—a one-in-two-thousand-years event. The El Niño of 1997–1998 is the most severe on record. A recent study found that the mean temperature of 1901–1990 was higher than that of any ninety-year interval since 914 C.E., and the decade of the 1990s was the hottest decade of the millennium.[17]

SIGNS AND EFFECTS OF GLOBAL WARMING

In a "State of the Planet" article in the September 2002 issue of *National Geographic*, the National Oceanic and Atmospheric Administration (NOAA) reported that the highest global average temperature on record for any January occurred in January 2002 at 54.9 degrees Fahrenheit.[18]

Currently the top climate scientists in the world are expressing grave concerns about the impact of global warming on the Earth. One such group is the Union of Concerned Scientists, whose membership includes over 1,700 scientists representing over one-half of the Nobel laureates worldwide. They were so alarmed in 1992 about the fragile balance of life on the planet that the group issued an unprecedented warning: we need to immediately change our stewardship of the Earth or face dire and permanent consequences that will lead to vast human misery.[19]

An IPCC panel in 2001 issued its most emphatic warning yet on global warming: world temperatures might rise much further and faster than seemed likely just five years before. The panel also abandoned its earlier hedging about human causation, asserting that the greenhouse gases from industry and autos "contributed substantially" to the observed warming over the latter half of the twentieth century. We now know more clearly than ever that the rising temperatures are the fault of industrial pollution, not natural causes such as changes in the sun. The average global surface temperature was projected to rise by 2.5 to 10 degrees Fahrenheit over the period of 1990–2100 and will trigger droughts, floods, and other disasters from shifts in the weather patterns. Global sea level in the past century has risen at a rate ten times faster than during any time over the last 3,000 years, and it is projected to rise by about 3.5 to 34.6 inches over the period of 1990–2100, causing many densely populated coastal areas to flood. Northern hemisphere snow-cover and sea-ice extent are projected to decrease further.[20]

The IPCC report continued to warn that rising temperatures threaten to disrupt fishing, farming, and forestry and are killing much of the globe's coral reefs. Rising seas could flood heavily populated coastal areas of China, Bangladesh, and Egypt, while in the United States, the coasts of the Gulf of Mexico and Chesapeake Bay, as well as other low-lying coastal areas, would be affected. Droughts and the expansion of deserts are likely to destroy wetlands and eradicate the plants and animals that live there. All of this, if it happens as predicted, would seriously disrupt food production, leading to starvation in many parts of the world. Sir John T. Houghton, co-chairman of the 2001 meeting, said in a news conference, "The rate of climate change this century is expected to be greater than it has been in the past 10,000 years."[21]

The most serious impacts will most likely include human health, agriculture, and natural habitats. Unfortunately, those who are elderly, along with the poor and their children, and those whose health is already compromised will be bearing the brunt of the impact, because they are less able to adapt. With the combination of global warming and poverty, we will have a new scale of catastrophe and misery.

KILLING WITH CARBON DIOXIDE

Further, the atmospheric level of carbon dioxide will be higher in the next century than it has been for 420,000 years. "Concentrations of carbon dioxide were, prior to the industrial revolution, about 275 parts per million and are currently at 360 parts per million," says Sir John T. Houghton, co-chairman of the 2001 meeting of the IPCC. These levels are expected to double near the middle of this century.[22]

The full effect of the planet's warming will not be felt until short-term cooling air pollutants fall out of the atmosphere in a few years, leaving carbon dioxide and its effects to last for at least another century. In 1994, the IPCC, citing new findings from ancient ice-core records, noted that the planet's temperature is demonstrably sensitive to changes in carbon dioxide concentrations in the atmosphere. The paleontological record shows that prehistoric changes in carbon dioxide concentrations correlate very closely with rapid, dramatic snaps in the climate.[23]

We humans are intimately related to the cycle of Nature's seasons— the rhythmic breathing of growth and decay. Life and breath depend upon the healthy "lungs" of a "living planet." When balance is maintained between the carbon dioxide, nitrogen, and oxygen in the biosphere, the rhythmic breathing of the planet enables life to flourish. But now the imbalance is making the living planet sick. Its breath is being extinguished by global warming. It is like a person suffering with chronic obstructive pulmonary disease (COPD). Because enough carbon dioxide cannot be exhaled and replenished with life-giving oxygen, the planet's body has become exhausted and is struggling for life.

THE RISING SEA

It is easy to discern the basic interdependence of living things, but it is much more difficult to grasp the delicate intricacy of that interdependence. Seemingly small changes can impact our planet in devastating ways. For example, we know that the ocean levels are rising ten times faster now than at any time in human history. The Atlantic is rising at a rate of about a tenth of an inch a year. According to Ross Gelbspan, author of *The Heat Is On: The Climate Crisis, The Cover-Up, The Prescription*, "One-tenth of an inch seems like a small amount until you stop to think that the oceans cover more than 70% of the Earth's surface. A sea level rise of even a few inches could wreak havoc to many of the world's coastal communities."[24]

Rising sea levels lead to more moisture in the atmosphere. In fact, atmospheric humidity has risen by 10 percent in the past twenty years, which in turn is producing more extreme weather events, such as intense downpours, hurricanes, and floods. The term "hundred-year storm" may no longer hold much meaning when storms that huge are occurring every other year. Untold human and wildlife losses stemming from these events are devastating, not to mention the insurance costs. Weather-related losses seem to be increasing. Claims totaling an average of $2 billion a year were paid out during the 1980s due to extreme weather, and that increased to more than $12 billion average per year in the 1990s. In 1998 the first ten months alone totaled $89 billion! Insurance executives are worrying that unless something is done to stabilize the climate, it could bankrupt the industry.[25]

The Canadian and Alaskan forests are the Earth's largest land ecosystem and hold a large part of the world's forests. Greenhouse gases have seriously stressed this huge ecosystem. The increased warmth has stunted growth and caused a loss of moisture, which in turn has weakened the trees and led to a serious increase in insect infestations.

DROUGHTS AND DOWNPOURS

Long droughts coupled with intermittent severe downpours have been eroding soils in southern Europe for the past generation. Such weather used to be the exception, but now it is the rule, creating desert-like conditions in Spain, Portugal, Greece, and Italy. The wheat fields of the western plains of the United States are facing similar conditions. Even small changes in the warmth from greenhouse gases will create droughts, floods, and shifting soils, putting the thin layer of grass that covers the plains at risk of becoming desert. Throughout our midwestern prairies, the paths of migratory birds are changing due to the drier conditions and loss of wetlands.

Evidence is now indicating that the timing of the seasons is changing. Spring in the northern hemisphere is now arriving one week earlier than it did twenty years ago, and rising atmospheric temperatures are the most likely cause. David J. Thomson of AT&T Bell Labs has discovered that after the beginning of World War II, when the levels of carbon dioxide emissions in the atmosphere began to significantly increase, the timing of the seasons began to shift. The seasonal patterns "of the previous 300 years began to change and now appear to be changing at an unprecedented rate."[26]

CHANGING OCEAN CURRENTS

Leading experts on global climate change have expressed concern that the buildup of greenhouse gases and warmer temperatures could lead to an abrupt collapse of the ocean's prevailing circulation system. If that system, known as "the Conveyor," were to shut down, land areas in the North Atlantic region (which would no longer be blessed by warmer water from the south) would plummet twenty degrees Fahrenheit or more within ten years. Dublin, Ireland, would acquire a climate like that of Greenland.

The Conveyor governs the Earth's climate by transporting heat and moisture around the planet. According to some scientists, the Conveyor is the Achilles heel of Earth's climate. The entire system is sensitive to small changes in temperature and has shut down or changed directions many times in Earth's history. Wallace S. Broecker, Newberry Professor of Earth and Environmental Sciences at Columbia's Lamont-Doherty Earth Observatory, a leading expert, warns that the consequences could be devastating: "Each time the Conveyor has shifted gears, it has caused significant global temperature changes within decades, as well as large scale wind shifts, dramatic fluctuations in atmospheric dust levels, glacial advances or retreats and other drastic changes over many regions of the Earth."[27]

The warming of the oceans is creating a potential wasteland, since plankton, a common food source that many species of fish depend upon, is vanishing. Reports show that due to a rise of two to three degrees Fahrenheit in water-surface temperature over the past four decades, there has been a 70 percent decline in zooplankton off the coast of southern California. That trend raises the question of the survival of several species of fish up and down the West Coast. A possible ripple effect appears in the coincidental 90 percent decline in a certain species of seabird and the disappearance of many varieties of fish in the same area.[28]

PERMAFROST: THE WORLD'S
CARBON DIOXIDE REGULATOR

New research indicates that the Arctic's permafrost—land that stays frozen year round—is melting, releasing carbon dioxide that could cause temperatures there to further increase. The vast expanses of permafrost throughout the Arctic and Antarctica play an invaluable role in the planet's health, in that for thousands of years the permafrost has mopped up carbon dioxide from the atmosphere and stored it in the soil. This cleanup happens because the decomposition of dead vegetation is extremely slow in such low temperatures. With today's rising temperatures, however, microbes are decomposing plant matter at a higher rate, releasing carbon dioxide that adds to the problems of global warming. There is evidence now to suggest that parts of the Arctic have switched from being "sinks" of carbon dioxide to sources.[29]

After four hundred years of relative stability, nearly 1,150 square miles of the Larson B and Wilkens ice shelves in Antarctica collapsed between March 1998 and March 1999. Rodolfo del Valle, an Argentine scientist, witnessed the disintegration of the ice shelves and later flew overhead to view where the ice, once up to a thousand feet thick in places, had broken up. "It was spectacular because what was once a platform of ice more than forty miles wide had been broken up into pieces that looked like bits of polystyrene foam smashed by a child. The first thing I did was cry. An enormous crack had opened from the edge of the shelf on the Weddell Sea up to the mountains."[30] Now the concern is that catastrophic flooding from rising global temperatures will occur—not over the course of several centuries, as previously thought, but much faster.

As noted earlier, the Earth's overall temperature has increased only about one degree Fahrenheit in the last hundred years. To put that number in perspective, only an average of about five degrees separates us from the last ice age. Consider "the year without a summer"—1816.[31] Atmospheric ash from a volcanic eruption in Southeast Asia that year decreased the amount of solar radiation that reached the Earth's surface, lowering the global mean temperature. As a result, frost occurred in July in New England, and crop failures occurred throughout the world. Yet the average temperature change caused by that eruption was less than one degree Fahrenheit over a period of one year. Furthermore, a thousand years ago, a temperature increase of only one to two degrees warmed the North Atlantic enough to allow the Vikings to colonize Greenland and perhaps even reach North America. Several centuries later, a two-degree decrease in global temperature during the "Little Ice Age" purportedly caused the Viking colonies to disappear.

Scientists worry that the public is focusing too much on who and what is at fault in global warming when what people should be focusing on is the instability of the climate system. If the world became, on average, ten degrees warmer in the winter and ten degrees cooler in the summer, the average global temperature would remain the same. But the economic, agricultural, and ecological effects would be disastrous.[32]

INDUSTRY OPPOSITION

Almost since the beginning of the scientific community's awareness of global climate change, strong industry opposition has contested scientific research methods, findings, and conclusions. Strong combined economic and political forces within the auto, coal, and oil industries have conspired to protect their mutual interests. Their intent appears (on the surface) to be the presentation of other sides of the issue, but their impact has been to sabotage efforts to keep the public informed. Altogether they are spending billions of dollars annually to keep the problem hidden, creating powerful lobbies in Washington, D.C., for that purpose.

Their main industry-lobbying group is the Global Climate Coalition (GCC). The GCC has not only questioned the validity of the science of internationally respected climate scientists, but has funded its own researchers to promote its monetarily self-interested views. Another group, the George C. Marshall Institute, a politically extreme conservative institute, maintains that the climate crises are basically a liberal plot to subvert the U.S. economy.

News organizations have given just as much time to coal, auto, and oil industry–funded scientists (a handful of greenhouse skeptics) as they have to more reputable climate scientists who have submitted their research to the critique of their peers. As a result, the public is largely unaware of the fact that industries gain financially from the professionally unsupported conclusions of their scientists—conclusions that promote industry biases. Although the GCC has recently suffered the major defections of British Petroleum, Shell, Ford, Daimler-Chrysler, Texaco, the Southern Company, and General Motors, the group has continued to spend millions in lobbying efforts throughout the mid- to late 1990s. The GCC still continues to represent such groups as the American Petroleum Institute, the Automobile Manufacturers' Association, and Western Fuels.[33]

Most problematic for the scientific community is the public perception that researchers are sharply divided—the myth of which has been created by the public relations apparatus of the oil and coal industries. But the Intergovernmental Panel on Climate Change (both 1995 and 2001) countered this perception when it released its conclusions based on independent (that is, not financially reimbursed) findings that it agrees show the "fingerprint" of global warming upon our "living planet."[34]

Up to this time the auto, oil, and coal industries have been able to create the false impression in the public eye that global warming research is either based on an incomplete understanding of the Earth's climate or simply inconclusive. They have even touted the benefits of global warming! Trying to appeal to the public's sense of humor, they have run ad campaigns such as "If the Earth is getting warmer, why is Minneapolis getting colder?" when data suggests just the opposite.[35] Industry lobbyists have used the immense financial resources at their disposal to attempt to sway congressional representatives against the funding of climate-change research during key congressional hearings. This has been very damaging to the truth about global warming and has delayed important action to reverse its effects.

For instance, in May 1996 the House Science Subcommittee on Energy and the Environment cut by one-third the funding earmarked for NASA's global warming research at the counsel of the politically conservative George C. Mitchell Institute. Subcommittee Chair Dana Rohrabacher left no doubt of the Institute's influence when he stated,

> I think that money that goes into global warming research is really money right down a rathole. The fact is that global warming, the more I've studied the issue, the more I've come to believe, at best it's nonproven and at worst it's liberal claptrap. This idea about global warming is more like a religion than it is a science. When we had people talking about global warming, they didn't make their case at all. And, as far as I could see, they [the climate scientists] were shot down totally by the [skeptics] who were presenting the other side of the argument.[36]

This attitude has had far-reaching effects: President George W. Bush, amid public outcry from world leaders, refused to sign the 2001 Kyoto agreement on global warming in Kyoto, Japan, stating that it was not in America's best interests.

GLOBAL WARMING AND NEW DISEASES

When we consider the sobering impact of global warming, nothing touches us more than health concerns. The warming-driven spread of infectious disease is a real threat. Just a few years ago the West Nile virus broke out in New York City and killed seven people. By the summer of 2001, it had spread to the midwestern states, carried by birds harboring the infectious parasite. As of the autumn of 2002 it had killed over fifty people and infected thousands in the United States, despite the fact that the odds of getting infected are like those of finding a needle in a haystack.

The point is that a previously tropical virus is now finding the United States a hospitable environment. It is simple to understand how with today's rapid travel a virus can easily spread across the world, but why *such* a virus would spread to an area that was previously inhospitable to it is not as clear-cut. Global warming may be the key to a chain of events that now finds the West Nile virus thriving in New York City.

Many of the mosquitoes that carried the virus in 1998 were able to survive in this country during the milder winter of 1998–1999. That spring, which arrived early, they were able to find excellent conditions for laying their eggs in damp basements, sewers, and open pools of water. Already thriving, the mosquitoes were helped by a drought in the spring and summer, which killed off many of the insects' natural predators. A heat wave then accompanied the drought and sped up the maturation process of the deadly virus inside the insects.[37]

Sadly, this is not the end of the story or of the threat. The intense hot spells of the past decade have coincided with outbreaks of locally transmitted malaria in the United States, occurring not only in the sun-belt states of Florida, Georgia, and Texas, but also in the northern states of Michigan, New Jersey, and New York. Clearly, malaria parasites are able to infect a traveler and find conditions warm and humid enough to thrive in the United States. Malaria has now returned to many parts of the world thought to be free of the disease. Some experts believe that by the end of the twenty-first century, ongoing warming will have enlarged the zone of potential malaria transmission from an area containing 45 percent of the world's population to an area containing about 60 percent.[38]

As warming speeds up the breeding rate of disease-bearing insects, it also drives them to altitudes and latitudes that were only a few years ago too cold to support their survival. Scientists estimate that if those changes continue at the current rate, mosquito-borne epidemics will double in the tropical regions and increase 100-fold in the temperate regions (including the United States and Europe)—leading to as many as eighty million new cases a year of malaria alone in the next century. The fear, according to Dr. Paul Epstein, Associate Director of the Center for Health and the Global Environment at Harvard Medical School, is that "infectious illness is a genie that can be very hard to put back in the bottle. It may kill fewer people in one fell swoop than a raging flood or an extended drought, but once it takes root in a community, it often defies eradication and can invade other areas."[39]

Extreme and unpredictable weather conditions, resulting in unusually large, intense downpours and floods, are on the rise worldwide. Sanitation problems often follow big storms and floods, leading to outbreaks of cholera and yellow fever. Insects breed in the subsequent standing water, devastation, and decay, increasing the potential for the spread of diseases such as malaria, meningitis, encephalitis, and dengue fever.

Moisture in the atmosphere also produces uneven heating, which in turn generates stronger and hotter heat waves throughout the world. Of greatest concern is the steady rise of overall temperatures in the nighttime, the winter, and at latitudes higher than fifty degrees. The inability of humans and wildlife to recover in the nighttime from the stress of the daytime heat will inevitably lead to more strokes, heart attacks, and other heat-related deaths and illnesses. Again, it will be poor children, those with already compromised health (such as the HIV-infected), and the aged who are most affected. Due to the climate's warming trend, the hundreds of children suffering and dying of AIDS each day in Zimbabwe and South Africa will be even more compromised in their ability to fight off infections. The number of deaths related to heat waves is projected to double by 2020.[40]

For those who are asthmatic, or suffering from allergies or lung disease, global warming threatens increased problems through its exacerbation of air pollution. Prolonged heat increases the production of smog and the scattering of allergens. Both effects have been linked to respiratory systems.[41]

RAPID CLIMATE CHANGE EVENT

An increasing number of scientific studies involve what scientists are calling "Rapid Climate Change Event." Many of the changes in the climate of the Earth have happened as sudden shifts rather than gradual transitions. The ecosystem is so delicately balanced that even small changes have triggered very large outcomes. The concern now is that some new outcome may be the first arc in a vicious circle that threatens to spin out of control. For instance, sustained warmer temperatures would promote drought and wildfires, which in turn could burn huge areas of forest and release more carbon dioxide, which would then accelerate the buildup of greenhouse gases, leading in turn to more warming.[42] This is what scientists are beginning to fear for the twenty-first century.

As the political debate continues over whether global warming is a real danger, the first direct evidence was released showing that greenhouse gases are building up in the atmosphere. Scientists were able to compare readings of infrared light from the Earth's surface taken in previous years with current readings. They found that less was escaping into space now, specifically in the wavelengths that greenhouse gases are already known to absorb.[43] This finding was announced two days after President George W. Bush rescinded a campaign promise to regulate carbon dioxide from coal-burning power plants, stating that mandatory controls would lead to higher electricity prices.

Some scientists are feeling hopeful that the public's general understanding of the chemistry of the atmosphere has improved. The public seems more familiar with the greenhouse effect and the role that gases emitted from power plants and automobiles play in global warming.

F. Sherwood (Sherry) Rowland, an atmospheric chemist at the University of California–Irvine, continues to express concern: "It's alarming to see our rising use of fossil fuels despite evidence that they are heating the planet."[44]

It's alarming indeed—especially when we consider that Heat, the first of Black Elk's four horses, represents just *one* of the environmental problems Mother Earth faces. In the chapter to come, we turn to the next of our four horses, Thin, to examine ways in which the ozone layer is harming Human as well as our animal brothers and sisters.

THIN

Lesson of Deer

The horse named Heat has alerted us to the building negative effects of global warming, and the alarm is still sounding. The short- and long-term effects are impacting all systems of Earth, and we need to not just adapt but, like the cottonwood, adapt with heart to make changes that will be in harmony with Earth.

Heat rides neck and neck with the horse named Thin, the second of the four horses in Black Elk's vision, a black horse that arrives gaunt and sick. These first two horses arrive together because they represent related problems: while Heat represents the danger of atmospheric pollution that threatens to overheat the planet, Thin represents the danger of our ozone layer getting so thin that it lets harmful radiation reach the Earth's surface for the first time in millennia.

Our animal friend Deer offers a good example of the destruction that can result on both sides of a boundary when that boundary becomes too thin. Various relatives of the deer clan can live in a lot of different environments, from elk in the African desert to reindeer in the frozen Arctic. Many deer live in the shrinking prairies and woodlands near urban areas. As farms, cities, and housing developments spread into wilderness areas, the deer are forced either deeper into the wilderness, where the concentration of animals becomes too high to sustain them all and many starve, or into the suburbs of cities, where they feed on shrubs and gardens and in some areas carry the ticks that spread Lyme disease.

Deer are somewhat nomadic, tending to seek a new feeding ground every few months. When food becomes particularly scarce, they sometimes eat tree bark, which can lead to the eventual death of the trees (and a further decrease in their wooded habitats). When deer are forced into smaller islands of wilderness, they interbreed too often and live too close together, both of which may be related to the increasing spread of a disease among deer called "chronic wasting disease"; once affected by this malady, similar to the so-called mad cow disease, the deer gradually become too thin and weak and eventually die.[1]

THE DEADLY THINNING OF THE OZONE LAYER

In large areas of the world, especially over Earth's poles, the ozone layer that protects us from harmful solar radiation is becoming dangerously thin. Over Antarctica the thinning is so extreme that scientists refer to a "hole" in the ozone—an unprotected expanse that in September 2000 was measured at a record 18 million square miles. That is almost 600,000 square miles greater than the record size reported only two years before. To give you a better sense of scale, the entire United States is about 3.5 million square miles (of which a little over half a million square miles is the state of Alaska). A possible second ozone hole, this one over the Arctic, is growing rapidly.[2]

At fifty-three degrees south latitude, Punta Arenas, Chile, sits under the South Pole's huge ozone hole. Preschoolers there recently attended a show featuring a seven-foot Paul the Penguin and his friends, who warned the kids that the sunlight would turn their skin red. However—said Paul—if they covered themselves with Eucerin sunblock, they could play outside as long as they wanted and not get burned.

Most of the world is oblivious to the fact that Chilean children are now being taught how to survive under the ozone hole that the rest of the world has created. These kids are living at what has been called "ground zero of a global ecological catastrophe," exposed to levels of ultraviolet-B (UV-B) radiation 40 percent greater than normal.[3]

The ozone layer is a band that varies between six and thirty miles up within Earth's middle atmosphere (the stratosphere), beneath which is the level of atmosphere nearest Earth's surface in which we live and breathe (the troposphere). Ironically, ozone near the Earth's surface is the most toxic component of air pollution, and ozone higher in the troposphere is a powerful greenhouse gas believed to play a role in global warming. Ozone in the stratosphere, however, serves as Earth's self-protective shield against radiation.

Intercepting the sun's harmful UV-B rays, the ozone layer exists as a continuous self-balancing process of ozone destruction and re-creation. In a nutshell, this process involves UV-B rays splitting the ozone into an oxygen molecule and an oxygen atom. The free oxygen atom easily hooks up with another oxygen molecule to form ozone again. We might imagine, given how easily ozone re-forms, that there must be tons of it up there to create a shield strong enough and large enough to protect all of Earth. "But the equilibrium is delicate," says a Web site for the Union of Concerned Scientists, "and ozone is rare even in the ozone layer. For every ten million molecules of air, two million are breathable O_2, and only three are ozone. Yet this small amount of ozone is enough to prevent most UV-B radiation from reaching the surface of the earth."[4]

CHLOROFLUOROCARBONS:
OZONE'S NUMBER-ONE ENEMY

Warnings to alert us to the existence and dangers of a thinning ozone layer in our atmosphere have been sounding for the past generation—since 1974, when two chemists discovered the potential for devastating effects on the stratospheric ozone of a very common class of compounds called chlorofluorocarbons (CFCs). This was a shattering discovery, for CFCs had been considered all but miraculous since they were first blended in 1928, and had become ubiquitous in the "stuff" of our modern lifestyle. They were efficient refrigerants that enabled refrigeration to become accessible to almost every home. Air-conditioners in vehicles and homes relied on them. They were propellants for aerosol sprays, as well as filler in foam packaging (Styrofoam) and insulation. In later years they were used as a cleaning agent in the making of computers.[5] Millions of tons of CFCs had been manufactured and sold by the time the world was alerted to their potential harm.

When the findings about CFCs were first published, no one seemed to pay much attention. After additional efforts on the part of environmental activists, however, the public eventually took notice. In fact, so many letters about CFCs poured into Congress that the government responded very quickly, "passing amendments to the Clean Air Act in 1977 that called for the regulation of any substance 'reasonably anticipated to affect the stratosphere.'"[6] The use of CFCs in aerosol sprays was banned in 1978.

Despite such quick governmental response, there continued to be many skeptics of the ozone issue who needed hard evidence before buying into the warnings. Evidence of a thinning ozone layer did not come until eleven years later, when in 1985 the huge "hole" in the ozone layer was discovered above Antarctica. When that news was supplemented by the finding that CFCs are also greenhouse gases that absorb heat radiating from Earth's surface, the need and urgency to halt production were magnified worldwide.

After years of chemical industry opposition, scientific disagreements, and differences in needs among developed and developing countries regarding the use of CFCs, in 1987 the first global environmental agreement was made among fifty-seven industrial nations under the United Nations Environment Programme (UNEP). They agreed to begin phasing out CFCs and other ozone-depleting chemicals on a specified schedule. All production of CFCs in developed nations was to be halted by January 1, 1996, with other nations to do the same in 2006 (later modified to 2010). In the United States this agreement (referred to as the Montreal Protocol) now has the force of law through the Clean Air Act of 1990 and is enforced by the Environmental Protection Agency (EPA).[7]

OTHER OZONE-DESTROYING COMPOUNDS

Human responsibility for ozone depletion was not proven until 1994, when a NASA satellite detected hydrogen chloride in the stratosphere. Hydrogen chloride is involved in ozone-destroying reactions that come only from human-produced sources.[8] Since the mid-1990s many human-produced ozone-depleting chemicals have been identified. Many of them are chemical compounds used in industry and are now either phased out completely or restricted considerably, with planned phase-outs by international agreement. In addition to the CFCs, these human-produced chemicals are carbon tetrachloride (released in the production of aluminum), other chlorocarbons (found in industrial solvents and degreasing compounds), halogens (chlorine and bromine) and halons (bromine-related gas found in fire extinguishers), and hydrochlorofluorocarbons (currently used as a CFC substitute).

Human-produced fertilizers and pesticides also contribute to ozone depletion. A report of "The Breathing Earth," a project of the NASA Ames Earth System Science Division, states that a significant part of the nitrogen used in agricultural fertilizer ends up in the air, dramatically changing atmospheric concentrations of nitrous oxide. When it finds its way into the stratosphere, it causes ozone-depleting reactions.[9]

In addition, soil and crop sprays contain the fumigant methyl bromide, which kills soil pathogens and is actually required as an insect treatment before fruits and vegetables can be imported into many coun-

tries. Despite its harmful potential, methyl bromide has been the fumigant of choice for farmers, nurseries, and importers/exporters because it
is easily applied, inexpensive, and highly effective. As mentioned earlier,
bromine is much more effective than its closest rival, chlorine, at eating
ozone, so even small amounts are worrisome. Though many people believe that the EPA does not do enough to promote the use of available
substitutes for methyl bromide, it has mandated the phase-out of U.S.
production and importation, to be completed by 2005. International
treaty members have agreed to a phase-out schedule for gradually reducing methyl bromide use by developing countries (25 percent by
2001 and 50 percent by 2005), and a cap has been placed on its use
worldwide. Unfortunately, methyl bromide isn't being eliminated as
quickly as CFCs have been, especially in developing countries that have
difficulty affording the substitutes.[10]

Chemicals released years ago are still present and at work, thinning
the ozone and contributing to high chemical concentrations. For instance, it is now known that CFCs and halons reach the stratosphere intact due to their extreme stability, and have lifetimes of between fifty
and several hundred years. This means that significant quantities of
their peak concentrations will linger in the atmosphere long after all
emissions have stopped.[11]

MYTHS ABOUT OZONE DEPLETION

A myth persists in the public mind that the major source of ozone-
depleting chemicals is natural occurrences rather than human activities.
People claim, for example, that when ocean spray evaporates, the salt
particles (a form of chlorine) are released into the air. That is true:
oceans do add ozone-depleting chemicals to the air we breathe and the
air higher up in the troposphere. However, because sea salt dissolves in
water, this particular form of chlorine is absorbed into clouds, ice, snow,

or rain and never makes it up to the stratosphere, where it could threaten the ozone layer.[12]

Volcanoes, in particular, have been highlighted as a major natural source of ozone-depleting chemicals—greater, some people claim, than that of CFCs. Skeptics point out that volcanoes such as Mount Pinatubo pose a far greater risk to the ozone layer than human activity. They claim that the Mount Pinatubo eruption (in 1991) released a thousand times more chlorine into the stratosphere than has ever been released by CFCs. But scientists report that the chlorine released in that event was in the form of hydrochloric acid, which (like the chlorine of salt) is water-soluble and thus rapidly absorbed by clouds, snow, and rain droplets and then deposited back onto the ground. This means that very little of the volcanic pollution ever reached the stratosphere to contribute to ozone destruction.[13]

RECIPE FOR AN OZONE FEAST

Although there continue to be questions as research persists, a basic "recipe" of essential ingredients for an "ozone feast"—an opportunity for ozone to be "consumed" in greater-than-usual quantities—seems to be widely accepted.[14] The first ingredients exist within the long polar winter night, when there is no sunlight. It gets so cold during those dark months that strong winds (called the "polar vortex") arise, circulating like a funnel at high velocity around the polar region in the middle to lower stratosphere. Because these winds block the normal mixing of warmer air from below, the cold air becomes isolated and even colder. When the cold gets to about -112 Fahrenheit, clouds unique to the polar stratosphere (called "polar stratospheric clouds") begin to form. As the cold increases, the clouds become larger droplets of water or ice.[15]

The next part of the recipe contains the active ingredients—the chemical processes—that lead to ozone depletion. It is widely accepted now that stratospheric chlorine and bromine compounds from human activities are what is destroying the ozone over the poles. It takes one or two years for these compounds to mix into the air masses and rise into the strato-sphere, where the UV-B light breaks them down into the molecules—chlorine and bromine—that eat the ozone. Eventually they fall at the poles and sit within the cold polar vortex, inactive and benign until they come in contact with the surface of the polar stratospheric clouds.

As soon as the spring sun begins to warm the polar vortex and split the chlorine molecules, the next ingredient—atomic chlorine—suddenly appears, and ozone suddenly *dis*appears. "Predator" has found "prey." The meal has begun. But this is only the appetizer.

Even with chlorine atoms hungrily eating ozone, there are many more ozone molecules than chlorine atoms. So how does the ozone thin so drastically? The final recipe ingredient is sunlight-driven "catalytic cycles"—cycles started when one chemical serves as a link (or catalyst) in a chain reaction that ends up enabling other chemicals to destroy in-creasing amounts of ozone (or regenerating the same chemicals, such as chlorine atoms), over and over. As long as conditions permit, catalytic reactions can simply go on and on.[16] It is believed that a single chlorine atom can thus destroy up to a hundred thousand ozone molecules. Sim-ilar reactions take place with bromine, which has an appetite for ozone fifty times greater than chlorine.

The Arctic polar vortex is not as strong as the vortex in the Antarc-tic, because the atmosphere in the north is warmer. As a result, the Arc-tic stratosphere neither gets as cold nor stays cold as long as the Antarctic, and thus has accordingly less ozone depletion. Nevertheless, the winter of 1999–2000 brought alarming information to light. Ac-cording to scientists atNASA/Jet Propulsion Laboratories, "Ozone losses of more than 60 percent have occurred in the Arctic stratosphere near 60,000 feet (18 kilometers) in one of the coldest winters on record. This is one of the worst ozone losses at this altitude in the Arctic."[17] An area larger than the entire United States was covered by cold deep enough to create polar stratospheric clouds—the largest such area recorded in more than forty years of analysis.[18]

NASA's SAGE III Ozone Loss and Validation Experiment (SOLVE), involving more than 200 scientists and support staff from the United States, Canada, Europe, Russia, and Japan studied this Arctic ozone depletion from December 1999 through March 2000. They saw "significant decline in ozone over the Arctic due to an increase in the size and longevity of polar stratospheric clouds."[19] The NASA project later shared another disturbing finding. Scientists found nitrogen "drizzling out of the clouds."[20] This is alarming, since nitrogen can be a moderating influence on the destructive activity of chlorine on ozone—an "appetite-suppressant," if you will.

Hidden global climate change is increasingly suspected of being indirectly involved in the depletion of ozone. Greenhouse gases in the troposphere hold and reflect more and more heat back toward the Earth's surface and away from the stratosphere, creating changes in Earth's climate and atmosphere. Some believe that global climate change is slowing the ozone layer's healing process. The warming of the atmosphere near the ground causes the stratosphere to become even colder. As mentioned earlier, cold stratospheric temperatures, particularly during the early Antarctic spring, catalyze processes that destroy ozone molecules.[21] It is possible that the polar stratospheric clouds are lasting longer due to global warming processes.

There are natural differences in levels of ozone in the ozone layer due to seasonal variations in the amount of sunlight, wind, and temperature. In addition, Earth's atmosphere is always in flux and constantly mixing in anything that has been added to it. So regardless of where ozone-depleting gases are emitted, they get mixed throughout the atmosphere. While ozone loss is greatest over the South Pole region due to the special weather conditions there, air throughout the stratosphere contains nearly equal amounts of chlorine and bromine. In other words, the danger does not exist only over Antarctica and surrounding latitudes; reduced stratospheric ozone is potential anywhere in the world—and with it the danger of more dangerous levels of UV-B rays reaching the surface of Earth.

Unfortunately, the areas of the world most responsible for emission of ozone-depleting chemicals have not necessarily been the ones feeling the impact or suffering the consequences. "Human emissions of chlorofluorocarbons (CFC's) and halons (bromine-containing gases) have occurred mainly in the Northern Hemisphere." The World Meteorological Organization reports that "about 90% have been released in the latitudes corresponding to Europe, Russia, Japan, and North America."[22]

With the current increase in ozone depletion in the Arctic, it appears that the impact is finally beginning to threaten the areas of the world guilty of emitting the chemicals. Patches of air containing high levels of ozone-depleting chemicals created by the polar stratospheric clouds may drift over other latitudes, and some may mix in to influence the ozone levels there. These patches of air may experience ozone thinning as they drift south over more populated areas in the mid-latitudes. Thus ozone loss is now occurring at disturbing levels not only at the poles but in the middle latitudes as well, with accompanying increases in ultraviolet radiation.[23]

The only place on Earth where the dangers of ozone depletion and consequent increases in UV-B radiation probably do not exist is the tropics. No significant trend in stratospheric ozone has been observed there.[24]

UV-B RADIATION AND SKIN CANCER

Humans need moderate exposure to sunlight (perhaps as little as fifteen minutes a day on face and hands) in order to function normally and to maintain sufficient vitamin D in addition to what we get from food. Less than 1 percent of total sunlight, ultraviolet light is divided into UV-A, UV-B, and UV-C radiation. UV-A radiation passes through the ozone layer to the surface of Earth. The very dangerous UV-C is completely absorbed by the oxygen and ozone in the stratosphere and never makes it to the surface. UV-B is almost completely absorbed by the ozone in the ozone layer, with only minimal amounts escaping the shield and traveling to Earth's surface.[25] Increased exposure to UV-B radiation challenges life's natural defenses, straining healing mechanisms beyond their capabilities and creating many adverse effects on life and health. Some of these effects can be seen almost immediately and some may not be apparent until decades later.

Sunburns—even suntans—are an immediate and visible danger to human health due to the potential damage to DNA that occurs with UV-B exposure. Reports admonish that there is no such thing as a "safe" tan, because even careful tanning kills skin cells, damages DNA, and causes changes in the skin's connective tissue that lead to wrinkle formation in later life.[26] "The ability of the sun to redden skin is believed to increase 1% for each 1% decrease in ozone," say scientists at Norfolk State University, "and damage to DNA is believed to increase 3%."[27]

Under the Antarctic ozone hole in Punta Arenas, where UV-B exposure is up to 40 percent greater than normal, there were thirteen "red alerts" in 2000. (A "red alert" means that UV-B is so high that some people's skin will burn in five minutes.) One Punta Arenas resident spent four hours at an outdoor sporting event in October of that year. That night his face burned "like fire" and his eyes became so inflamed he could not open them. The pain lasted for three months, and the blotchy effects on his face still show. The man's dermatologist reports that thirty-one patients came to him with sunburns that year, while only one person per season came in with sunburn in the entire thirteen years prior.[28]

A clear association between sun exposure and skin cancer has been known for many years. But now molecular biology has demonstrated evidence that genetic changes found in human skin carcinomas are indeed caused by UV-B radiation, with the greatest risk being for lighter-skinned humans.[29] NASA reports that with as little as a 1 percent decrease in the ozone layer, UV-B will increase an estimated 2 percent, which in turn will lead to a 4 percent increase in basal carcinomas and a 6 percent increase in squamous-cell carcinomas. Ninety percent of skin carcinomas are attributable to UV-B exposure. These carcinomas are relatively easy to treat, if detected in time, and are rarely fatal. But the much more dangerous malignant melanoma is not as well understood. There appears to be a correlation between brief, high-intensity exposure to UV-B radiation and the eventual appearance (as much as ten to twenty years later!) of melanoma.[30]

As harmful as an increase in potential sunburns is for adults, it is much more so for children. Experiences in early life with increased UV exposure, especially sunburns, can increase the risk for melanoma later in life, as noted above, but they also increase the risk of less lethal skin cancers.[31]

OTHER HARMFUL EFFECTS OF UV-B RADIATION

There are other long-range adverse effects from increased exposure to UV-B radiation due to ozone depletion. When the eyes of any living thing are exposed to too much UV-B radiation, they are at risk for developing cataracts. With increased exposure, cataracts—already a wide-ranging problem—will begin to evolve at earlier ages. Unlike skin, which can adapt to a certain extent through thickening and darkening, the eyes have no defense. The number of people experiencing cataracts and other eye disorders will certainly increase if ozone depletion continues. According to the *Encyclopedia of Atmospheric Environment*, "A 1% decrease in stratospheric ozone may result in 100,000 to 150,000 additional cases of blindness due to eye cataracts worldwide."[32]

Immune systems are also negatively affected by UV-B, which gradually impairs the body's ability to fight off disease. Darker skin suffers almost no skin cancer; nevertheless, tumors of other kinds find it easier to take hold and spread if the immune system is suppressed—regardless of skin color. If the immune system is suppressed, the body may not produce the antigens and antibodies needed to fight off a variety of diseases. Even vaccinations encounter diminished effectiveness when the immune system is not functioning at peak capacity.[33]

If Earth's surface is exposed to increased amounts of UV-B radiation because of ozone depletion, there will be increased amounts of noxious ozone lower down, in the air we breathe, leading to respiratory problems. According to the EPA, 10 to 20 percent of all summertime respiratory-related hospital visits in the northeastern United States are associated with ozone pollution. Ozone damages the cells that line the respiratory tract, causing irritation, burning, and breathing difficulty. When inhaled, even at very low levels, ozone can cause acute respiratory problems, aggravate asthma, cause inflammation of lung tissue, and impair the body's immune system, making people more susceptible to respiratory illness.[34]

With our bodies' immune systems—and the effectiveness of vaccines—increasingly compromised by greater exposure to UV-B, it is obvious that children will bear the brunt of the bodily harm caused by increased radiation. Major children's diseases are currently held at bay due to widespread immunizations. If the radiation levels climb dramatically, it seems likely that we would see an increase in children's diseases as a consequence of slowed or changed responses to vaccinations, not to mention slower recoveries following medical emergencies and surgeries.

Whereas irritation from smog might produce only a slight response in an adult, it can create a significant obstruction in the developing lungs of a child. Kids breathe faster than adults; thus they breathe a proportionately greater volume of air, inhaling more pollutants per pound of weight.[35] Ozone is of concern anywhere, but especially in the poorer industrial areas. We can already see the negative effects of increased breathable ozone on the children: half the pediatric asthma population under the age of eighteen lives in areas plagued by smog.[36]

WAMASKASKAN AND UV-B RADIATION

Wamaskaskan, our animal brothers, are also at risk for increased skin cancer. Although UV-B radiation does not directly affect densely haired body parts of animals, even furry creatures can develop tumors on the exposed parts of their bodies.[37] Amphibians in many parts of the world are in alarming decline, and experiments show that UV-B radiation may be one of many stresses acting together to threaten them.[38]

Land-based animals face the greatest risk, but lakes, rivers, and oceans offer no guarantee of safety. If water is pure, UV-B radiation can damage cells at depths up to around half a mile. Most natural water, however, has dissolved organic matter that absorbs UV-B and to a certain degree protects living organisms in it.

Human swimmers should beware of the continued risk of UV-B damage in water, but they should be even more concerned by what penetrating radiation means for organisms, such as plankton, that live in the surface waters of the ocean and other bodies of water. These minute plants and animals—the very foundation of the aquatic food cycle—are constantly exposed to UV-B radiation that (even at current levels) can and does easily damage them. The risk is there, as well, for any aquatic life that nurtures its early stages in the surface waters. This is of huge consequence for Earth's aquatic web of life, because any change in plankton numbers and species variety will negatively impact the production of fish and shellfish all over the world, which in turn will directly affect the food supply. Plankton, in their intake of carbon dioxide and output of oxygen, are also a major contributor to the planet's healthy "breathing." A decrease in their numbers would directly impact not only the fight against global warming, but the very air we breathe.

The *Encyclopedia of Atmospheric Environment* reports that it is possible that many species of plankton are already at or near their maximum tolerance of UV-B. "If ozone layer depletion reached 15% over temperate waters in the mid-latitudes, it would take fewer than five days in summer for half the zooplankton in the top metre of these waters to die from the increased radiation." Studies have already shown that plankton in the waters off Antarctica have been reduced by between 6 percent and 12 percent due to increased UV-B.[39]

UV-B also causes damage to the early developmental cycles of many fish, shellfish, amphibians, and others. The most severe effects are decreased reproductive capacity and impaired larval development. Even small increases in UV exposure could result in a significant reduction in the size of the population of animals that eat these smaller creatures. If ozone depletion reached 15 percent, large amounts of young fish, shrimp, and crabs would die before reaching their reproductive age.[40] There would be less food for living things higher in the food chain, and therefore less food for human consumption. Given that more than 30 percent of the world's animal protein comes from the sea, this would dramatically affect the web of life.[41]

RADIATION'S EFFECTS ON PLANTS AND TREES

Land plants are also at risk. Almost all green plants are stunted in their growth if they receive too much UV-B radiation. Scientists are concerned that some plant species may die out, negatively impacting the world's food supply. A decrease in plants would also mean more soil erosion and water loss. Oxygen production would be threatened, as would the process that removes carbon dioxide.

Some of the crops we grow may be sensitive to UV-B radiation and lower their yields. For instance, some research has suggested that ozone depletion of 25 percent could result in a comparable reduction in total soybean crop yield. Increased exposure to UV-B has also been observed to reduce the quality of certain types of tomatoes, potatoes, sugar beets, and soybeans. Some species of rice have been found to suffer from even minor increases in UV-B radiation.[42]

Luckily, there are also varieties tolerant to UV-B light, so there is a possibility of genetic engineering to produce more tolerant varieties of crops and trees. However, this capability will not necessarily help natural forests and growth, because some plants that appear to be UV-tolerant may accumulate detrimental impacts slowly from year to year. Half of the known species of conifer seedlings have been studied, and all were found to be adversely affected by increased UV-B radiation. Old needles are able to protect themselves by strengthening their outer coating and increasing the amount of protective pigment, but young needles are vulnerable. Indirect changes caused by UV-B radiation—such as flowering and germination rates, changes in plant form, and changes in how nutrients are distributed within the plant—may be more important than the damaging effects of the radiation itself.[43]

As the primary players in the healthy "breathing of the Earth," forests serve as the "lockboxes" of Earth's carbon "stock." In light of all the environmental threats to the world's forests, tropical and temperate, it is indeed disheartening to see them vulnerable to the silent and all-pervasive threat of increased UV-B radiation as well.

UV-B RADIATION AND MANMADE MATERIAL

UV-B causes many building materials to degrade. With increased ozone depletion, those materials will degrade faster. Windows, door frames, pipes, and gutters that have PVC in them, as well as products made with nylon and products made of polyester, will all show impaired integrity or shorter lifetimes.

Most materials used outdoors or otherwise exposed to UV-B radiation are already treated with additives that protect them, so the effect we now see is usually discoloration. Ozone depletion, however, will lead to faster breakdown and more limited usefulness.

Questions remain regarding how other essential materials (rubber, paint, paper, and textiles, for example) might be affected, and regarding the high costs of prevention, especially in developing countries.[44]

PROTECTION AND REPAIR

Some may argue that the Earth has always been exposed to the damaging effects of UV-B radiation, and that the danger from UV-B is something to which life on Earth will simply adapt. This is true. In fact, life on earth has already evolved "cellular repair mechanisms" that heal damaging effects from UV-B and help living things adapt. Several repair mechanisms exist for plants, for example—mechanisms that help them repair damage to their DNA as well as other injuries.

Human beings have defenses and repair mechanisms as well. Even under a balanced and effective ozone shield, humans naturally enhance their defenses by limiting exposure to sunlight or by ensuring that the rays are blocked. For example, eyes have brows and muscles for squinting. Human skin cells may also continually repair damage caused by UV-B rays to the nucleic acids of genes.[45] Skin gets thicker and darker, as a general rule, to efficiently adapt and protect against UV-B light. In addition to these natural forms of protection, humans have developed some artificial aids as well: for example, UV indices warn entire cities and regions to avoid solar exposure to help keep UV-B damage at a minimum.

These protections are not enough, however, when unusually large amounts of UV-B radiation reach Earth. With the thinning and weakening of Earth's protective shield, the penetrating UV-B radiation produces damage greater than can be naturally repaired, especially with repeated exposures over time. The freedom that humans enjoy with their lifestyles in the sun may become constrained with the need for extra protection and more limited time outdoors, especially for children. In some regions, as has happened already in Chile under the Antarctic ozone hole, there may be a number of days when no time can be safely spent outdoors.[46]

RECOVERY EFFORTS AND OBSTRUCTIONS

The dangers of ozone depletion are real and present, but there is reason for hope, albeit guarded. For instance, in 2002 the maximum area of the ozone hole over Antarctica was a dramatically reduced 8.1 million square miles, compared to the maximum area of 11.5 million square miles in 2000. Unfortunately, in 2003 the maximum area was back up to 10.9 million square miles, the second largest ever observed.[47]

We can't yet rest on our laurels, however. "While enormous progress has been made over the past decade in phasing out ozone-destroying chemicals, the health of the ozone layer remains critical," said Klaus Toepfer, executive director of UNEP, at the world meeting in Nairobi in December 2000.[48] Experts predict that ozone recovery may not be complete by 2050, as hoped when protective regulations were first introduced.[49]

There are several human and environmental realities slowing the process of recovery:

First, global warming is offsetting the progress made in phasing out the use of ozone-depleting chemicals. As mentioned earlier, greenhouse gases are not directly dangerous to ozone, but they instigate global climate changes that impact the ozone layer in the stratosphere. Yearly variations in cold temperatures related to climate change—especially around Antarctica—are affecting ozone loss. In fact, the stratosphere as a whole will most likely cool in response to climate change, according to the United Nations Environment Programme, "therefore preserving over a longer time period the conditions that promote chlorine-caused deletion in the lower stratosphere, particularly in polar regions."[50]

Second, ozone-depleting chemicals that were released half a century ago or more are still active. With atmospheric lifetimes of fifty to hundreds of years, they can continue at peak concentrations long past the cessation of all emissions.

Third, human activities continue to send out ozone-depleting chemicals. For instance, hydrochlorofluorocarbons (HCFCs) and hydrofluorocarbons (HFCs) are two substitutes for CFCs that are continuing to affect ozone directly and indirectly. HCFCs still contribute chlorine to the stratosphere, though in much lesser amounts than do CFCs. Both HCFCs and HFCs indirectly contribute to ozone depletion by trapping heat in the lower atmosphere as effective greenhouse gases. New ozone-depleting chemicals continue to enter the market, while there are many who continue to profit from the smuggling, selling, and use of the old ones.

And fourth, developing countries need more financial and technological assistance to reduce their dependence on ozone-depleting chemicals. More help is needed to strategize the discontinuation of the use of these chemicals, and more money is needed to help make substitutes more affordable.

The ozone layer is out of our direct sight, so it is also out of mind unless we make an effort to keep the issue paramount. In 1996, Dana Rohrabacher, chair of the House Science Subcommittee on Energy and the Environment, said, "The ozone scare turned out to be another basically the-sky-is-falling cry from an environmental Chicken Little, a cry we have heard before when the American people were scared into the immediate removal of asbestos from their schools."[51]

Despite such accusations of fear-mongering, the horse Thin is calling us to become more aware of how we directly contribute to ozone depletion through the chemicals we use, as well as how we indirectly contribute through actions that support global warming. Deer teaches us the importance of separation and wider boundaries to protect our way of life.

We need to learn the truth about what is occurring in Nature so we can make wise changes. Unfortunately, we need to be unusually mindful of the sun, probably for the next hundred years—or more. We especially need to wake up to how we affect that which is out of our direct sight—whether it be the ozone layer, the ozone hole, or the children in Punta Arenas, Chile—and how even what we cannot directly see impacts us. As the Sioux remind us, we are one.

Chapter 10 brings us to the horse called Gone and the lesson of Buffalo, building on how we are all interrelated, connected to the point that the loss of too many of our plant and animal brothers may lead to the loss of Human as well.

GONE

Lesson of Buffalo

Buffalo are one of few animals that can survive a Great Plains blizzard out in the open. Their huge coats covered with clinging snow, they stand together and face into the wind, tramping the ground to preserve their access to emergency grass beneath. They heed the whistling of the white north wind, which lets the world know that bounty can disappear and provisions must be stored and carefully nurtured. Modern beef cattle cannot survive severe blizzards out on the plains as can the buffalo. They do not have the buffalo's ability to "make do" by developing emergency resources.

Buffalo were plentiful, as were many other resources in the western hemisphere, when representatives of the now Dominant Society first arrived. Millions roamed the Great Plains, contributing to the health of all the other creatures who shared residence. The Sioux believed that the animal was a special gift from the Great Spirit and treated it with reverence. It was referred to as "the all-providing one." Buffalo were provision, sustenance, shelter, warmth, and life to the Sioux. They represented the bounty of Mother Earth, because one buffalo could clothe and feed many.

I have read the white man's books claiming that early America was a land of "endless resources"—oil, gas, iron, timber, and more. We can see now that through waste and overexploitation, many of our natural resources are starting to run out. What we were told in school was not the truth. Nor is what we are being told by politicians owned by corporate institutions. Their claims regarding the health and resources of our planet differ considerably from the untainted information offered within these pages from concerned scientists. The endless resources are soon to be no more.

When we look at the great white horse of Black Elk's vision roaring down from the north—the horse called Gone—we think of all the resources and opportunities and cultures that are gone, but the horse is also a reminder, as is Buffalo, that we had better conserve what is left and learn new values. The white horse also carries a reviving medicine. That medicine, if effective, will make us realize how to save our resources and adjust our lifestyles. The white horse will attempt to save those species that are endangered, as it revived the black horse in the vision, but it will need help from Human.

THE SIXTH EXTINCTION

Mother Earth, over her eons of existence, has already seen five large-scale drops in biodiversity—for example, during the Ice Ages. Anthropologist Richard Leakey predicts another: "[The so-called sixth extinction is] the next annihilation of vast numbers of species. It is happening now, and we, the human race, are its cause."[1]

We are now seeing, in our lifetime, the greatest mass extinction of species to ever occur on Earth. Buffalo is only one of many living things to be threatened. Biological diversity is vanishing at a breathtaking rate due to the destruction of habitats and the overexploitation of species. Those extinctions have shown us how easily diseases spread and kill in animals and plants with a very narrow genealogical background, and they remind us such diseases can lead both to the failure of crops and to the spread of animal diseases to humans.

THE SAD FATE OF MOTANE ISLAND

Up until a couple hundred years ago, Motane was a thriving island in the lush South Pacific, rich in both flora and fauna (including people). By the time Thor Heyerdahl visited it just before World War II, it no longer had human inhabitants, and the remaining life was severely out of balance. Heyerdahl recorded his observations in the book *Fatu-Hiva: Back to Nature*. What happened on that island is a small-scale model of how we are damaging our only home, Mother Earth, by taking over her natural areas and exploiting her resources too fast.

Early European settlers saw Motane as an island where modern man had beaten nature. They had entered this South Sea paradise intent on improving conditions for themselves and their uncivilized local hosts. They brought in plants and domestic animals that they thought would be a benefit, but in so doing they upset the whole balance of a life lived in accord with local conditions. Eventually, those settlers brought diseases, the local inhabitants sickened and died, and the white men left again—but they didn't take their sheep with them.

When Captain Cook first encountered the Marquesa Islands and their inhabitants in 1773, he estimated the Polynesian population in the region at one hundred thousand. After him came European settlers, whalers, and missionaries. A good century later, in 1883, the census for the islands as a whole was a mere 4,865. By 1920, the population was down to 3,000, mainly due to European germs and deteriorating living conditions. On the island of Motane, eventually not a single survivor remained to tell the story of what had long since become a ghost island.

With no humans, the domestic animals ran wild and the sheep were the survivors. With meat-eating man gone, the sheep of Motane multiplied. Hordes of wild sheep consumed all within reach, and when famine hit them, they devoured the roots of the grass and the bark of the trees, turning Motane into a desert. It was thus that Heyerdahl found it.[2]

SUICIDAL WHALES?

The afternoon of March 15, 2000, must have arrived like any other afternoon in the Bahamas. Tourists lounged quietly, lulled by the sounds of the surf punctuated by chattering seabirds searching for prey. Suddenly enormous and apparently desperate mammals appeared in the water, struggling toward shore. One by one these whales and dolphins stranded themselves mysteriously upon the beaches of Abaco Island.

A number of tourists and local residents quickly gathered in disbelief, standing in helpless horror as these noble creatures lay gasping at their feet. Several marine biologists were eventually summoned to assist the local folks, who were pushing a few whales back to sea. Yet seven of the creatures died there that day in a logic-defying, seemingly suicidal act. What would compel them to such behavior?[3]

It was all too similar to an incident in May 1996 off the coast of Greece, when twelve Cuvier's beaked whales also beached themselves and died. They were each young and healthy with no signs of illness or disease. They belonged to a species that rarely gets beached. Still another mysterious occurrence happened in March 1998 off the coast of Hawaii, when members of the Ocean Mammal Institute (OMI) found two abandoned whale calves and a baby dolphin in a U.S. Navy testing area. OMI's Marsha Green told the *Earth Island Journal*, "We have never heard of anyone observing an abandoned calf in our nine years of research off the Hawaiian Islands."[4]

Officials found that six of the seven dead whales on the beaches of Abaco Island had suffered hemorrhages of the inner ear. This kind of

damage is likely to be caused by a sonic blast. It is interesting to note
that in each of the incidents related above, the U.S. Navy was in the area
testing a new high-powered sonar system (called Low Frequency Active
Sonar) that has the ability to create sounds underwater at decibel levels
over 240. (For comparison, a jet engine is about 120 decibels at the
source. Since each decibel increases exponentially from the level before,
240 is vastly louder than 120.)[5]

A DEAF WHALE IS A DEAD WHALE

The Navy test levels that presumably caused the hemorrhaging in the
beached whales were billions of times louder than sounds already
known to disturb whales. Much, much lower levels cause whales to di-
vert from their migratory routes and become aggressive. Certain levels
of sound are known to cause humpback whales to stop their singing. It
is unknown just how adverse such gross sound is for ocean life in general. According to the Ocean Mammal Institute, "Aquatic animals are
very vulnerable, especially those with air filled lungs and swim blad-
ders. Whales and dolphins are especially vulnerable because they are
acoustic animals. Powerful underwater sounds can kill them by causing
internal bleeding from ruptured tissues, or deafness. If a mammal's hearing is impaired this causes difficulties in navigation, feeding, communication, and mating. So, therefore, a deaf whale is a dead whale."[6]

Sound can harm human divers at 160 decibels, which is the level
that was used by NATO ships in the 1996 incident off Greece. The Natural Resources Defense Council (NRDC) is concerned that the Navy intends to use up to 240 decibels throughout 80 percent of the world's
oceans in the future—levels up to a million times more intense than
those tested in 1996—to search for elusive and quiet enemy submarines.
The new Low Frequency Active Sonar system enables searchers to flood
a single sound source through several hundreds of thousands of square
miles of ocean at one time, and is among the loudest human-made

sounds ever deployed. The deafening sounds from which the whales and dolphins attempted to painfully and desperately flee were well below its peak of 240 decibels.

An NRDC report reveals the potential for harm:

According to the Navy's own study, scientists briefly exposed a 32-year-old Navy diver to LFA sonar at a level of 160 decibels. [The Navy tests on the whales off the coast of Hawaii in March 1998 were at varying levels up to 203 decibels.] After 12 minutes, the diver experienced severe symptoms, including dizziness and drowsiness. After being hospital-ized, he relapsed, suffering memory dysfunction and seizure. Two years later he was being treated with anti-depressant and anti-seizure medications.[7]

It is logical to assume that if humans, whales, and dolphins are trau-matized or severely damaged by sonar, other parts of the marine ecosys-tem may be as well. Ego-centered human actions and thoughtless use of technology often disregard the delicate balance of Earth's ecosystem.

This pattern of self-centered behavior lay at the heart of European expansion into the New World, and it is still evident today. It is the major cause of the current crisis in biodiversity, which many are calling the sixth great mass extinction of species.

HUMAN SURVIVAL IN A TIME OF MASS EXTINCTIONS

On April 20, 1998, the American Museum of Natural History in New York City released the results of a nationwide survey of 400 biologists entitled "Biodiversity in the Next Millennium." According to that sur-vey, seven out of ten biologists believe that we are living within a mass extinction of living things, and that this dramatic loss of species threat-ens human existence in the next century. One-third think that as many as half of all species on the Earth will die out in the next thirty years. This mass extinction is the fastest in Earth's 4.5 billion–year history and, unlike prior extinctions, is mainly the result of human activity and not of unusual natural events.

Scientists clearly are fearful about the future, but the general public is relatively unaware of the loss of species and the threats that it poses. Scientists overwhelmingly believe that we must act now to address the biodiversity crisis. The majority of them believe that the crisis could be averted by a stronger stance by policymakers and governments and by individuals making changes in their daily lives.[8]

We must remember the lesson of Buffalo—now—and change the direction we are headed. We must look at our disharmonious relationship with Mother Earth and resolve to make things right. We can no longer wait to examine and address our neglectful and greedy wastefulness.

EARTH'S COMPLEX WEB OF LIFE

Our planet relies on the interdependent relationship of all living things for life to flourish. Biodiversity is the delicately balanced ecosystem of wildlife, birds, marine life, plants, forests, insects, microorganisms, and fungi in its enormous diversity. There are more than 1.7 million known species and an estimated 3 to 30 million more unknown (mostly rare) species yet to be discovered. Of the known species, only 4,000 are mammals, 9,500 are birds, and over half are insects. Most of the planet's biodiversity is in the tropics. Tropical rain forests, which take up only about 7 percent of the Earth's land area, house about half its species. According to the Union of Concerned Scientists (UCS), "In a single tree in Peru, for example, 43 species of ants were found—about the same number as live in the entire British Isles."[9] In addition to the tropical rain forests, the wetlands and coral reefs are the most biologically dynamic ecosystems on the Earth. The importance of these three primary ecosystems cannot be overemphasized, for together they support the overwhelming majority of the species on the planet.

All living things are now imperiled by the impact of human activity on Earth's ecosystems. The "sixth great extinction" is underway, escalating beyond the five prior great mass extinctions that have occurred since the evolution of life on the planet. Extinction of species is a natural process of the biosphere, but its natural rate has increased an incredible 100 to 1,000 times in the last 500 years. Richard Leakey predicts that "fifty percent of the Earth's species will have vanished inside the next one hundred years."[10]

Water and air pollution from a whole host of sources is destroying the habitats of many plants, animals, fish, birds, and insects. Not only are the streams, rivers, lakes, wetlands, and forests upon which these living things rely for their survival being poisoned, they are being obliterated through the encroachment of human beings. Rather than seeking harmony with their fellow creatures, people force the ecosystems they invade to adjust, move, or die out. Tuxill and Bright report that "some ecosystems, such as tall-grass prairies and tropical dry forests, have almost entirely disappeared; others, such as wetlands, have greatly diminished. Over the past 200 years, 53 per cent of the wetlands in the continental United States have been destroyed, mostly drained and converted to agricultural land."[11]

And it is not only the wetland inhabitants that suffer. With wetlands diminishing, farm waste runoff loses an important natural means of filtering. As a result, ground water, aquifers, and rivers become contaminated by human pollutants. In addition, migratory birds are declining due to destruction of breeding grounds, wintering areas, and "refueling" sites.

OCEANS IN TROUBLE

Other human practices have indirect effects on ecosystems. One major example is the pollution of the oceans. Biologists at the Monterey Bay

Aquarium say that few Americans realize that individuals, not industry, pose the biggest threat to the health of the world's oceans. They emphasize that individuals cause most of the oceans' pollution by contaminated runoff from yards, parking lots, and roads. In fact, "street runoff and individual dumping into municipal storm drains is responsible for 15 times more oil reaching the ocean than the [35,000 tons] the Exxon Valdez dumped in 1989." Nearly one ton out of every thousand tons of oil produced every year ends up polluting the oceans.[12]

An unparalleled call for action to the world's governments and citizens came in 1998—the United Nation's International Year of the Ocean. Over 1,600 marine scientists and conservation biologists representing sixty-five countries warned that the sea is in trouble and called for immediate, decisive action to prevent further severe, irreversible damage to the sea's biological diversity and integrity.[13]

Echoing the harm to the buffalo, which were ruthlessly hunted for so long that they almost disappeared, the impact of this irreversible damage is already affecting ocean life. Many of the Earth's coral reefs are dying or have died. An estimated 90 percent of coral reefs worldwide have experienced moderate to severe damage through bleaching caused by downstream runoff of soils and nutrients from recently deforested land.[14] Runoff is washed into river systems and emptied into the oceans, creating algal blooms.

Algal blooms use up the oxygen in the water and contribute to "dead zones," areas where aquatic life cannot live due to the lack of oxygen. In the Gulf of Mexico, the runoff of excess nitrogen and phosphorus flowing down the Mississippi River has created the largest aquatic dead zone in the western hemisphere. During the summer of 1999 that dead zone stretched over 7,700 square miles (the size of New Jersey) in the Gulf of Mexico. There are now fifty known dead zones in the world's coastal areas due to such pollution.[15]

People living in the midwestern United States who aspire to lush green lawns contribute unknowingly to the growing dead-zone problem. Their fertilizer runoff from home use eventually drains into the Gulf of Mexico, over a thousand miles away, via the Mississippi, Missouri, and Ohio River systems. Crop farms in this region are another source of dangerous fertilizer runoff.

In addition to crop farms and suburban lawns, giant livestock farms are even larger contributors to the growing dead-zone problem. These "factory farms" can house hundreds of thousands of pigs, chickens, turkeys, or cows and generate more waste than an entire city. Livestock produce almost 2.7 trillion pounds of manure a year, and yet farms do not have adequate waste management systems. While waste treatment systems are required for human waste, livestock waste from factory farms goes untreated. Rivers and ground water end up polluted and contaminated as a result. According to the Environmental Protection Agency, 35,000 miles of U.S. rivers have been affected. "Animal waste contains disease causing pathogens, such as salmonella, E. coli, cryptosporidium, and fecal coliform, which can be ten to 100 times more concentrated than in human waste. More than 40 diseases can be transferred to humans through manure." In fact, manure from dairy cows is thought to have caused the 1993 contamination of the drinking water in Milwaukee, Wisconsin, that killed more than 100 people and made 400,000 sick.[16]

In addition, the large open-air, clay-lined lagoons—some as big as many football fields—that most farms create to store the waste are often prone to leak or spill. In North Carolina in 1995 an eight-acre hog-waste lagoon burst and spilled 25 million gallons of manure into the New River, killing, according to the Natural Resources Defense Council, "10 million fish and [closing] 364,000 acres of coastal wetlands to shellfishing."[17] In 1996, the Centers for Disease Control established a link between spontaneous abortions and high nitrate levels in the contaminated drinking water wells of people living near feedlots in Indiana. Livestock farms are also responsible for 10 percent of the emissions of methane worldwide—a greenhouse gas mentioned earlier that contributes to global warming.[18]

THE IMPORTANCE OF A DIVERSE BIOSYSTEM

The Earth needs a diverse and healthy biosystem in order to thrive, just as it has for eons, with its intricate and rhythmic balance intact. All living things benefit from Earth's biodiversity in many ways—especially humans. Creator has given plants and animals to Human to provide food, shelter, raw materials, companionship, and products that enhance our quality of life. Few of us give much thought to the fact that these natural beings play roles from which humans, in particular, benefit. For instance, birds, insects, and bats pollinate flowering plants and agricultural crops. Birds, fish, and frogs provide natural pest control. Mussels and other aquatic organisms cleanse water supplies and create habitats for other sea creatures and plants. Microorganisms and plants create soils. Worms and other burrowing creatures break up the soil so that young plants can grow.

Wetlands are one of the most helpful gifts Creator has given us. Swamps, marshes, and mangroves clean our water supply by intercepting surface runoff and filtering out sediment, nutrients, and large quantities of contaminants. Like a sponge, wetlands store floodwaters and slowly release them, reducing the potential for erosion. As the UCS notes, "They also serve as breeding grounds for thousands of species of wildfowl, fish, and shellfish, and thus are vital to the productivity of our lakes and oceans." The U.S. Fish and Wildlife Service estimates that nearly 43 percent of threatened and endangered species rely upon wetlands for their survival.[19]

Forests, which cover a third of the Earth's land surface, remove carbon dioxide from the atmosphere and replenish it with life-giving oxygen. Forest ecosystems contain about 80 percent of the global biomass and are the major storehouse of Earth's carbon—the basic ingredient of life in the biosphere. By removing the pollutants caused by industries and vehicles, forests keep the air breathable and reduce damage caused by acid rains. As these forests dwindle (which they are at the rate of more than 1 percent a year), carbon dioxide builds up in the atmosphere, contributing to global warming.[20]

Known as the "Amazon of the oceans," coral reefs are among the strongest and most ancient living systems on the Earth, dating back 225 million years, with some as many as 2.5 million years old. They are among the most biologically active ecosystems on the planet, supporting an enormous variety of species. Though they cover only 0.2 percent of the ocean floor, they support nearly one-fourth of all marine species. Their importance to the planet is similar to that of the tropical rain forests, in that they thrive under nutrient-poor conditions yet support rich communities through incredibly efficient recycling processes. They also exhibit very high levels of species diversity.[21]

Coral reefs, however, contain more varied life forms than do the tropical rain forests. All but one of the thirty-three major phyla (or kinds of organisms) is found in the coral reefs, and fifteen are found there exclusively. Reef-building corals are responsible for constructing some of the largest and oldest structures on the Earth, providing shelter for numerous creatures. Capturing almost one-half of the ocean's calcium each year, reefs cooperate with certain types of algae to create these calcium carbonate structures. They are the products of thousands of years of growth.[22]

Even the smallest organisms are gifts from Creator and play key (though often unacknowledged) roles in biodiversity. Who would have thought that an obscure heat-stable bacterium living in the hot springs of Yellowstone National Park would spawn a major breakthrough in genetic engineering? And other largely unnoticed bacteria are equally as important, if not more important, to life on Earth. Bacteria in the soil, for example, give an incredible gift to plants (and us). Although nitrogen is a very plentiful gas, and a necessary nutrient for flora, plants cannot absorb it directly from the air; rather, they draw it from the soil. In a process known as "fixation," rhizobial bacteria convert nitrogen into nitrate, a form of nitrogen that plants can use. This process is responsible for the fixation of 80 million tons of nitrogen into the soil each year, twice as much as that produced by nitrogen fertilizer. Also important are the insects, fungi, and microorganisms that decompose manure, dead animals, and plants, thereby returning minerals to the soil.[23]

Commercialization of plants and animals tends to exploit one or a few species at the exclusion of the others and at the risk of weakening the gene pool. For instance, breeding only the species that brings the highest market value, whether it is cattle or strains of crops, makes that species vulnerable to being wiped out by a single disease. The planting of genetically diverse varieties provides built-in barriers against devastations of entire crops.

But breeding new strains of crops and livestock depends upon the availability of wild strains, as well as the strains that have been "invented" and grown by farmers all over the world. A report from the Union of Concerned Scientists tells us that the importance of such genetic diversity was proved by the southern corn leaf blight outbreak of 1970, which destroyed 15 percent of the crop—the greatest economic loss of a single crop in a single year in the entire history of agriculture. This devastating blight spread rapidly across the United States because of the lack of genetic diversity in U.S. corn varieties.[24]

PRIMARY REASONS FOR BIODIVERSITY LOSS

There seem to be four main reasons why Nature is losing its biodiversity, and all of them are related to human activities.

Loss of Habitats

The most common reason is the loss of habitats, such as the destruction of wetlands to make room for urban sprawl. The World Resources Institute tells us that habitat loss and habitat degradation affect 89 percent of all threatened birds, 83 percent of threatened mammals, and 91 percent of threatened plants assessed. Lowland and mountain tropical forests are habitats with the highest number of threatened mammals and birds.[25] Bird habitats are especially threatened due to pesticide pollution. In fact, nearly one-third of all threatened species are birds.[26]

Covering 7 percent of the Earth's land surface, the rain forests are home to over one-half of the world's species, and as such are the very "cauldron of evolutionary innovation," as Leakey puts it.[27] So destruction of the tropical rain forest ecosystem destroys the habitats of more species proportionally than anywhere else on Earth. In addition, global warming sets the stage for fires and the ravages of insect infestations that also create loss of habitats.

Overexploitation

Overexploitation is the second most common reason for loss of biodiversity. Overhunting and overharvesting, collecting, commercial fishing, and trade in species and species' parts constitute a major threat for birds (37 percent), mammals (34 percent), plants (8 percent of those assessed), reptiles, and marine fishes. Hunting and collecting impact the threatened 338 bird species, 212 mammals, and 169 plants, while trade, in addition, affects 13 percent of both threatened birds and mammals.[28]

Buffalo in the United States were exploited and brought to near extinction by mass slaughters during the nineteenth century. In 1872, there were 15 million buffalo (American bison) roaming the Great Plains, and a decade later only a thousand were left.[29] But that is only one example. Similar near-extinctions have been caused by hunters and fishers all over the world.

Elephants in Africa have been hunted almost to extinction for their ivory tusks alone. Tigers, who once roamed throughout Asia to the Middle East, continue to be killed by poachers throughout that range. In India, certain of a tiger's body parts—used for aphrodisiac potions, medicinal products, and other uses—are potentially worth five million dollars per animal. This market has propelled illegal hunting to overwhelming numbers. Their total world population has drastically declined. By 2001 there were merely three to five thousand tigers remaining worldwide, mostly in small, isolated populations.[30]

Sturgeons are one of the most ancient fish lineages, and yet now fourteen of their species are highly endangered due to the overharvesting of their eggs—the world's premier caviar. The African mountain gorilla, wolves, rhinos, polar bears, great whales, and sea lions, among numerous other creatures, have all been legally and illegally overhunted to the point that their very survival is threatened. Unfortunately, once a species becomes rare or protected, the profit in smuggling generally increases; international illegal trade of poached and endangered species is a business worth two to three billion dollars a year. The human appetite for collecting trophies, eating exotic foods, and otherwise economically exploiting wildlife is so voracious that numerous species may disappear forever.

The Island Effect

The "island effect" is the third reason for loss of diversity. It occurs when there is a concentration of many species confined to a small area, like an island. It also happens when ecosystems are fragmented by the rapid expansion and development of civilization. Should disease or complete loss of habitat threaten the confined species, migration is not an option, and species begin to vanish. In the Pacific islands this problem has led to the extinction of as many as two thousand species of birds (nearly 20 percent of known bird species worldwide) since humans first settled there.[31]

Specialized ecosystems need a minimum amount of space to support their particular web of life, and if fragmented, species will die off or otherwise disappear. The disappearance of one species may begin a domino effect of other species disappearing or dying off. For example, in one South American location three species of frogs quickly vanished from a 250-acre plot because their habitat was too small to support peccaries (a sort of wild American pig), whose wallowing in the mud created ponds. Without the ponds, the frogs died off.[32]

Fragmentation has other negative effects. Small ecosystems may be vulnerable to extinction due to disease or storms, while larger populations can weather such events. In fact, even in large forest areas species are still vulnerable for up to a half mile into the forest. This is due in part to changes in climate from grasslands to forests, the impact of hunters, and incursions by non-forest animals. This vulnerability is especially important in light of logging activities in areas such as the Amazon tropical rain forests, where forest boundaries are changing daily. The Union for the Conservation of Nature and Natural Resources (UCNN) warns that implications for biological diversity are not encouraging and provide added impetus for the minimization of tropical deforestation.[33]

The Introduction of Foreign Species

Finally, loss of diversity occurs when foreign species are introduced into an ecosystem where they have never been found before, as with the earlier example of Motane Island's sheep. Almost half of imperiled species in the United States are threatened by non-indigenous species.[34] In many instances the new species will thrive, but the introduction of exotic species can be harmful to the existing ecosystem.

Fire ants were introduced into the southeastern United States and are now notorious for their severe sting and for devouring planted grain.

Zebra mussels traveled through the Great Lakes waterway on foreign ships and are now found in the upper Mississippi River, where they have established large populations. Besides threatening the food web of native species, they are clogging intake pipes for cities' water supplies, covering up the spawning reefs of certain fish and amphibians, and fouling boat hulls.[35]

Another example throughout the southeastern part of the United States is kudzu, a plant introduced from Japan and China. Kudzu is a woody, somewhat hairy twining vine that has large leaves and may grow sixty feet in one growing season. It was introduced with the best of intentions: to anchor steep banks of soil and thus prevent erosion. In a short period of time, however, it began to dominate the landscape, covering trees and shrubs as well as exposed soil. Eventually it crowded and choked out many of the indigenous species. Its beauty and charm certainly belie its dominance and negative impact.[36]

Africa's Lake Victoria is the site that Boston University ecologist Les Kaufman calls "the Hiroshima of the biological apocalypse." More than 200 species of fish have disappeared from its waters. The culprit is the voracious Nile perch, which was introduced to the lake for commercial fishing nearly four decades ago.[37]

Occasionally exotic species are introduced simply to see the effect that they have. One seven-year study introduced non-native lizards to an archipelago of lake islands in Northern Sweden. Researchers found that the lizards quickly devastated both the diversity and the abundance of spiders (a main meal of the lizards). Spiders were twelve times more likely to go extinct on these islands than on the islands without lizards.[38]

It is clear from these four causes of the loss of biodiversity that Human has been at best ignorant and neglectful, and at worst irresponsible to Nature. Plowing under prairies to grow crops, filling in wetlands, and clearing forests for developing cities have now substantially altered nearly one-half of the Earth's land surfaces. The vast majority of species must now continue to live on a greatly reduced and increasingly fragmented natural landscape. Plants and animals are dying off at such a rapid rate that many are very likely disappearing before they are even discovered by people.

Scientists tell us that each year 17,000 to 100,000 species vanish, a rate likened to destruction from the impact of a giant asteroid.[39] A great deal of alarm has been generated in our society in response to the possibility of being struck by a giant asteroid. Though the odds of this happening rank lower than the likelihood of being abducted by aliens, contingency plans nonetheless have been drawn up to deal with that kind of event. Given our response to that unlikely scenario, it is ironic that we remain blind to the cataclysmic events occurring in Nature and unresponsive to the devastation happening in our own backyards!

It is almost impossible to realize the total impact of lost biodiversity upon our planet, because we do not know how the lost species fit within the delicate balance of Nature. This situation is not helped by the fact that 80 percent of the world's biologists live in developed countries, where only 20 percent of the world's species live.[40] But whether we know the total impact yet or not, we *do* know that the imbalance is caused by humans and can be stopped.

THE PLANET WE ARE LEAVING OUR CHILDREN

Chief Seattle tells us, "If men spit upon the ground, they spit upon themselves."[41] The hard part of what it means to be interrelated to all things is that our neglect comes back full circle to affect us as negatively as it affects other species. *Our* existence is being threatened too. We are held accountable for our actions (or lack thereof) toward the Earth, even to generations unborn.

As individuals we can no longer afford to be quiet and complacent; now is the time, for example, to write letters to politicians about preserving and increasing wetlands or protecting wildlife areas. Be outspoken against suburban sprawl within your community and state. Decrease or stop the use of fertilizer on your lawn. Pay attention when you are boating on lakes and rivers to see if you have picked up and are inadvertently spreading an invading aquatic species such as the zebra mussel or Eurasian milfoil (a foreign water-plant that is choking out our lakes). Start or continue your financial support of those organizations working to preserve the rain forests or any of the many other endangered ecosystems throughout the world. There are many, many ways you can apply your ideas, resources, and creative energy to help us prevent or slow down the loss of our biodiversity.

THE DISAPPEARANCE OF
USABLE SOIL, WATER, AND AIR

Loss of biodiversity is not the only loss that the horse named Gone is warning us about. We also face the loss of our natural resources in general, the very basics of the Earth herself, the bounty that Creator has provided for all living things. Buffalo reminds us of Earth's bounty but also of the reality of the loss of resources.

In the future, we will see not only a continued loss of plant and animal species, ultimately affecting the human food supply, but a decrease in the world's food production due to loss of soil. The frequency and intensity of droughts throughout Asia and Africa probably will lead to more starvation for those who live in poverty. A new study by the International Food Policy Research Institute (IFPRI) and the World Resources Institute (WRI) is telling us that the world food production is "at risk from farming methods that have degraded soils, parched aquifers, polluted waters, and caused the loss of animal and plant species."[42] Soil degradation—nutrient depletion, erosion, and salinization—is a widespread problem. It has seriously affected two-thirds of the world's agricultural lands in the past fifty years. In fact, annual plowing in the United States alone leads to the erosion of over two billion tons of topsoil into the Mississippi, Ohio, and Missouri River system, which eventually empties into the Gulf of Mexico (where the fertilizers trapped in the soil leave a dead zone).[43] Many of Human's attempts at self-preservation in the short run seem to threaten his survival in the long run.

Adding to the problem, 70 percent of the freshwater used yearly by humans is devoted to agriculture. Water tables are falling, due to irrigation practices that use more water than is replenished by rainwater. We are facing decreasing water supplies for this and other reasons, including poor sanitation and the runoff of waste pollution. Dirty water from poor sanitation is a problem detrimental to millions the world over. The World Health Organization reports that more than 1 billion people have no access to clean water and 3.4 million people die each year from diseases related to lack of sanitation. In fact, the poor pay more of their income, up to 20 percent, than the rich for worse water and are more at risk from water-borne illnesses.[44]

Freshwater lakes, oceans, and rivers polluted by waste result in contaminated food sources for animals, fish, and humans. Exposure to mercury, for instance, puts 375,000 babies born each year at risk of neurological problems. A new report by the Centers for Disease Control states, "One in 10 women of childbearing age in the United States are at risk of having newborns with neurological problems due to in utero mercury exposure."[45] Consumption of contaminated fish by pregnant mothers exposes the fetus to mercury in the womb. Mercury is a very toxic heavy metal that, when taken into the body in even very small amounts, can cause devastating effects to the nervous systems of children and newborns. It can also damage the brain, lungs, and kidneys, and even cause death.

The main sources of contaminating mercury are power plants, incinerators, and industrial processes that send the metal directly into the atmosphere. Eventually it falls into the oceans, lakes, and streams, where humans and wildlife ingest it by eating contaminated fish. Even dredging a lake can stir mercury sediments back into the water. Women of childbearing age and young children are being publicly warned not to eat certain predatory fish, including shark, swordfish, king mackerel, and tilefish. Six states are also warning pregnant women not to consume more than one or two cans of tuna a week. Mercury levels present in these women's bodies are far greater than what is healthy for their unborn children.[46]

Air pollution signals, of course, the growing loss of clean air. Smog sends nearly 53,000 people to hospital emergency rooms and leads to more than six million asthma attacks in the eastern United States each summer. A study authorized by the Environmental Protection Agency blames ground-level ozone from coal-fired power plants for what they are calling a nationwide public health crisis.[47] Ozone, the main component of summer smog, is a highly reactive gas. It can cause damage to lungs and airways as the gas burns through cell walls. Coal-fired power plants are the single largest contributor of this type of ground-level ozone. Rebecca Stanfield, a clean air advocate for the U.S. Public Interest Research Group (PIRG), says, "An accident or national disaster that sent this many people to emergency rooms would be front page news. Although the effects of ozone are spread out over the course of the summer, the suffering of people with respiratory problems is no less real."[48]

A THOUSAND YEARS IN A FEW SECONDS

And yet, perhaps there is no consequence of our neglect of the Earth greater than the energy crisis that is facing us. The loss of the natural resources that we depend on to fuel our energy needs is a matter of prime urgency. And it is another example, like the buffalo, where we have had bountiful supply that in the public mind still seems unending. In reality, though, our energy resources are dwindling, threatened by gluttonous overconsumption and deliberate ignorance of truth. As with his treatment of the buffalo, the white man refuses to recognize his greedy and wasteful disrespect for the Earth's gifts. The horse named Gone is showing us, for example, how oil that took thousands of years to develop from decaying plants is being used up in a few seconds of energy consumption. The lesson of Buffalo is simple mathematics: do not take a resource faster than it is replaced, or it will disappear. Though we try to apply that lesson to certain resources (planting as many trees as we cut down, at least in some cases), we come nowhere near applying it to our energy resources

President Ronald Reagan's energy secretary, Donald Hodel, said of the coming oil crisis, "We're sleepwalking to disaster."[49] The United States is by far the largest consumer of fossil fuels in the world, using fossil fuels for 85 percent of its energy needs. It took Earth one million years to produce what the United States consumes in one year! The United States itself has already used 65 percent of its own oil reserves, and our oil industry is working mightily to gain access to the last known undeveloped reserve of oil, on the Arctic Circle in Alaska. Tapping that reserve would delay the inevitable by only a few years—at best a decade. This means that the United States is more dependent on foreign sources than ever before.[50]

Currently two-thirds of the world's oil is concentrated in five Middle Eastern countries: Saudi Arabia (25 percent), Iraq (10 percent), Kuwait (9 percent), United Arab Emirates (9 percent), and Iran (9 percent). The United States is their largest consumer at 25 percent of sales, with Japan a distant second. Since the Gulf War in 1991, the U.S. military has been constructing "fortified air bases" in the deserts of Saudi Arabia—presumably to protect the Saudis, but also to protect U.S. oil interests. Each year the Pentagon is spending $50 billion to protect the supply of Persian Gulf oil—that is, to protect our own supply of cheap-for-now oil.[51]

A 1995 oil industry report stated that world oil production and supply probably would peak as soon as 2000 and would decline to half the peak level by 2025. However, many people believe that the oil companies and oil-exporting countries have been giving out false information. Ted Trainer, a sustainability advocate, explains why:

It is in their interest to state that remaining resources are in good shape, because their business agreements limit them to pumping and selling a

proportion of their remaining resources. In fact, the rate of oil discovery
is falling sharply. The world consumes 23 billion barrels a year, but the
oil industry finds only 7 billion a year.[52]

As Colin J. Campbell and Jean H. Laherrere, two former oil industry
scientists, write in their famous article on oil depletion, "There is only so
much crude oil in the world, and the industry has found about 90 percent of it."[53] In the very near future, when world oil production peaks
(sometime between 2010 and 2020), we will begin to feel the problem in
our pocketbooks. The world's dwindling oil supplies will result in much
higher prices not only for transportation and heating, but for all products that use oil in either production or distribution.

THE ADDITIONAL STRAIN OF WAR

And if the situation of daily energy consumption were not enough of a
crisis, think about how much more energy is consumed in waging a
war! How much oil was consumed in World War II? How much in the
Korean War? How much in the Vietnam War? How much has been consumed in the two Gulf Wars and the Afghanistan War in between? How
much oil did Saddam Hussein burn off when he set fire to the oil wells
back in 1991 (a crime for which our commander in chief, George H. W.
Bush and the United Nations let him go free)? How much oil and iron
ore, along with natural gas and timber resources, have we used for
wartime projects during the past century?

More important, how much longer can we afford to bear the expense of war—expense measured not so much in dollars, or even human
lives destroyed, but in resources wasted? Spain used her vast forests to
build her armadas centuries ago; now that country is relatively poor, her
forests turned to scrubby desert. Disaster has likewise befallen numerous other nations that were once world powers. At present, our country

is the Tiger of the Jungle, the Orca of the Sea, the Eagle of the Air, the Owl of Technology, the Bear of Modern Medicine, and one of the better respecters of Balance on the planet. All this is due mainly to the Great Buffalo of Plenty that our land and climate are blessed with—as long as we have the resources. The question is: How much longer will they last?

Unconventional oil (that is, oil obtained by means other than traditional methods) is stored in the world in great reserves, which some believe can be substituted for crude oil when it becomes profitable to do so (that is, when the price of crude oil rises high enough). However, obtaining and processing this kind of oil can be damaging to the environment, because it often involves strip-mining and a great deal of air pollution.

FUELING OUR AUTOMOBILES

As the population of the world has exploded from three billion in 1950 to beyond six billion in only fifty years, the number of cars has shot up from 50 million to 500 million in the same period of time. In other words, we are producing cars five times faster than we're producing people. Despite the advent of hybrid cars (fueled both by gasoline and by electricity), most vehicles use gasoline only. Astoundingly, almost 85 percent of the gasoline used in a car is lost to the engine, drive-train, and wind resistance. Yet no matter how fuel-efficient we make our vehicles, we are only delaying the unavoidable. We will eventually run out of oil.[54]

What of the touted hydrogen car, which proponents promised would free us forever from petroleum reliance? At this point, it is still in the "Star Wars" stage—but then, at one time so was the airplane. Hydrogen seems to be the only power source that is capable of coming into real fruition within a decade or two. An April 2003 article in *Wired Digital* magazine, "How Hydrogen Can Save America," authored by Peter

Schwartz and Doug Randall, maintains that hydrogen is the ultimate answer to freeing ourselves from foreign oil dependence:

> Hydrogen stores energy more effectively than current batteries, burns twice as efficiently in a fuel cell as gasoline does in an internal combustion engine (more than making up for the energy required to produce it), and leaves only water behind. It's plentiful, clean, and—critically— capable of powering cars.
>
> Today, power from a fuel cell car engine costs 100 times more than power from its internal combustion counterpart; it'll take a lot of R&D to reduce that ratio. More daunting, the notion of fuel cell cars raises a chicken-and-egg question: How will a nationwide fueling infrastructure materialize to serve a fleet of vehicles that doesn't yet exist and will take decades to reach critical mass? Even hydrogen's boosters look forward to widespread adoption no sooner than 30 to 50 years from now. That's three to five times too long.[55]

NASA's Apollo program developed early hydrogen fuel cells. As critical as our alternative energy search is, why not shut down NASA to further space-flight research and concentrate its funding on hydrogen research? Yes, that is how extremely serious the dire need for alternative fuel has become.

Those who are sounding the alarm regarding the oil crisis often offer simultaneous reassurance, saying that with sufficient preparation the transition to a post-oil economy need not be traumatic. They say, for example, that if advanced methods of producing liquid fuels from natural gas could be made profitable and scaled up quickly, natural gas could become the next source of transportation fuel.[56] But here is an awful truth: there is not enough natural gas. In very simplified calculations, if energy consumption were to continue at its present pace and natural gas were to replace oil completely in order to maintain the current level of oil consumption, and if the current consumption of natural gas were to continue unabated, then global natural gas supplies would be exhausted in a mere thirty-five years. If the combined consumption of oil and natural gas were to be held down to the present level of oil consumption, then natural gas could continue for fifty-six years. Humanity can only postpone the inevitable by substituting natural gas for oil.[57]

Ironically, the natural gas industry is positively projecting growth of production far into the future. And the energy future of the United States is clearly being built on this premise. For in addition to hopes that natural gas will be the next source of transportation fuel, it is being counted on also to provide our non-transportation energy needs. According to some observers, nearly all of U.S. electrical generating capacity anticipated to be installed in the near future is projected to be fired by natural gas.[58]

OTHER ENERGY SOURCES

Coal-fired and nuclear power plants produce most of our basic electric power, with a smaller amount produced by hydroelectric power. Consumption of electric power has been growing at 3 percent a year since the mid-1980s, driven by the increase in the U.S. population, the increase in air-conditioning, and the advent of the Internet. Ironically, global warming, with its "hotter hots" and "warmer cools," is exacerbating air-conditioning use. Overpopulation is straining energy resources as well, with the rubber hitting the road in highly populated areas. Several states have suffered seasonal electric energy crises. California, for example, instituted "rolling blackouts" in the late winter of 2001, controlling overconsumption statewide by shutting off power to random areas on the grid in an effort to save energy and equalize shares in the loss. However, many believe that the United States is in a major electric power crisis. Peak power demand is exceeding reliable generation and transmission capacity, especially in California and on the West Coast. The industry is trying to overcome the crisis by installing gas turbines just when the supply of natural gas in North America has reached a peak, creating in turn a natural gas supply crisis.[59]

The organization Hubbert Peak, devoted to educating about the coming energy crisis, concludes that using natural gas as the primary substitute for oil is at best a temporary solution for a short-term gain. At worst it is a diversion of time and resources greatly needed to create a lasting solution, as well as a waste of a natural resource that may have greater potential value to future generations.[60] When our grandchildren and great-grandchildren ask where all the oil and natural gas went, how will we answer them?

CONSERVATION AS A SPIRITUAL MATTER

It is easy to feel overwhelmed by the magnitude of the threat to Earth's abundance. There are steps we can take, though, to counter that threat. It is possible for individuals—and cities and countries—to make different choices in their relationship with Mother Earth and with Creator's gifts. The Indians preserved their bountiful Buffalo before the white man arrived by living in harmony with it and by not wasting out of ignorance or greed. It was a spiritual matter for them to honor Buffalo and use all of it as a way to honor its gifts and Creator.

We can do the same: we can begin to be grateful for our resources, appreciative to Creator for Nature's gifts. That is not an empty gesture, for when we cultivate gratitude for something, we find it more difficult to ignore or waste that thing. As our gratitude is reflected in a desire to not be wasteful or greedy, we can pay more attention to peak electrical-use time and spread out our consumption more evenly throughout the day. We can buy and use energy-efficient appliances, lawnmowers, and vehicles. We can encourage landlords and office-building owners to reduce energy use and establish healthier buildings that are environmentally sensitive. We can be more mindful about leaving grass clippings on lawns so as to decrease water pollution by decreasing fertilizer use. We can stop ourselves from dumping trash or waste in our lakes, rivers, and oceans. We can begin to find our own energy to speak out in our communities against community practices that hurt the Earth, such as the use of salt as a winter de-icer on our streets and highways. We can use economic pressure for change by not buying from companies that do not have ecologically sound fishing or farming practices. And we can make our politicians aware that addressing the matter of the loss of biodiversity and natural resources, including the energy supply, is of the utmost importance. We can choose a pet issue and become an expert and advocate, helping the horse named Gone to wake up Earth's citizens.

Scientists who study loss of biodiversity and natural resources are seeing a dramatic increase in public awareness of the issues. New areas of concern are coming to the fore, such as human impact on the oceans, once considered unendingly bountiful and immune. The fact that international conventions are addressing the problems is hopeful, because such conventions start the ball rolling toward the construction of global mechanisms to respond constructively to ecological issues.

The next and last chapter of the book confronts the overpopulation crisis, the alarm for which is riding in with the horse named Too Many, guided by the lesson of Rat.

ELEVEN

TOO MANY

Lesson of Rat

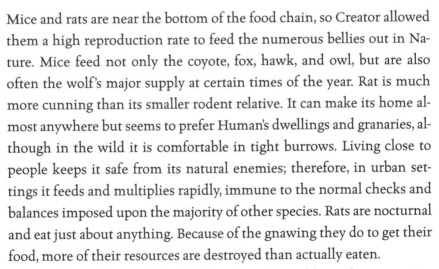

Mice and rats are near the bottom of the food chain, so Creator allowed them a high reproduction rate to feed the numerous bellies out in Nature. Mice feed not only the coyote, fox, hawk, and owl, but are also often the wolf's major supply at certain times of the year. Rat is much more cunning than its smaller rodent relative. It can make its home almost anywhere but seems to prefer Human's dwellings and granaries, although in the wild it is comfortable in tight burrows. Living close to people keeps it safe from its natural enemies; therefore, in urban settings it feeds and multiplies rapidly, immune to the normal checks and balances imposed upon the majority of other species. Rats are nocturnal and eat just about anything. Because of the gnawing they do to get their food, more of their resources are destroyed than actually eaten.

The fourth horse of Black Elk's vision, the red horse known as Too Many, is now riding among us. Red represents knowledge. Each day the sun comes up from a red dawn and brings us new wisdom, if we have the spiritual depth to look for it. The red horse would like us to gather the desperate knowledge of the peril of overpopulation before it is too late.

Nature has built into every species some safeguards against over-populating themselves, but many species still overpopulate a particular habitat, and some of those that do so simply vanish. Human is not immune to this tragedy. A great tragedy for millions of people, perhaps billions, waits in the future if we continue our present course. The whole world is overpopulating, and this tragedy could be Human's end song. The message that Too Many carries is now true of both us and our semi-domesticated rat guests. The population of two-leggeds is growing at an exponential rate, taxing the Earth's ability to provide food and other resources. The dilemma of harvesting enough food and fuel to maintain a vast world population is not the only dilemma unfolding, however. We learned in previous chapters some of the great destruction that humans are bringing upon our planet. Overpopulation increases that destruction dramatically, threatening to turn it into annihilation.

GROWING BY LEAPS AND BOUNDS

While Earth is facing the sixth great extinction of its plants and animals, Earth's human population is competing with non-human species for survival. Amazingly like rats in our choice of populated habitat, 20 percent of the world's people live on the 12 percent of the land surface with the highest densities of non-human species. Human population is growing at an annual rate of 1.8 percent in these biodiversity hotspots—significantly faster than the 1.3 percent rate in the world as a whole—and is threatening habitats and endangering species.[1]

The Iroquois people consider such human overpopulation to be irresponsible toward our plant and our animal relations. Throughout many generations since the late 1500s the population of the Iroquois in New York has remained constant at about 200,000 people. They have a saying: "The frog does not drink up the pond in which it lives."[2]

As Linda DeStefano notes in an article for the *Syracuse Herald-American*, it took all of recorded history until 1830 for world population to reach one billion; by 1930 we were at two billion; by 1960, three billion; 1975, four billion; 1986, five billion; and in 1999 we crossed the six billion mark. The world is adding about 78 million more people every year.[3] The United Nations Population Fund has projected that the world population will grow by another 50 percent by 2050.[4] By that time 85 percent of the world population will live in developing countries, where most of the projected growth will be taking place. In fact, according to the United Nation's Population Fund, "The 48 least-developed countries will nearly triple in size."[5] Even in the United States, the population has increased by 70 million people just since 1970 (primarily along the coasts, where coincidentally the ecosystems are the most fragile). At 1 percent, the United States has the highest annual growth rate of any developed nation and could double its population within seventy-two years.[6]

LIFE EXPECTANCY

But overpopulation isn't just about fertility rates. We're also living longer. As Nicholas Eberstadt, a demographer at the American Enterprise Institute, puts it: "It's not because people started breeding like rabbits. It's that they stopped dying like flies."[7]

All over the world the average life expectancy is rising—from forty years in 1950 to sixty-one years in 2001.[8] The discovery and use of sanitation practices and modern medicines, such as antibiotics, have led to the increase of human life spans and have drastically reduced the infant mortality rate during the past century. Big increases in certain groups within Western population segments, such as the "baby-boomers" born between World War II and the early sixties, are changing the demographics of the population in developed nations.

As the baby-boomers now begin to enter retirement years, we are seeing an explosion of older adults, with their numbers expected to increase well into the next few decades. Older adults in developed countries currently have access to better medical care and medicines than ever before, contributing to better health and longer life spans. Those who are sixty-five years or older now make up 10 to 15 percent of the world population; in just fifty years, they are expected to make up 20 to 30 percent.[9] The elderly population has already surpassed the child population, according to the United Nations, and by 2050 there will be two elderly persons for every child.[10] In 1998, one of every 100 individuals worldwide was aged eighty or over; in 2050, four in every 100 people will be over eighty.[11] Centenarians (age 100 and over) are already one of the fastest growing age groups in the Western world.

These statistics are averages, of course. While the elderly and older adult populations are larger proportionally in developed countries, in the less developed regions the proportional weight is on the two billion people under the age of twenty-five. The poorer areas of the world are experiencing a "youthquake." In the sub-Sahara, 45 percent of the population is under fifteen years of age. Every year 18 percent of women ages fifteen to nineteen give birth in Middle Africa, compared to 1 percent in the Western world.[12] Lori Ashford, a senior policy analyst at the Population Reference Bureau, explains what this means:

> *Decades of rapid growth mean that there are now more young men and women of childbearing age than ever before; just behind them is another large generation of children who will enter childbearing age in the next decade. This huge generation of young people provides the momentum for continued population growth well into the 21st century.*[13]

Many concerned people worry that there are now two parallel worlds: one world in which the fertility is lower and declining as economic development advances, and another world where fertility remains higher and where much of the population is mired in poverty.[14]

POPULATION CONTROL POLICIES

Family planning programs have been a common response in most countries. However, family planning is not an easy answer, either within a single country or internationally. Rightwing Christians, especially in the United States, are aggressive in curtailing aid to any domestic programs or foreign countries that allow abortion; they are a powerful influence on Congress in suppressing family planning funding not in league with their attitudes. Even when family planning is implemented, there is no guarantee of success. Many of the countries in the deepest demographic trouble have imposed aggressive family planning programs, only to see them go badly—even criminally—awry. One such example is India, which recently surpassed the one billion threshold for population, with nearly 16 million births registered each year. Though the need for population control is great, earlier planning efforts failed, as *Time* magazine reports:

> In the 1970s, Indian Prime Minister Indira Gandhi tried to reduce the national birthrate by offering men cash and transistor radios if they would undergo vasectomies. In the communities in which those sweeteners failed, the government resorted to coercion, putting millions of males—from teenage boys to elderly men—on the operating table. Amid the popular backlash that followed, Gandhi's government was turned out of office, and the public rejected family planning.[15]

China too has experimented with population control. With a population of nearly 1.3 billion people, it adopted a one-child policy. This has slowed population growth, but not without problems of another kind. "In a country that values boys over girls," notes *Time*, "one-child rules have led to abandonment, abortions and infanticides, as couples limited to a single offspring keep spinning the reproductive wheel until it comes up male." Abandoned girls are a huge issue in China: experts speculate there are 500,000 girls in orphanages.[16]

These failed efforts suggest that Alex Marshall of the United Nations Population Fund is correct: "We've learned that there is no such thing as population control. You don't control it. You allow people to make up their own mind."[17] I wonder if this statement will hold much water when the world has doubled its present population in a very short time span.

Even disease is not always an effective control of population. A 1998 United Nations report shows that although AIDS will cause 15.5 million more deaths in the next five years than would otherwise be expected in the forty-eight developing countries, the overall population of those countries will nonetheless increase. Their population is growing faster than the mortality rate attributed to AIDS, primarily due to high fertility rates for women and girls and the accompanying lack of access to reproductive health care.[18]

REDUCING OVERPOPULATION BY ADDRESSING WOMEN'S NEEDS

Endemic poverty, low levels of education, and weak family planning programs contribute to a fertility rate of over six children per woman in poor regions of the world. Studies have shown that one-third of the population growth in the world is the result of incidental or unwanted pregnancy.[19] Furthermore, over 600,000 women die every year because of complications from unwanted pregnancy and abortion—deaths that could have been avoided through family planning.

Unprotected intercourse results in not only pregnancy but disease for many women. There are an estimated 333 million new cases of sexually transmitted diseases (STDs) each year. Worldwide, the disease burden of STDs in women is more than five times that of men. Sadly, the total worldwide annual cost of better reproductive health care is about $17 billion—less than one week of the world's expenditures on armaments![20]

The United Nations is attempting to address these pressing issues, recommending the actions put forth by its 1994 International Conference on Population and Development in Cairo. These are universal access to reproductive health care, including voluntary family planning, by 2015; greater access to education for girls; and action to promote gender equality. Survey data suggest that some 120 million additional women worldwide would be using a modern family planning method if information and affordable services were easily available, and if their families and communities were more supportive.[21]

We in the Western world tend to see information and support as givens. Many of us consider it incomprehensible that rational adults should choose to bring babies into lives that face the daily threat of starvation, and yet many men and women living in underdeveloped countries are unaware that they can do anything about controlling fertility. Traditional values and culturally reinforced gender inequality are powerful forces that keep people from being open to change. Religion plays a role as well.

It is apparent that women need to be brought into balance with men so that they have more and better opportunities for education, a greater voice in decisions that impact their lives, and more support. The first step in that transition is the transmission of truthful information. If women know where to go to get help, if they can become better informed about opportunities and services available, and if they pursue better schooling and find fulfilling employment, they may make life decisions that have a positive impact on the problem of overpopulation for years into the future. The World Population Fund estimates that the number of children in many developing countries would fall by a third if there were access to the kinds of services that people need.[22]

FOOD AND WATER FOR THE BILLIONS OF US

If efforts at population control fail and we continue to grow dramatically as a species, we will find ourselves facing various shortages. Our supply of water for sustenance and for agricultural use, for example, will be drastically reduced. By the year 2025, the number of people living in either water-scarce or water-stressed conditions could quadruple to between 2.4 billion and 3.2 billion people, depending on future rates of population growth. Water shortages are likely to grow especially acute in the Middle East and in much of Africa.[23]

For many people in the world, the overpopulation situation is already nearly impossible and getting worse. An estimated 420 million people live today in countries that have less than 0.17 of an acre of cultivated land per person. (That figure is the estimated minimum parcel capable of supplying a vegetarian diet for one person without use of costly chemicals and fertilizers.) By 2025 the number of people living in such countries is expected to increase to between 557 million and 1.04 billion.[24] As it is now, more than three billion people worldwide are suffering from malnutrition, according to the World Health Organization—the largest proportion of malnourished persons in history. Malnourishment compounds suffering because it makes already vulnerable humans more vulnerable to other diseases, such as diarrhea, malaria, and AIDS.[25]

In contrast, a person living in a First World city requires the equivalent of about 11.1 acres of productive land for food, water, housing, and goods. As well-known population activists Paul and Ann Ehrlich note,

Applying this "ecological footprint" standard to a city such as Sydney, Australia, shows that it would need an area of productive land 35 times as big as the city to sustain itself. For the projected world population in 2050 to live like people in Sydney, we'd need about 124 billion acres of

productive land—around six times all the productive land on the planet.[26]

It is astounding to realize how much of the world's productive land, not to mention natural resources in general, is necessary to sustain the way of life that developed countries are used to—while billions are hopelessly relegated to starvation. It is a complete impossibility to feed the entire world population in the manner to which First World countries have become accustomed.

If there is one major thread to understanding why overpopulation matters, it is the need to balance numbers relative to sustainable resources. Like Rat, it appears that we are soon to be gnawing through and destroying everything around us just to survive. It is not population density alone that matters, but the number of people in an area relative to its resources and the capacity of the environment to sustain human activities—that is, to the area's carrying capacity. "In short," says the organization known as Zero Population Growth, "if the long-term carrying capacity of an area is clearly being degraded by its current human occupants, that area is overpopulated."[27]

REDUCTION OF LIFESTYLE

One would reason that the 18 million more people added to the world's population by India last year would make a far greater negative impact on the Earth than the 2.5 million added to the United States last year. If considered in light of sheer numbers, this would be true, of course. But when we consider the impact of each person's lifestyle and the resources used to sustain it, we reach an entirely different conclusion. Most of the 18 million newcomers to India will live in extreme poverty; not so the newcomers to the United States. Gregory Mankiw, Allie S. Freed Professor of Economics at Harvard University, points out how dramatically lifestyles in America differ from those in India (and elsewhere):

*Although Americans comprise only five percent of the world's popula-
tion, we use 25 percent of its resources and produce more trash and pollution than citizens of most other nations. The average American's
energy use is equivalent to the consumption of two Japanese, six Mexi-
cans, 13 Chinese, 32 Indians, 140 Bangladeshis, 284 Tanzanians or 372
Ethiopians. Because Americans consume much more of the Earth's resources than do people in India, 2.5 million additional Americans have
the environmental impact of nearly 80 million Indians. In this light,
U.S. growth might be considered more costly to the planet than India's
growth.*[28]

Those who are concerned about overpopulation share the insight
that because resources are scarce, the only way to improve living standards is to limit the number of people we share them with. There are
some who look at the same statistics about births and deaths and do not
see a population crisis. They believe that people *create* resources. In
order to determine whether the world population is a problem or not,
they say, we need to ask whether an extra person added to the planet
uses more or less resources than he or she creates. As long as people pay
for what they consume, there is no problem.

To these critics, it is a market economy that "ensures that no one can
consume resources without first creating some of equal or greater value,"
says Mankiw. For instance, the best solution to the overuse of fossil fuels
that create greenhouse gases, which in turn damage the environment, is
a tax system in which the individual pays for the harm he or she causes.
The best way to protect the environment, in the eyes of this market-
based perspective, is not to deal with overpopulation itself, but to ad-
minister a "well-designed tax system." Efforts to limit population growth
do not mean much in this view, because the market will determine the
limits.

INCREASED ODDS FOR AN EINSTEIN?

One outspoken advocate of increasing population states that the best way to get geniuses is to have more people. If enough new babies are born, an Einstein, Newton, or Darwin may be among them. Calling himself a serial procreator, he makes no apologies, and defends the birth of his third child "without a shred of guilt. I don't guarantee that he will find a cure for cancer or a solution to global warming, but there is always a chance. And in that chance lies the hope for our species."[29]

This statement appeals to Human's foolish ego, in my opinion. Basing one's hope on a mere chance is like a gambler risking everything at a blackjack or craps table. It ignores the unbending laws of math. Hoping that Lady Luck will defy sheer math at organized gaming is complete stupidity! So too the hope that a brilliant baby today will solve Earth's problems tomorrow. No one human being, no matter how brilliant, can single-handedly solve the ongoing environmental dilemma. Think about Einstein: one of my heroes, he was brilliant, but he was powerless to save six million of his own countrymen during World War II. Only large numbers of informed and active people all over the world, working in unison, will have a chance to stave off the cruel fate that Nature would otherwise unleash to counter the imbalance that we have caused.

Maybe the more-babies-are-better folks are taking a tongue-in-cheek approach to the dangers of overpopulation. If not—if they are serious—they are advocating a theory that adds up (or multiplies!) correctly on paper only; although it seems quite logical, it is out of touch with the reality of the Third World, where a different logic rules and a different math applies. In other words, it does not make sense in struggling countries, and in the streets of mega-cities such as Calcutta or Mexico City, where overcrowding is already critical. Proponents of this view sometimes argue that even famines in developing countries are rarely due to overpopulation; civil war is a more common cause, they say. That argument fails to recognize the fact that a powerful contributor to civil war and its attendant political and economic instability may be overpopulation!

Perhaps the market theory has more relevance in stable economies. No one should feel guilty for bringing a child into an environment where children can thrive. And certainly we all should hope for the next Einstein. But dismissing those who are concerned with overpopulation and subverting efforts toward positive change are actions that are both irresponsible and insular. The market theory simply is not helpful for countless women in Third World countries who are malnourished and give birth to children who face inevitable starvation. Many of them want to have as many children as possible so that a few might survive to take care of them later in life. An Einstein is not what they hope for, and it is not what we should count on to save us.

DIFFERENT COUNTRIES, DIFFERENT SOLUTIONS

Approaching overpopulation from another perspective, Garrett Hardin, recipient of the 1989 Humanist Distinguished Service Award, advocates a contextual response among the nations. He believes that we are faced not with a *global* population problem, but with numerous *national* population problems. Each nation has an individual set of circumstances to address when facing national and international population issues. According to Hardin, "There are three processes that determine the extent of environmental impact that population has on a particular region, 1) fertility, 2) immigration, and 3) resource consumption. A region characterized by low fertility/high immigration will obviously seek different solutions than a region with high fertility/low immigration."[30] In order to be successful, Hardin says, solutions need to be adapted to fit that area's context. When issues are looked at more closely from within their contexts, it becomes clearer that the problem of overpopulation is more than an academic exercise. The consequent pain and suffering of all affected living things are real.

There are myriad untold human struggles within the various regions and contexts affected by overpopulation stresses. The brief stories
in the following section, from disparate areas of the world, are related by
David Paxson, president of Population Balance, who has traveled exten-
sively throughout Third World countries listening, observing, and experiencing the impact of overpopulation.[31] These stories reflect human
dilemmas created by too many people. These are not isolated events,
tragically, but are all too common. They are snapshots of a larger reality—
the reality of life in the rats' nest.

LIFE IN THE RATS' NEST

In Mexico City, it actually snows fecal matter. Mexico City is the fourth
most populated urban area in the world, at almost 20 million people.
Tens of thousands of the city's residents live next to a trash dump or
under a cardboard box, almost 10 percent of the population surviving
on less than one U.S. dollar per day. With so many people having no
sanitation facilities, their human waste dries, gets picked up by the
wind, and then is breathed by everyone else.

In India, an American nun was riding on a train stuffed with people
inside and out, with many riding and hanging on to the roof outside.
While standing in the densely crowded aisle and trying to keep her balance, she suddenly felt pressure and saw that an apparently abandoned
baby had been left on her arm. (Don't be tempted to assume that "it
doesn't happen here." Approximately five thousand infants are abandoned in the United States each year.)[32]

In Nepal, the farmers struggle to grow food wherever they can. In
some places they grow it on three-foot-wide terraces, each terrace separated from the next by a ten-foot rise. The land is so steep that some of
the precious topsoil washes away every time it rains. And despite the
vanishing farmland, mothers in Nepal keep having babies a year or less

apart. Of those babies, many die because there is not enough food for everyone.

In Malawi, villagers must now spend four hours doing a task that previously took only one hour. Having harvested too many trees without replanting, they must walk an hour and a half to a forest preserve each day, spend an hour looking for sufficient sticks of wood to cook their daily meal, and then walk back home again carrying the wood.

Given the prevalence of stories such as these, why is it that we have so much trouble making the connection between runaway population growth and environmental crises? "It seems plain that the issues that matter most to us—biodiversity, urban sprawl, loss of rainforests and old-growth trees, air and water pollution—have their roots in the incredibly successful propagation of the human species," writes Jim Motavelli in *E/The Environmental Magazine*.[33] Success usually brings celebration and joy, but human overpopulation on Earth is bringing untold misery to most living things and threatening our very existence as a species.

And this is only one side of the problem—the human side. Over-population is profoundly impacting Earth's entire web of life. How will the stately and critically endangered tiger be able to peacefully coexist with humanity in modern India, whose population is expected to reach 1.5 billion and surpass China by 2050?[34] Whether of human or non-human living things, the stories of the consequences of overpopulation are grossly unacknowledged, dismissed, and ignored. The horse named Too Many warns us to wake up to the runaway population growth that is happening *now*. Overpopulation is not a distant issue. Its overwhelming problems are already upon us.

NATURE'S SELF-REGULATING EFFECTS

Although humans have been largely unsuccessful at controlling their own population, the same is apparently not the case with Nature herself.

Recent studies have led some to suggest that Nature and her varied ecosystems work together to curb overpopulation. But certainly not in the way we might think. Charles Darwin assumed that it was external causes, such as predators, starvation, severities of climate, and disease that would keep population in check in all species. But large numbers of field studies suggest otherwise. They suggest that the population of a species is maintained by internal adjustments of the onset of maturity of its females. These adjustments also seem to operate with a consideration of the entire ecosystem.

For example, birth rates are generally lower when overcrowding occurs. Numerous species of animals have been observed and linked to this finding, such as white-tailed deer, elk, bison, moose, big-horn sheep, ibex, wildebeest, Himalayan tahr, hippopotamus, lion, grizzly bear, harp seal, southern elephant seal, spotted porpoise, striped dolphin, blue whale, and sperm whale. This outcome has also been found among various small mammals.[35]

A large number of animal species also internally regulate their population according to the abundance or scarcity of food within their environment. The short-eared owl and the nutcracker lay fewer or produce more eggs, and the arctic fox and the lion bear more or less young in relationship to the availability of food.[36] Kangaroos actually halt the development of their embryos when food or water is scarce, and the development resumes when those resources are available again.[37]

It appears that Nature itself innately understands the larger picture and regulates itself accordingly. Humans probably also once instinctively understood their role in the larger ecosystem, but as our daily lives have increasingly separated us from Nature, we have lost such self-regulating mechanisms and today are bearing the consequences.

As mentioned in previous chapters, the Earth too has self-regulating mechanisms—among them the greenhouse effect, which ensures that Earth's atmosphere maintains a life-enhancing equilibrium of temperature and gases. A significant fluctuation in either direction from equilibrium would mean disaster for the entire planet. If we are to avoid that disaster, we need to recognize that the Earth is more than the sum of its parts. Something that we used to think of as a metaphor may be an even more essential truth: the parts appear to demonstrate an awareness of the whole ecosystem and work for its ultimate betterment and balance. The Earth appears in this fundamental nexus of relationships to be alive!

Will Nature eventually be forced to rid itself of Human, as antibodies attack a spreading, life-threatening infection? A disturbing thought—yes indeed! The dinosaurs are an example that such a response did happen (and no doubt there are other examples that we are not aware of).

INTER-SPECIES COOPERATION

We see a crucial principle at work in Nature: species cooperate with other species in order to ensure that multiple species survive. For instance, five carnivores of the African savannah—lion, leopard, cheetah, hyena, and wild dog—all depend upon the same prey (zebra, gazelle, and wildebeest) in order to survive. Yet these predators coexist because they have developed five different ways to live off the prey species without directly competing with one another.[38]

The same behavior is observed among herbivores: competing species use scarce resources in a cooperative manner. The development of certain evolutionary traits has also benefited these particular species. The authors of The Non-Local Universe explain:

> Zebras take the long dry stems of grasses for which their horsy incisor teeth are nicely suited. Wildebeest take the side-shoot grasses, gathering with their tongues in the bovine way and tearing off the food against their single set of incisors. Thompson's gazelles graze where others have

been before, picking out ground-hugging plants and other tidbits that
the feeding methods of the others have overlooked and left in view.
Although these and other big game animals wander over the same
patches of country, they clearly avoid competition by specializing in the
kinds of food energy being taken.[39]

In Central Africa, several species of yellow weavers live on the same
sandy shore, yet each survives on a different diet. One species eats only
hard black seeds, while another eats only soft green seeds, and yet a third
eats only insects. Newly hatched garter and green snakes display the same
tendencies: one pursues the scent of the cricket, while the other prefers the
scent of worms in the same environment, yet each *could* eat the same
prey.[40]

These examples are repeated over and over in Nature. Such cooperation is particularly obvious in the plant world, where certain plants
thrive in differing types of soils, temperature ranges, and moisture content. All this leads biologist Lynn Margulis to conclude: "All organisms
are dependent on others for the completion of their life cycles. Never,
even in space as small as a cubic meter, is a living community of organisms restricted to members of a single species."[41]

Our human species is also dependent on the balance of the whole
ecological system. Overpopulation remains the most serious threat of
all our grievous offenses toward the Earth. The frog may not "drink up
the pond in which it lives," but the human does indeed. All of the other
crises facing our planet (global warming, thinning of the ozone, and the
loss of biodiversity and natural resources) reach their crisis level because
of the overpopulation of the human species. Of all the billions of species
alive today on the Earth, only the human lives in ignorance, not only of
the consequences of our choices and actions, but also of the path that
leads toward healing.

For humanity, the implications are obvious. As part of a living community, we have the ability to see the sum of the parts and understand our role in the emergent consciousness of the Earth. We can live in a responsible and cooperative manner, using the Earth's available resources wisely to ensure a healthy ecosystem for all. Nature's memory is deeply embedded within our collective consciousness, waiting to be rediscovered. A simple commitment to learn and experience more of Nature's Way in our daily lives is a spiritual practice that may lead to the salvation of our living planet.

GETTING PRACTICAL

Each of us needs to think about what sorts of things we can do to commit to following Nature's Way. Here are some suggestions:

Perhaps you will think about conserving energy, even now while you can still afford your utility bills, and even before the rolling blackouts come to your neighborhood.

Perhaps you will ask your family to cremate you when you die, to save money for them and space on Ina Maka (Mother Earth).

Perhaps you will walk to the grocery store today instead of taking the car, in order to get a little healthier, save a little gasoline, and keep one more car out of an overcrowded street.

If you are like most people, your reaction about now is to doubt how much these small sorts of changes can have on the world. Let me reassure you: when small changes are multiplied by many people, they become powerful, significant changes. As an example, think about how radical even a small change in your buying habits can be when multiplied by everyone else reading this book:

Say you begin to think twice about buying (and putting on your plate) more food than you need. Because you're purchasing less food, the grocery store stocks less, farms get lower prices for the food they grow, and they therefore cut production and use up fewer of Earth's resources.

Maybe a few acres of precious rain forest will be saved. And with the better health that comes from better eating, the productivity of lower-income families will increase, and they will feel less urgency at having a large family to serve as their support network when they retire or can no longer work. And on and on go the benefits!

The possible steps on Nature's Way go on and on too. For example, perhaps you will go out in Nature more often, developing a greater reverence for Wamakaskan (the animals) and what they can teach us about how to live our lives:

Maybe you will watch an eagle circling above you and be inspired to observe the world from a higher perspective. Or maybe you will catch a glimpse of a bear digging up some roots with its claws and ponder what sort of "medicine" you should be searching for in your life.

Maybe you will plan a trip to a Nature preserve or to Africa. As you watch a powerful lioness bringing food back to her pride, maybe you will think about the importance of both males and females in caring for each other and their offspring. Or maybe you will come across a wolf pack working together to bring down a larger animal and think about how much more effective we are when we cooperate instead of acting alone.

Maybe you'll find yourself on an ocean-going ship or at an aquarium and see a big killer whale with whom you sense an unexplainable bond of friendship or family. Maybe you will hear the hoot of an owl that seems to follow you as you walk, making you think about other things you know are there but cannot see. Maybe you'll see a mountain lion, tiger, or some other predatory cat and marvel at the freedom it expresses—freedom you need to find in your own life.

Or maybe you'll come across a tree, perhaps a cottonwood, standing alone in an arid landscape, and wonder how it manages to get water in the burning heat. Maybe you'll notice you're getting a sunburn rather quickly and remember what the experts said about ozone depletion and the use of aerosols. That thought may prompt you to throw out that old box of aerosol spray paints in your garage. As you lift the rickety box, maybe you'll notice a couple of rats (more likely mice), scurrying out when you uncover their home. Maybe then you'll think about where those mice will go now that you've taken away their home, and what happened to the other animals that used to live where you do now. Maybe you'll imagine the buffalo and all the other many animals that are no longer here because we've killed too many of them and eliminated too many of their habitats in the name of economic progress.

Or maybe you will just think a bit more about the repercussions of your actions!

The Earth-respecters of the past were not computer-age people, and yet they developed their intuition to perceive Earth's saving depths, which Nature instills in all its harmonic subjects. No doubt modern Human has this very same trait, this intuition, but our egos block it. Yes, for millennia some societies managed to preserve and maintain this intuitive spirituality—a spirituality that Dominant Society has proven it can no longer perceive. The people of Dominant Society are depending on God to save them, though their deity is an idol of false materialism with no track record of past intervention. Creator has not saved the many societies that have fallen into obscurity. With billions of planets surrounding their respective suns (stars), and with each of the inhabited planets no doubt endowed with the same basic freedoms Earth's citizens have been granted, is vast Creator going to intervene on *our* planet? I doubt it.

For 4,500 years, the Native Indians of North America managed to carry on and preserve an entire hemisphere. The Pilgrims were not repelled, as one might have expected, but instead were treated with generosity, although as the Indians would later find out, the newcomers carried steel "bang sticks" that would eventually subdue the Natives. Maybe with an initial repelling of those first Pilgrim immigrants by the tribes (who might later have united to strengthen their defense), colonization of the Americas would at least have been set back a few centuries. If the colonization had been thus postponed, maybe enough time could have been bought to save resources, and hence we would have been at a more Earth-honoring, human-supporting stage than we are now.

Maybe we would have had a stronger platform from which to educate the white man on the power of Eagle's observance, Wolf's sharing, and Owl's truth. Dominant Society was receptive only to freedom, however. While I yearn for the day that the wisdom of our animal brothers and sisters is heard and heeded, I am thankful for the freedom that we have. In this great land of Iroquoian-spawned freedom—Tiger's freedom—books and great ideas can still speak out.

Vaclav Havel, writer and president of the Czech Republic, had this to say: "It is my deep conviction that the only option is a change in the sphere of the spirit, in the sphere of human conscience, in the actual attitude of [humans] toward the world. But it seems to me that responsibility for the world has become a very low priority."[42] We need to place responsible partnership with one another and the Earth at top priority. Every plant, animal, and human being of future generations will be directly affected by what we cease now to greedily exploit and by what we choose now to give away for the population balance of the Earth. Remember: the frog does not drink up the pond in which it lives!

Given the information contained in these last four chapters of *Nature's Way*, we can believe without hesitation that the Four Horses of the Apocalypse are truly on the horizon—or worse, now riding among us.

Pilamiya, *Kola* (Thank you, my friend), as you walk on in partnership upon your planetary journey!

NOTES

INTRODUCTION

1. Dr. Beatrice Medicine, Sihasapa Lakota. *Learning to Be an Anthropologist and Remaining "Native"* (Urbana and Chicago: Univ. of Chicago Press, 2001), p. 188.

2. This conversation appears in Thomas Mails, *Fools Crow: Wisdom and Power* (Tulsa, OK: Council Oak Books, 1991), p. 42.

CHAPTER TWO

1. Joseph Epes Brown, *Animals of the Soul* (Rockport, MA: Element Books, 1997), p. 22.

2. Vince Shute Wildlife Sanctuary, "Bear Facts," www.americanbear.org, p. 1.

3. Brown, *Animals of the Soul*, pp. 21–22.

4. Union of Concerned Scientists (UCS), "Global Environment," www.ucsusa.org. FAQ about Biodiversity: "Why Is Biodiversity Important?"

5. UCS, "The Science of Biodiversity," www.ucsusa.org.

6. Dirk Bryant, Daniel Nielsen, and Laura Tangley, "The Last Frontier Forests," World Resources Institute, www.wri.org, 1997.

7. John Tuxill and Christopher Bright, "Sharing the Planet: Can Humans and Nature Coexist?" *USA Today* magazine, Jan. 1999.

8. Virginia Morell, "The Sixth Extinction," *National Geographic*, Feb. 1999.

9. John Neihardt, *Black Elk Speaks* (Lincoln, NE: Univ. of Nebraska Press, 1961), p. 225.

10. Bob von Sternberg, "Olson Gets Plea Deal in SLA Killing" *Minneapolis Star Tribune*, Nov. 8, 2002.

11. Thomas Mails, *Fools Crow: Wisdom and Power* (Tulsa, OK: Council Oak Books, 1991), p. 43.

12. Max Charlesworth, Howard Murphy, Diane Bell, and Kenneth Maddock, *Religion in Aboriginal Australia* (St. Lucia: University of Queensland Press, 1984), p. 5.

CHAPTER THREE

1. Riane Eisler, *The Chalice and the Blade* (San Francisco: HarperSanFrancisco, 1987), p. 258, fig. 5.

2. Ibid., fig. 5, pp. 24, 25.

3. Ibid., p. 86.

4. Ibid., p. 87.

5. Merlin Stone, *When God Was a Woman* (New York: Harcourt, Brace, 1978), p. 217.

6. Timothy Freke and Peter Gandy, *Jesus and the Lost Goddess: The Secret Teachings of the Original Christians* (New York: Harmony Books, 2001), p. 44.

7. Bernard Lewis, "What Went Wrong?" *Atlantic Monthly,* Jan. 2002, pp. 43–45.

8. Ibid., p. 45.

9. Tom Cowan, *Fire in the Head* (San Francisco: HarperSanFrancisco, 1993), p. 4.

10. Peter Ellis, *The Celtic Empire* (London: Constable, 1990), p. 16.

11. Anne Ross, *The Pagan Celts* (Totowa, NJ: Barnes & Noble Books, 1986), pp. 103, 104.

12. Cowan, *Fire in the Head,* p. 6.

13. Michael Parfit, "Hunt for the First Americans," *National Geographic,* Dec. 2000, p. 46.

14. Barry Fell, *America* B.C. (New York: Pocket Books, 1976), p. 218.

15. Ed McGaa, *Rainbow Tribe* (San Francisco: HarperSanFrancisco, 1992), p. 53.

CHAPTER FOUR

1. Ed McGaa, *Native Wisdom* (San Francisco: Council Oak Books, 2002), pp. 61–65.

2. John Neihardt, *Black Elk Speaks* (Lincoln, NE: Univ. of Nebraska Press, 1961).

3. Ibid., pp. 32, 33.

4. Jack Weatherford, *Indian Givers* (New York: Crown, 1988), p. 123.

5. Ibid., p. 128.

6. John Bryde, *Modern Indian Psychology* (Vermillion, SD: Univ. of South Dakota Press, 1971), p. 30.

7. For evidence of Pilgrims "stealing" or "finding" the Indians' food cache, see William Elliot Griffis, *The Pilgrims in Their Three Homes* (Boston and New York: Houghton Mifflin, 1898), pp. 74–75.

8. Clyde Holler, *Black Elk's Religion* (Syracuse, NY: Syracuse Univ. Press, 1995), p. 227.

9. Ibid., p. 124.

10. Bryde, *Modern Indian Psychology,* p. 239.

11. Ibid., p. 234.

12. Brian R. Croone and Dennis W. Harcey, *White-Man-Runs-Him* (*Crow Scout with Custer*) (Evanston, IL: Evanston Publishing, 1993), pp. 10, 15.

13. Bryde, *Modern Indian Psychology,* p. 259.

14. Ibid., pp. 238, 270.

15. Chief Eagle Feather and Ben Black Elk, Indian Mystique Conference (Vermillion, SD: Univ. of South Dakota (July 29–Aug. 2, 1968).

16. Chief Eagle Feather and Ben Black Elk, Indian Mystique Conference.

17. Bryde, *Modern Indians*, pp. 349–52.

18. Holler, *Black Elk's Religion*, p. 120.

19. Hilda Neihardt, ed., *Black Elk Lives: Conversations with the Black Elk Family* (Lincoln, NE: Univ. of Nebraska Press, 2001), Appendix: "Black Elk Family Tree."

20. Discussion with Wacama Tribal Chairwoman, Apr. 1991. Wacama Reservation, NC.

21. Holler, *Black Elk's Religion*, p. 132.

22. James Carroll, *Constantine's Sword: The Church and the Jews* (Boston: Houghton Mifflin, 2001), p. 384.

23. Bishop John Shelby Spong, *Why Christianity Must Change or Die* (San Francisco: HarperSanFrancisco, 1998), p. 37.

CHAPTER FIVE

1. William Stolzman, *The Pipe and Christ* (Chamberlain, SD: Tipi Press, 1986), pp. 9–10.

2. Ibid., p. 12.

3. Mikkel Aaland, *Sweat* (Santa Barbara: Capra Press, 1978), pp. 15–16.

4. Ed McGaa, *Mother Earth Spirituality* (San Francisco: HarperSanFrancisco, 1990), p. 61.

5. Ibid., p. 51.

6. Deborah Chavez, *Fallen Feather: A Spiritual Odyssey* (Minneapolis: Four Directions Publishing, 1997).

CHAPTER SIX

1. William Stolzman, *How to Take Part in Lakota Ceremonies* (Pine Ridge, SD: Red Cloud Indian School, 1986), p. 63.

2. Thomas Mails, *Fools Crow: Wisdom and Power* (Tulsa, OK: Council Oak Books, 1991), p. 42.

3. Stolzman, p. 61.

4. Ibid., p. 62.

5. Ibid.

6. Stolzman, *The Pipe and Christ* (Chamberlain, SD: Tipi Press, 1986), p. 12.

7. Ibid., *The Pipe and Christ*, p. 9.

8. William Powers, *Yuwipi, Vision and Experience in Oglala Ritual* (Lincoln, NE: Univ. of Nebraska Press, 1984), p. 94.

9. Ed McGaa, *Mother Earth Spirituality* (San Francisco: HarperSanFrancisco, 1990), p. 105.

10. "Allegory of the Cave" from *Plato's Republic*. John M. Cooper, *Plato's Complete Works* (Indianapolis, IN: Hackett Publishing Company, 1997), pp. 1132–34.

CHAPTER SEVEN

1. Jim Corbett, *Man Eaters of Kumaon* (New Delhi, India: Oxford Univ. Press, 1944), p. xii.

2. Ibid., pp. xi–xii.

3. Charles Van Doren, *A History of Knowledge* (New York: Ballantine Books, 1991), p. 12.

4. http://www.mexika.org/Heritage.html.

5. Bishop John Shelby Spong, *Why Christianity Must Change or Die* (San Francisco: HarperSanFrancisco, 1998), p. 98.

6. Ibid.

7. Andrew Sullivan, "They Still Don't Get It," *Time*, Mar. 4, 2002, p. 55.

8. Ibid.

9. "Alleged Abuse Prompts Lawsuit," *Yankton (SD) Daily Press and Dakotan*, June 7, 2003, p. 1.

10. James A. Haught, *Holy Horrors: An Illustrated History of Religious Murder and Madness* (Buffalo, NY: Prometheus Books, 1990), p. 62.

11. Ibid., p. 64.

12. Ibid., p. 68.

13. Heinrich Kramer and James Sprenger, *Malleus Maleficarum* (New York: Dover Publications, 1971).

14. Haught, *Holy Horrors*, p. 76.

15. James Carroll, *Constantine's Sword: The Church and the Jews* (Boston: Houghton Mifflin, 2001).

16. John Cornwell, *Hitler's Pope: The Secret History of Pius XII* (New York: Viking, 1999).

17. Carroll, *Constantine's Sword*, p. 524.

18. Awake, *Could the Holocaust Happen Again?* (Wallkill, NY: Watchtower Bible and Tract Society, May 8, 2001), p. 12.

19. Carroll, *Constantine's Sword*, p. 524.

20. Ibid., p. 524, 525.

21. Ibid., p. 381, 382.

22. Ibid., p. 29.

23. "In Focus, Middle East," *National Geographic*, Dec. 2001, p. 130.

24. Muslims, Turkey (Frontline WGBH, Boston); http://pbs.org/frontline/.

25. Bernard Lewis, "What Went Wrong?" *Atlantic Monthly*, Jan. 2002, p. 45.

CHAPTER EIGHT

1. Carolyn Merchant, *The Death of Nature: Women, Ecology, and the Scientific Revolution* (San Francisco: HarperSanFrancisco, 1989), p. xvi.

2. Ian G. Barbour, *Religion and Science: Historical and Contemporary Issues* (San Francisco: HarperSanFrancisco, 1997), p. 7.

3. Ibid., p. 6.

4. Merchant, *The Death of Nature*, p. 20.

5. Ibid., p. 8.

6. Ibid., p. 9.

7. Ibid., pp. 2–3.

8. Provided by Vincent Ferraro, Ruth Lawson Professor of International Politics, Mount Holyoke College, South Hadley, MA.

9. John Gribbin, *In the Beginning: The Birth of the Living Universe* (Boston: Little, Brown, 1993), pp. 110–11.

10. Andrew C. Revkin, "Glacier Loss Seen as Clear Sign of Human Role in Global Warming," Reuters, Feb. 19, 2001.

11. Ibid.

12. Gribbin, *In the Beginning*, pp. 110–11.

13. Intergovernmental Panel on Climate Change, 1990, p. xxxvii.

14. Ross Gelbspan, *The Heat Is On: The Climate Crisis, the Cover-Up, the Prescription* (Cambridge, MA: Perseus Books, 1997), p. 18.

15. Andrew Revkin, "Who Cares About a Few Degrees?" *New York Times on the Web*, November 27, 1997.

16. Associated Press, "UN Increases Global Warming Projection," Jan. 22, 2001.

17. Ibid.

18. "State of the Planet," *National Geographic*, Sept. 2002, p. 102.

19. Ross Gelbspan, "The Heat Is Online," www.heatisonline.org.

20. Intergovernmental Panel on Climate Change 2001, Climate Change 2001: The Scientific Basis, "Highlights From 'Summary for Policy Makers'—Working Group I," www.atmos.umd.edu/~owen/METO123/IPCC2001/.

21. Associated Press, "UN Increases Global Warming Projection," Jan. 22, 2001; Sir John Houghton, "Overview of the Climate Change Issue 'What Is Global Warming?'" Presentation to Forum 2002, St. Anne's College Oxford, July 15, 2002, www.jri.org.uk/resource/climatechangeoverview.htm.

22. Associated Press, "UN Increases Global Warming Projection," Jan. 22, 2001.

23. Gelbspan, *The Heat Is On*, p. 17.

24. Ibid., p. 6.

25. Gelbspan, "The Heat Is Online."

26. David J. Thomson, "The Seasons, Global Temperatures, and Precession," *Science* 268, Apr. 7, 1995.

27. *Science Daily*, www.sciencedaily.com, from a Columbia University press release, Dec. 1, 1997.

28. Gelbspan, *The Heat Is On*, p. 136.

29. New York Times Online, Science, Feb. 8, 2001, www.newyorktimes.com.

30. Gelbspan, *The Heat Is On*, pp. 1–2.

31. H. Stommel and E. Stommel, "The Year Without a Summer," *Scientific American*, June 1979, pp. 176–86.

32. Gelbspan, *The Heat Is On*, p. 22.

33. Gelbspan, "The Heat Is Online."

34. Associated Press, "UN Increases Global Warming Projection," Jan. 22, 2001.

35. Gelbspan, The Heat Is On, p. 34.

36. Ibid., p. 77.

37. Paul Epstein, "Is Global Warming Harmful to Health?" Scientific American, Aug. 2000.

38. Ibid.

39. Ibid.

40. Ibid.

41. Ibid.

42. Ross Gelbspan, "A Global Warming Crisis," Yes! A Journal of Positive Futures, fall 1999.

43. Associated Press, "Study Sees Greenhouse Gas Buildup," Mar. 15, 2001.

44. Sherry Rowland, University of California at Irvine, shared the Nobel Prize for chemistry in 1995 with his associate Mario Molina for their groundbreaking work on CFCs and ozone, which led to the landmark ban of CFCs from aerosol cans.

CHAPTER NINE

1. Laura Lee Online, LL Broadcasting, www.lauralee.com.

2. United Nations Environment Programme (UNEP), "Ozone Layer under Intense Stress as Governments Meet to Plan Next Steps," www.unep.org, Dec. 1, 2000.

3. Dawn MacKeen, "Life under the Hole in the Sky," www.salon.com, Nov. 3, 2000.

4. Union of Concerned Scientists (UCS), "FAQs about Ozone Depletion and the Ozone Hole," www.ucsusa.org.

5. Natural Resources Defense Council (NRDC), "The Ozone Depletion Story," www.nrdc.org.

6. Sasha Nemecek, Scientific American, "Profile: Mario Molina," Nov. 1997, www.sciam.com.

7. Friends of the Earth, "Ozone Depletion and the Flat Earth Myths," www.foe.org.

8. NASA Ames Research Center, Earth Science Division, "Respiration of the Global Biosphere 'The Breathing Earth'," http://geo.arc.nasa.gov.

9. Union of Concerned Scientists (UCS), "The Science of Stratospheric Ozone Depletion," www.ucsusa.org.

10. World Meteorological Organization (WMO), "Scientific Assessment of Ozone Depletion: 1998, WMO Global Ozone Research and Monitoring Project," report no. 44, Geneva, 1998.

11. Friends of the Earth, "Ozone Depletion and the Flat Earth Myths."

12. Center for Atmospheric Science (CAS), Univ. of Cambridge, "The Science of the Ozone Hole," The Ozone Hole Tour, www.atm.ch.cam.ac.uk/tour/part3.html.

13. Ibid.

14. Ibid.

15. NASA/Jet Propulsion Laboratory, "NASA-European Measurements See Significant Arctic Ozone Loss," www.sciencedaily.com, Apr. 6, 2000.

16. Ibid.

17. NASA/Jet Propulsion Laboratory, "Arctic Ozone Depletion Linked to Longevity of Polar Stratospheric Clouds, Say Studies," www.sciencedaily.com.

18. Ibid.

19. UNEP, "Ozone Layer under Intense Stress as Governments Meet to Plan Next Steps," www.unep.org, Dec. 1, 2000.

20. WMO, "Scientific Assessment of Ozone Depletion: 1998, WMO Global Ozone Research and Monitoring Project."

21. UCS, "The Science of Stratospheric Ozone Depletion," www.ucsusa.org.

22. UNEP, "FAQs about Ozone to the Environmental Effects Assessment Panel," www.unep.org.

23. UCS, "The Science of Stratospheric Ozone Depletion."

24. WMO, "Scientific Assessment of Ozone Depletion: 1998, WMO Global Ozone Research and Monitoring Project."

25. NASA Ames Research Center, "Ultraviolet Radiation," www.nas.nasa.gov/About/Education/education.html.

26. Ibid.

27. Norfolk State University, "Skin Cancer and UV Radiation," http://vigyan.nsu.edu.

28. MacKeen, "Life under the Hole in the Sky."

29. NASA Ames Research Center, "Ultraviolet Radiation."

30. Ibid.

31. UNEP, "FAQs about Ozone to the Environmental Effects Assessment Panel."

32. "Ozone Depletion: Eye Disorders," *Encyclopedia of the Atmospheric Environment,* www.doc.mmu.ac.uk.

33. "Ozone Depletion: Immune System," *Encyclopedia of the Atmospheric Environment,* www.doc.mmu.ac.uk.

34. Natural Resources Defense Council (NRDC), "Our Children at Risk: The 5 Worst Environmental Threats to Their Health," chap. 4 ("Air Pollution"), www.nrdc.org.

35. Ibid.

36. Ibid.

37. UNEP, "FAQs about Ozone to the Environmental Effects Assessment Panel."

38. Ibid.

39. "Ozone Depletion: Sea Life," *Encyclopedia of the Atmospheric Environment,* www.doc.mmu.ac.uk.

40. Ibid.

41. Ibid.

42. "Ozone Depletion: Land Plants," *Encyclopedia of the Atmospheric Environment,* www.doc.mmu.ac.uk.

43. Ibid.

44. "Ozone Depletion: Materials Damage," *Encyclopedia of the Atmospheric Environment,* www.doc.mmu.ac.uk.

45. Kefei Kang, M.D., Seth Stevens, M.D., and Kevin Cooper, M.D., "Pathophysiology of Ultraviolet Irradiation," American Academy of Dermatology, www.aad.org/education/uvirradiation.htm.

46. MacKeen, "Life under the Hole in the Sky."

47. NASA/NOAA Ozone Hole Press Release, Sept. 25, 2003, http://jwocky.gsfc. nasa.gov/news/press 2003.html.

48. UNEP, "Ozone Layer under Intense Stress as Governments Meet to Plan Next Steps."

49. D. W. Faley, "Twenty Questions and Answers About the Ozone Layer," University of Alabama at Huntsville, http://nsstc.uah.edu/atmchem/recent_events/upperstrato3_recovery.html.

50. UNEP, "FAQs about Ozone to the Scientific Assessment Panel," www.unep.org.

51. Ross Gelbspan, The Heat Is On: The Climate Crisis, The Cover-Up, The Prescription (Cambridge, MA: Perseus Books, 1997), p. 64.

CHAPTER TEN

1. Richard Leakey and Roger Lewin, The Sixth Extinction (New York: Doubleday and Company, 1995), chap. 13, www.well.com/user/davidu/sixthextinction.html.

2. Thor Heyerdahl, Fatu-Hiva: Back to Nature (New York: Doubleday and Company, 1974), pp. 198–202.

3. "Sonar from Navy Likely Killed Whales in the Bahamas," USA Today, Dec. 21, 2001.

4. Natural Resources Defense Council (NRDC), "We Need Sound Sensibility on California Coast," www.nrdc.org.

5. Ocean Mammal Institute (OMI), "FAQ about LFA Sonar," www.oceanmammalinst.org.

6. Ibid.

7. NRDC, "We Need Sound Sensibility on California Coast" and "Navy Sonar System Threatens Marine Mammals," www.nrdc.org.

8. American Museum of Natural History (AMNH), press release, www.amnh.org, Apr. 20, 1998.

9. Union of Concerned Scientists (UCS), "The Science of Biodiversity," www.ucsusa.org.

10. Leakey and Lewin, The Sixth Extinction.

11. John Tuxill and Christopher Bright, "Sharing the Planet: Can Humans and Nature Coexist?" USA Today Magazine, Jan. 1999.

12. Environmental Network News (ENS), "Individuals Called Biggest Threat to Oceans," Dec. 3, 1999, www.enn.com.

13. Marine Conservation Biology Institute, "Troubled Waters: A Call for Action" (news release), www.mcbi.org.

14. NRDC, "Pollution from Livestock Farms," www.nrdc.org.

15. Ibid.

16. Ibid.

17. Ibid.

18. UCS, "The Science of Biodiversity."

19. Ibid.

20. Ibid.

21. World Resources Institute (WRI), "Coral Reef Ecosystems: Amazon of the Oceans," www.wri.org.

22. Ibid.

23. UCS, "The Science of Biodiversity."

24. Ibid.

25. ENS, "Red List of Threatened Species Reveals Global Extinction Crisis," Sept. 28, 2000, www.ens-news.com.

26. Tuxill and Bright, "Sharing the Planet."

27. Leakey and Lewin, *The Sixth Extinction*.

28. World Wildlife Fund, www.wwf.org.

29. "Bison," *Encyclopedia Britannica*, 1994–2001.

30. "Tiger," *Encyclopedia Britannica*, 1994–2001.

31. Leakey and Lewin, *The Sixth Extinction*.

32. Ibid.

33. International Union for Conservation of Nature and Natural Resources (IUCN), "2000 IUCN Red List of Threatened Species" (news release), www.iucn.org/redlist.

34. Tuxill and Bright, "Sharing the Planet."

35. "Zebra mussels," *Encyclopedia Britannica*, 1994–2001.

36. "Kudzu," *Encyclopedia Britannica*, 1994–2001.

37. Leakey and Lewin, *The Sixth Extinction*.

38. "Devastation of Prey Diversity by Experimentally Introducing Predators in the Field," T. W. Schoener and D. A. Spiller, *Nature* 381, June 20, 1996, pp. 691–94.

39. Wilcove, Rothstein, Dubow, Phillips, and Losos, "Quantifying Threats to Imperiled Species in the United States," *BioScience* 48, no. 8, Aug. 1998, pp. 607–15.

40. Leakey and Lewin, *The Sixth Extinction*.

41. Elizabeth Roberts and Elias Amidon, eds., *Earth Prayers from Around the World* (San Francisco: HarperSanFrancisco, 1991), p. 10.

42. WRI, "New Study Reveals the Environmental Damage Threatens Future World Food Production," www.wri.org.

43. "The Gulf of Mexico Dead Zone and the Red Tides," Elizabeth Carlisle, http://www.tulane.edu/~bfleury/envirobio/enviroweb/DeadZone.htm.

44. Robin Pomeroy, "Millions Dying Needlessly from Dirty Water," Environmental News Service, Reuters, www.enn.com.

45. ENS, "Mercury Poses Risk to One in 10 U.S. Pregnancies," Mar. 5, 2001, www.ens-news.com.

46. Ibid.

47. ENS, "U.S. Hospitals Choked with Smog Victims," Oct. 6, 1999, www.ens-news.com.

48. Ibid.

49. Randy Udall, "When Will the Joy Ride End?" 1999, www.hubbertpeak.com.

50. Ibid.

51. Ibid.

52. Ted Trainer, "Running on Empty: The Death of the Oil Economy," *Earth Island Journal*, Mar. 1, 1997.

53. Colin J. Campbell and Jean H. Laherrere, "The End of Cheap Oil," *Scientific American*, Mar. 1998.

54. Udall, "When Will the Joy Ride End?"

55. Peter Schwartz and Doug Randall, "How Hydrogen Can Save America," *Wired Digital*, Apr. 2003.

56. Ibid.

57. Udall, "When Will the Joy Ride End?"

58. Brian J. Fleay, "USA's Triple Energy Whammy," Jan. 10, 2001, www.gulland.ca/depletion/fleay.htm.

59. Ibid.

60. The Hubbert Peak of Oil Production, "Natural Gas," www.hubbertpeak.com.

CHAPTER ELEVEN

1. Population Action International (PAI), "Scarcities of Water, Crop, and Forest Land Projected," Aug. 23, 2000, www.populationaction.org.

2. Linda DeStefano, "Human Over-Population and Wildlife," *Syracuse Herald-American*, Sept. 18, 1994.

3. The Population Institute, "1998 World Population Overview and Outlook 1999," Oct. 1998, www.populationinstitute.org.

4. United Nation Population Fund, "1998 Revision of the World Population Estimates and Projections," www.unfpa.org.

5. "Population of Poorest Countries Will Triple by 2050: United Nations," press release, Feb. 28, 2001, www.unfpa.org.

6. *Population-Environment Balance*, "The Sprawl Problem," www.balance.org.

7. "A Thousand Years of World Population: How Many People Does It Take to Change the World?" *Christian Science Monitor*, June 21, 2000.

8. U.S. Census Bureau, "World Population Gradually Slowing But Total to Hit 9 Billion in Next 50 Years," Jan. 1999, www.census.gov.

9. Ibid.

10. UN Population Division Issues, "World Population Prospects: The 2000 Revision," www.un.org/News/Press/docs/2001/dev2292.doc.htm.

11. The Population Institute, "1998 World Population Overview and Outlook 1999."

12. Population Reference Bureau, "1998 Population Reference Sheet," www.prb.org.

13. Lori Ashford, "Is the 'Population Explosion' Over?" Population Reference Bureau, Mar. 2001, www.prb.org.

14. Ibid.

15. Jeffrey Klinger, William Dowell, and Meenakshi Ganguly, "The Big Crunch," *Time*, Apr. 25, 2000.

16. Ibid.

17. Ibid.

18. United Nations Population Fund, "1998 Revision of the World Population Estimates and Projections," www.unfpa.org.

19. German World Population Fund, Dec. 28, 1998, www.overpopulation.org.

20. The Population Institute, "Facts and Figures," www.populationinstitute.org.

21. Ibid.

22. "Too Many People," *National Geographic*, July 28, 2000.

23. Population Action International, "People in Balance," www.populationaction.org.

24. Ibid.

25. World Health Organization, www.who.int.

26. Ted Trainer, "Running on Empty: The Death of the Oil Economy," *Earth Island Journal*, Mar. 1, 1997.

27. Paul and Ann Ehrlich, *The Population Explosion* (New York: Simon & Schuster, 1990).

28. Zero Population Growth, "More FAQs about Population," www.zpg.org.

29. N. Gregory Mankiw, "Be Fruitful and Multiply" *Fortune*, Sept. 7, 1998.

29. Ibid.

30. Population-Environment Balance, "The Sprawl Problem."

31. David Paxson, "World Population Balance," Mar. 2001, www.worldpopulationbalance.org.

32. Ibid.

33. Jim Motavelli, "Countdown to Six Billion," E/*The Environmental Magazine* 10, no. 4, July-Aug. 1999.

34. Ibid.

35. Robert Nadeau and Menas Kafatos, *The Non-Local Universe: The New Physics and Matters of the Mind* (New York: Oxford Univ. Press, 1999), p. 116.

36. Ibid.

37. PBS, *Voyage of the Odyssey, Papua New Guinea Logs*, http://www.pbs.org/odyssey/odyssey/20010905_log_transcript.html.

38. Nadeau and Kafatos, *The Non-Local Universe*, p. 117.

39. Ibid.

40. Ibid., p. 118.

41. Ibid.

42. Vaclav Havel, "Faith in the World," *Civilization*, Apr./May 1998.